The Blood on My Hands

The Blood on My Hands

AN AUTOBIOGRAPHY

Shannon O'Leary

ISBN-13: 9781519695871
ISBN-10: 151969587X

Contents

Prologue

I HAVE FELT THE COLD steel of a gun in my mouth and against my temple.

I have tasted warm blood on my lips and witnessed horrific scenes of mutilation, where nameless people took their last breaths. In my life, I have experienced poverty, met people who had plenty, and lived through fire, floods, and drought. I have befriended the intellectually challenged and physically impaired and have known the mentally ill and misfits who were geniuses. I also assumed anonymity with my mother and brothers without people realizing we had disappeared.

In my youth I was exposed to many facets of raw emotion.

I've seen a living heart, beating and pulsating for its last time; seen broken fingers tossed in the wind; and watched a severed head dance. Tormented by recurring memories, I have chosen to write this book and put these ghosts to rest.

I first contemplated suicide at the age of four.

I devised my death plan down to the very last detail but never had the courage to see it through to completion. Instead, my mother's face would keep interceding, begging me to stay alive. Faced with the fact that I could not inflict my death upon her, I'd pray for miraculous intervention. During hysterical bouts of entreaty, I would beg Jesus to strike us dead at exactly the same moment so that neither of us would feel the pain of enforced separation or the prolonged agony of death.

As a child, I dreamed of better things to come and lived in spiritualistic hope that one day my world would change. I thought my trauma was normal and didn't know what other families experienced. I thought fear, sadness, and horror were just the by-products of a barely tolerable childhood. My self-esteem was nonexistent, and after a while I sought approval through the creative arts. I loved to sing, and as my voice was strong, I sang to cover my feelings of inadequacy and desolation. To me, music represented true happiness, a make-believe world where I could cling to melodious sounds instead of the tortured screaming of my nightmares.

As an adult, I have felt exhilaration when audiences clapped and called my name. At the same time, I have felt myself torn in two, experiencing the immobilizing fear of personal exposure when not protected by the proscenium arch of a stage. When I present myself without camouflage or without a scripted character to protect me, my gut wrenches itself into a catatonic knot, an all-enveloping state of fear. If I feel I am being examined on a personal level, my arms and legs become frozen, and I feel my soul moving toward automatic pilot. I smile and behave in the correct manner, but I'm mentally blank and devoid of all feeling.

I know what it's like to be branded, to be labeled, and to work within the confines of a title. As a child I was called brilliant, genius, a child prodigy, and a precocious little troublemaker. I was also called an actress, liar, and evil. My teachers admitted they didn't understand me and often left me to myself. As an adult, I experienced national fame as a children's TV personality. I have brought joy to thousands of children by teaching them the elements of performance.

It brings me great fulfillment to see children experiencing happiness. It puts my own life in perspective.

I cannot find the words to describe my childhood. Words such as "passionately naive," "emotionally lacerated," and "holistically experiential" all pale in significance, in the shadow of living itself. My childhood was so creatively textured that it carried into adulthood without allowing me to become consumed by the insanity playing havoc around me. I am sane and strong, and for that I am eternally grateful. I have felt and seen extreme emotion. I have smelled my own flesh burning. I know what it feels like to have baby snakes wriggle across my body, to smell decay, and to see an eyeball popped between someone's fingers. Alone, I have spent what seemed like hours in a blackened hole, a makeshift grave with a steel curtain, waiting for death.

Through all this, I stayed courageous and strong.

I treasure the power of love and the absurdity of shock, and I deal with these emotions on a day-to-day basis.

This is the story of my childhood.

CHAPTER 1

THE NAME SHANNON MEANS "SMALL and wise." I have always been small. I was the shortest in my class at school, and I was younger than my fellow pupils by two years. I also never grew taller than five feet, so the "small" part of my name suited me. Yet my name also implied that I was "wise." As an adult, I have often wondered if wisdom is an acquired, inherited, or learned skill. In some ways I feel it was foisted upon me. Did my home environment force me to become wise beyond my years? Yes, I was a wise child, but many people made a point of telling me I was also "unnaturally old," almost "adult," and "beyond my years."

My mother conceived me in 1959. She was dismayed to discover she was pregnant, as she had recently had a miscarriage. When she broke the news to my father, he became angry. The last thing he wanted was another baby.

"Maybe you'll lose it," he said optimistically.

By the time my mother was four months pregnant, she was suffering from anemia and chronic morning sickness. During this time my parents and my older brother, Michael, were living with my father's mother, Ethel O'Leary. Grandma O'Leary ran a tight ship. It was my mother's responsibility to complete all the household chores and have dinner prepared by the time Grandma returned from her work as a scrubbing woman in Pymble, New South Wales. On one occasion, she was unable to complete her daily chores and look after Michael at the same time. She panicked because dinner wasn't ready and everyone was on the way home. She bundled my brother into his pram and headed up the steep hill toward the shops. A sudden flash of inspiration left her with the idea that she could buy some pies from the cake shop.

"Maybe they'll enjoy a change from my cooking," she thought.

Suddenly, a stab of pain ripped through her lower abdomen. Clutching her stomach, she clambered up the hill, the fear of an argument with Grandma O'Leary and my father driving her on and far outweighing the pain she felt. The pain continued until she returned home. Unknown to her, she was carrying twins. The pain worsened during dinner, and later that evening, my mother miscarried one of the babies. It was her second miscarriage in six months, and the doctor had told her that "if it happens again," she was to "bring the fetus in for tests." Distraught, my mother wrapped the premature fetus in a plastic bag, put it in the freezer, and went to bed.

She awoke the next morning to the sound of my brother crying. Exhausted, she went into the kitchen to make Michael his bottle. My father was in the kitchen cooking breakfast.

"Watch my kidneys," he said as he went to dress for work.

Smelling something strange, my mother looked into the frying pan.

The frozen lump was thawing. Crying out in dismay, her stomach churning and gulping for breath, she grabbed the pan and hurled the contents back into the plastic bag. My father had nearly eaten my twin.

After my twin's death, I lived on in my mother's womb without anyone suspecting she was pregnant. My mother was six months pregnant when her maternal grandmother died of a cerebral hemorrhage. It was a great loss because she loved her grandmother, Amy, dearly. Amy was the perfect Victorian grandmother—a beautiful mixture of chocolates, Eau De Cologne, and piano music. As I was growing up, Mum often said that I reminded her of Amy and that her "spirit has returned to earth" in me. She said that Amy had been "prone to nervous breakdowns and has come back to experience strength" in me.

Amy bequeathed her house on the North Shore to my mother's parents. Their own home was only a few doors away, so they decided to let my parents and Michael live there. My mother felt great relief at the prospect of moving into Amy's house, as living with Grandma O'Leary had been an extremely difficult experience. My father was prone to erratic mood swings, and his mother's interference often made these worse. Grandma O'Leary disliked my mother and blamed her for my father's "unfortunate behavior" and his "terrible choice" in marriage.

Grandma O'Leary was a small, stocky woman. Her strong personality geared people to attention. Fanatical about cleanliness, she ruled her roost with the snap of her fingers and a twisted, sharp tongue. Her cunning compensated for her lack of education, and secrets and superstition plagued her adroit survival instinct. She was born on March 20, 1898, in Sussex, and was named Ethel June Curtis. Her father, John Curtis, was a grocer's porter, and her mother performed household duties. When Ethel was thirteen, Ethel's parents took the liberty of arranging their daughter's future, making the decision that she should leave England rather than face the ridicule of an unwanted pregnancy. In 1911, she boarded the *Coraki* and set sail for Australia. Her papers were falsified, recording her marital status as widowed and her age as twenty-one. She carried in her arms a three-month-old baby boy, who was listed as her only traveling companion and closest relative.

"His father's dead," Ethel told everyone on the ship. "That's why we're here. My boy and I are looking for a new life in Australia." The whispered responses must have been frequent and muttered in hushed, embarrassed tones. She was a child with a child, the resilient fire of youth burning deep in her soul, pushing her around the world so she might flee postnatal rejection.

Ethel looked out from the ship's deck at the turbulent sea and then down at the baby in her arms. He was sleeping now, his fitful wakening in the night behind him. The journey on the *Coraki* had been long and tiresome. Upon her arrival in Sydney, Australia, Ethel O'Leary set about looking for a job. At this time, Australia was a developing nation, and incoming immigrants still knew little about the country.

Between 1911 and 1921, Australia's population grew rapidly. The Commonwealth Census recorded that Sydney's population grew from 629,503 to 5,435,700.[i] Communications systems in the great, wide land were changing, and a uniform penny postage system came into operation. The New South Wales Farmers and Settlers Association had launched the Australian newspaper *Land*.[ii]

Australia was also caught up in a flurry of artistic ventures. Dame Nellie Melba[iii] had begun to tour Australia with the Williamson Opera,[iv] and the performing arts flourished in Melbourne and Sydney. The Australian film industry had begun to flourish, with *Sweet Nell of Old Drury*[v] and *The Fatal Wedding*[vi] being released and viewed on the silver screen.

Mr. John O'Leary, a gardener by trade, had advertised for a housekeeping position. The money was not considerable, but the successful applicant would receive room and board. Ethel read the add and was sure she could fill the position. She knew it was the devil's own choice between starvation and a foundling home for her son. Ethel thought that her future life with John, an embittered Irish Catholic who lived by the bottle and ruled with his fists, was her only route for survival.

"Cleaning's good for the soul," she remembered her mother saying to her as a young child. "It helps to wash away the sins we sometimes forget to account for."

John O'Leary allowed Ethel to shelter in his run-down home. Surrounded by rugged beauty, the property boasted a few grassy paddocks surrounded by wild orchards and thick bushland. A creek with clean water ran through the middle of the land, which supported a huge vegetable garden. Blessed with sunshine over his head, baby Jack thrived while Ethel managed to shield him from John's drinking binges by lacing the child's bottle with alcohol. Ignoring the difference in their years, everyone in the district began to accept the odd couple as married. John O'Leary was twenty-five years older than Ethel and had previously been married to a girl of the same name. After his first wife had disappeared, John's staunch Irish Catholic beliefs prevented him from divorcing her and marrying the Protestant girl who had turned up on his doorstep.

Ethel had ten children, her first son who travelled with her from England and nine more fathered by John O'Leary; three babies died at birth, and the remaining six were baptized into the Catholic faith. Her first baby, Jack, was never baptized, but he managed to slip through the Catholic system to receive all the subsequent sacraments.

John was an extremely cruel man. A strong Labor supporter, he was prone to rapid mood swings and loved to fight. John's Irish temper took fly in numerous brawls, and Ethel became subject to his alcoholic rages. John's fists often battered her, and she learned to suffer the humiliating act of having excrement poured over her head. Ethel hoped God would rescue her from her private hell, and eventually, her prayers were heard. Three months after Ethel became pregnant with my father, John O'Leary dropped dead of cerebral thrombosis. He left Grandma O'Leary with eight children to support, the last child being my father, Patrick, who was born in 1935.

My mother, Emma, met Ethel O'Leary for the first time in 1957. My mother was sixteen years old and tongue tied. The older woman's severe demeanor and waspish tongue shocked her into a frightened silence. Emma had attended a private girls' school on Sydney's North Shore. She was unused to the blatant disapproval Ethel shed in her direction, fueling her prophetic apprehension.

"You will call me Mrs. O'Leary," she said to the girl on meeting. Ethel's face was lined from years of hard work. Her hands were chipped and roughened, bleached a bluish white from years of working with detergents and cleaning fluids. From the moment she saw Patrick dragging Emma down her path, she knew he was up to no good.

"Tell my mother," he demanded.

Ethel O'Leary glared at the young woman standing in front of her. "Tell me what?"

"I'm pregnant," Emma half whispered. She saw the older woman's eyes narrow into slits, puncturing what little confidence she had left.

"Well, that's that, then," she replied cryptically. "You've made your bed... now lie in it."

Emma had no reply. It was not the reaction she had been expecting. A stream of abuse, a hysterical outcry, a painful deluge of recriminations would have been easier to deal with. Ethel O'Leary's statement fell flat and leaden on her ears, shocking her, the way Patrick's reaction had previously.

"That's good!" he had said. "Now you belong to me."

My mother told me later that telling her parents that she was pregnant with my older brother, Michael, had been one of her most painful experiences. She decided to tell her mother first, waiting until they were alone, feeding the chickens. My grandmother, Sophie, was devastated. At that time Sophie also had a thirteen-month-old baby, and the thought of her eldest daughter becoming pregnant was unthinkable.

"I'll have to tell your father," she said. "And you'll have to see my doctor."

My mother silently agreed. My grandmother thought of a few different solutions to the problem, the first being that she could take my mother on an extended holiday, interstate. After the baby was born, Sophie would claim it as her seventh child and return to Sydney. My mother, however, wouldn't hear of adoption; she felt she owed it to everyone to marry Patrick.

The wedding date was set for October 26, 1958. On that day, my grandmother Sophie called through the locked bathroom door.

"It's not lucky to be late for your own wedding. You're meant to be at the church, Emma. You're late."

Emma didn't move. She sat in the warm, soapy water with her eyes half-closed and hummed to herself. Today was her wedding day!

"The people at the church can wait," she told herself. "They've got nowhere else to go." She imagined Patrick O'Leary. "I suppose I love him," she thought. "He's witty, charming, and unpredictable." Emma frowned. If only she could stop the nagging feeling caught in her chest. It happened at odd moments when they were alone and made her heart skip a beat. Emma shivered. The bathwater was getting cold. She placed her hands on her abdomen and felt the baby growing within her. She was beginning to like the idea of having a child.

Later, as she walked down the church aisle, her father gripped her arm tightly and whispered, "You don't have to do this, you know; you've got time to change your mind."

At that moment, Emma felt an overwhelming sense of love for her father. Her mixed feelings of doubt and love were totally entwined with a self-propelling guilt. She didn't have the courage to walk away; too many people were watching her make her way through the church. How could she leave her family to face the embarrassment of her daughterly misconduct? Her family would be disgraced, and she would be labeled an unmarried mother. Grandma O'Leary stood in the front row, stony and unsmiling, her blue-white knuckles gripping a well-worn set of rosary beads. This sight fixed my mother's resolve to go through with the marriage.

"I've made my bed," she thought, gritting her teeth into an endearing smile. "Now I'll have to lie in it."

My father promised my mother a honeymoon she would never forget. With ten pounds in his pocket, he whisked her off to Toukley.

"We're here for two days," he said happily.

When Emma walked into the unlined shed, she thought he was joking. Patrick pointed to the gas cooker in the corner of the room. "You can use that to cook on," he said.

"What's happening after we leave here?" Emma asked.

"Don't worry about that," Patrick reassured her. "I'll take you on a tour in the truck."

The honeymoon in the shed proved to be a nightmare for Emma. There were lice and sand fleas in the bed, and my father spent his time drinking, walking, and fishing by himself. When it was finally time to leave the shed, they drove around in the truck until night fell, and Patrick parked under a bridge.

"We'll sleep here," he said to my mother, who was trying not to cry. "I haven't enough money for a hotel, so this will have to do." The night air was cool, and Emma had brought only one jacket with her. It was her old school jacket, but it was warm.

"Just think how romantic it is being under the stars," Patrick told her, but Emma silently disagreed. She was four months pregnant, feeling sick, and craving the comfort of a real bed. Making love under the stars with pebbles digging into her back was not her idea of marital bliss. She hated camping, and they didn't have any blankets.

"I want to have a bath," she said, and she shuddered when Patrick glared at her.

"Tomorrow, we'll go to the pub for lunch," Patrick said, changing the subject.

Emma had never been in a pub before, as her father and the law forbade it.

"Not so fast, girl," the publican called as they ventured toward the counter. "You've got to be eighteen to come in here."

Patrick started to protest that Emma was eighteen, and a ravenous Emma tried to back him up.

"Sure, you're eighteen." The publican laughed as he pointed to her school blazer. "And my mother is fifteen." He was laughing so much he didn't see Patrick's fist flying into the air and smashing into his jaw. The man fell backward with a cry and called to his mates, "Call the police! Hurry up! They're getting away."

Patrick grabbed Emma's arm and dragged her out to the truck. "You stupid idiot!" he shouted. "Why did you wear that ridiculous jacket? Get it off at once!" He started the truck and headed off down the road. Emma quietly slipped the jacket off and asked him where they were going.

"We're going back to Sydney, you stupid cow!" came his angry reply, and Emma inwardly breathed a sigh of relief.

CHAPTER 2

ABOUT ME

I was born prematurely on December 31, 1959. The nurses placed me in a humidicrib and forgot about me until the New Year's Eve celebrations were over. My mother was unconscious after my birth, and she raised the alarm when she woke up. I was lost. It took the staff thirty minutes to find me, and, fortunately, I was none the worse for my adventure. I had been placed in the wrong ward without any identification, my mother's name written in the file near my crib. After the birth, my mother was too ill to feed me herself, so my diet was supplemented by bottled milk. I sustained a chronic allergic reaction and broke out from head to toe with eczema welts. Instead of an angelic newborn, I was a red, wailing creature, failing to enamor or charm any of those close to me.

Luckily for me, my mother had met a goat breeder called Marge Banning at an agricultural show many years before my birth. The meeting had taken place when Emma was fourteen years old, around the time of the birth of her youngest sister, Tara. Tara was a frail baby who was allergic to all dairy products. Her inability to keep food down had left everyone thinking she was going to die. My grandparents, Paddy and Sophie, heard about the medicinal properties of goat's milk and realized it could be used as a substitute for cow's milk products. In a last-ditch effort to make Tara well, they decided to answer an advertisement and buy milk from a goat breeder. After drinking the milk, Tara slept for the first night in her life. Gone were the projectile vomiting attacks, and she was on the road to recovery.

My mother's family decided to buy their own goat from a recognized breeder, but unbeknownst to them, the doe they bought was in kid. This meant the milk source would soon be dry. Luckily, the breeder felt sorry for baby Tara and gave my grandparents another doe for nothing. This meant Mum had her own little goat herd. Both goats were registered as breeders, but even with her untrained eye, she could tell the does were not show goats. She decided to enter the Brookvale Show[vii] to learn more about them.

An authority on goat breeding, Marge Banning was enthusiastic and always full of interesting tales. She and Emma immediately took a shine to each other, despite their difference in age; Marge took Emma under her wing. Marge was a short, plump woman who wore her hair in the style of traditional Austrian peasant women, with two gray plaits crossed over her head. At forty years of age, she divided her time among her goats, her cats, her dogs, and a husband she rarely saw. Howie, Marge's husband, was very eccentric and wealthy. Their relationship was the product of an arranged marriage, and they lived in separate residences. As Marge had no children, she decided to teach Emma everything she knew about the goat industry. As a result, my mother became a very successful goat breeder and, at fifteen, the youngest goat judge in Australia at the time.

When she brought me home, Mum immediately replaced my diet with goat's milk, and my health improved immediately. I stopped projectile vomiting and began to put on weight. My crying ceased, and I grew into a personable baby—a giggling, wide-awake baby who developed interactive skills quickly and scooted around on my bottom because it was faster than walking. When I was ten months old, my grandmother got the surprise of her life. After answering a knock on the door, she was presented with me, naked and screaming with indignant baby anger.

"Is this your little boy?" a strange man demanded angrily. I squirmed around chortling as he held me out at arm's length.

"No," she answered, "but *she* does live here."

"Well do your job, woman, and look after her; she was crawling across the road, and I nearly ran her over with my truck." The man turned to leave and added, "You might think about putting some clothes on her too…she'll catch her death…"

"Thank you," my grandmother stammered, embarrassed and not knowing exactly what to say.

It was winter, and despite my indifference to the passing danger, I was nearly blue with cold. Mystified, my grandmother took me inside and bundled me up warmly. It was a mystery. This story became the butt of jokes for many years to come. I had ventured out onto the road without a stitch of clothing on, and a stranger had called me a boy.

"Either he had very poor eyesight, or he'd never seen a naked baby before," everyone would comment as the story was told. My brothers told the tale to anyone who would listen, as my nudity gave it the embarrassing quality of a rude story.

"Did you know what Shannon did?" they would shout gleefully, and this became my cue to hide my head and wait for the ensuing laughter. As I grew older, I learned to laugh with them. I began to realize that my nakedness was part of the joke. It became obvious that the man should have known my gender. One problem remained, however, mystifying everyone. How did I manage to crawl through closed doors, past a multitude of obstacles, and out onto the road? The answer was never discovered, and after a while, no one really cared. It became "just one of those things." Strange incidents always occurred in our family.

When I was about fourteen months old, my parents moved my cot out to the glass-enclosed veranda, next to their bedroom. It was from my cot that I saw the flames reflected in the glass. The pretty yellow-and-orange tendrils danced through the glass in front of me. I stretched my hands out of the cot and placed them on the glass. With a wail, I recoiled instantly, my hand burning from the projected heat.

"Fire!" The shout rang out through the house. "The veranda's on fire."

Grandfather and my mother's older brother, Spud, ran to get water to put out the flames while Mum ran to get me out of my cot.

"Out of the way!" she shouted to the two little boys who were playing near the flames. "Move, or you'll get burned."

My uncle Benjamin, who was only four, helped Michael off the veranda and down onto the grass. The two boys stood and watched the men put out the fire. At last the flames were extinguished, and Grandfather tried to find the fire's source.

"Here it is!" he exclaimed, looking under the old lounge chair, which was opposite my cot. Everyone examined the charred remains of sticks and paper.

"Benjamin."

The little boy received a resounding smack on his behind and cried out, protesting his innocence.

"He's the only child old enough to have done it," Uncle Spud shouted as my mother took me squealing back to my cot.

"What's going on?" It was my father's voice, and everyone began talking at once. In the midst of garbled conversation and excitement, Spud felt something wasn't right.

"Why didn't you hear the commotion?" he said under his breath. "The noise was loud enough to wake the dead."

Spud had first met Patrick O'Leary during a family picnic. It wasn't a conventional meeting; it was more a collision of wills. Uncle Spud was celebrating his eighth birthday, and he had received a new cricket bat as a present. He was playing a game with Emma when they noticed a scrawny child watching them from behind a tree. Spud spotted a glimpse of snowy hair as the boy peeped around a tree trunk. Every time Emma caught the boy's eye, he'd pull faces at them. Emma was shocked.

"Such bad manners," she thought with a seven-year-old's disdain.

The ten-year-old boy looked like an urchin with his blond hair cropped into a basin cut.

"He's one of the O'Leary kids," her brother whispered. "They're really poor and always fighting. Don't pay him any attention." Spud put the cricket bat down near the wicket.

"Come on," he said to Emma. "Let's get something to eat."

The two children were walking over to their parents when suddenly Patrick O'Leary sprang from behind the tree and grabbed the cricket bat.

"Hey! Give it back!" screamed Spud, and he went to chase the boy, but it was too late. Patrick O'Leary raised the bat high in the air and, with a hefty whack, slammed it against the tree trunk. The bat splintered and gave a thunderous crack. Then the urchin flung it aside and ran off in the direction of home. Spud began to cry. Tears of rage and disappointment ran down his face as he raced to retrieve his broken present. Emma didn't know what to say or how to comfort her brother. She couldn't comprehend why the boy had broken the bat in such a willful and malicious way.

"He must be a very unhappy child," her mother, Sophie, said, trying to comfort Spud. "All you can do is feel sorry for him."

"I don't feel sorry for him," Spud sobbed. "I didn't do anything to him."

"Try and forget about him, dear…we'll get a new bat."

But Spud couldn't forget, and under his breath he muttered to his sister, "He's horrible and spiteful, and I hate him."

Later, when Emma was sixteen and she was dating Patrick, a sullen Uncle Spud chaperoned her outings. Try as he might, he couldn't bring himself to befriend Patrick, and although Emma tried to persuade him to be reasonable, he wouldn't listen.

"I don't like or trust him," Spud told Emma when they were alone.

"You're just being overprotective," Emma retorted. This resulted in Spud clamping his mouth shut and refusing to say any more. In return, Patrick goaded him, his rudeness infuriating Spud so much that my uncle deemed any type of reconciliation impossible.

"I said, what's going on?" My father's voice brought Uncle Spud back to the present. The fire was out, and my mother, who was heavily pregnant, was comforting me.

"Where have you been?" Spud asked my father.

"In the bedroom sleeping."

Spud looked at his little brother, Benjamin, who was sobbing in the corner. "I didn't do it," the boy kept crying over and over again.

Spud wondered, "How could Patrick have slept through the fire? There was so much shouting. How could anyone have slept through such a disturbance?"

The mystery fire was blamed on Benjamin and then subsequently forgotten, extinguished by time, as life continued on.

That same year, my father hoped to finish a plumbing course at a technical college.

"I've got an exam tomorrow," he told my mother.

"For what?"

"For my plumber's and drainer's license."

My father had nearly completed the course but had failed his final calculus exam. In order to get his certificate, he had been forced to study the subject again. My mother was confused. She hadn't realized Dad had gone back to technical college, let alone attended a course for the whole year.

"Good luck, then," she replied encouragingly, wondering all the while if he had told her about his course and she had forgotten about it. Afterward, she asked, "How did your exam go?"

My father replied, "It went really well," and the subject was quickly forgotten.

About three weeks later, Mum saw Dad's best friend, Jimmy Jones, when she was out shopping. Jimmy Jones was sporting an ugly black eye. Apparently, he had engaged in a fierce argument with my father, and they were no longer friends. When my mother asked what they had fought over, Jimmy didn't want to tell her.

"It was about the exam," he finally said.

"How did it go?" Emma asked.

"They failed Patrick."

Emma was surprised. "But he seemed so confident he'd pass."

"I had to inform the examiners," Jimmy told her quietly.

"About what?"

"He cheated."

"But how? Surely the examiners wouldn't have let him…"

Jimmy took a deep breath. "He didn't even turn up."

My mother didn't understand. "That doesn't make sense, Jimmy. How could he cheat if he wasn't even there?"

"I don't know how to tell you this…" Jimmy ventured. "Patrick didn't do the exam…he paid someone else to do it for him."

Emma wished Jimmy hadn't told her about the exam. Patrick O'Leary had always been a wild-tempered child with an almost feral instinct for survival. As his father had died before he was born, Grandma O'Leary had reared her five youngest children at home. When Patrick was little, her two older boys were fighting in the war overseas, and he was left to his own devices. Patrick was a loner by nature, and he often found himself in trouble. When he was fifteen, Patrick reported a dead body to the police. On that occasion, he was playing truant from school with his classmate, Allan.

"We'll have a smoke here; no one will see us," Patrick persuaded Allan as they walked down toward the bridge at Northbridge.

Allan was scared. "Are you sure it will be all right?"

"It will be fine," Patrick assured him. "I'll go along first and check no one's there."

Allan was nervous. He didn't know whether the illicit cigarette was worth it. They would be expelled from school if anyone in authority saw them. He shifted from foot to foot and watched his friend running down the track toward the water.

"Hurry back," he shouted, and he sat down to wait. Patrick had been gone for five minutes when Allan spotted him running back toward him.

"Come quick! Look what I've found."

The boys hightailed it down the track to the water's edge. Then they ventured under the cement pillars that held up the bridge. A tramp was lying dead on the ground. Allan was terrified, while Patrick seemed thrilled.

"We'd better call the police," Allan called frantically, running up the hill to the main road. "Come on, Pat."

Patrick's mood changed in an instant, his excitement swept from under him. "You stupid fool," he called after Allan, "now we'll get reported for wagging school."

Patrick O'Leary attended an all-boys private school in North Sydney. The Marist Brothers[viii] had relaxed their school fees in an effort to be charitable to his mother and her widowed status. Known for his volatile temper, sarcastic tongue, and quick replies, the boy was both ingenious and bright.

"His lessons suffer. Not through lack of intelligence," his school reports read, "but through his tendency to be too preoccupied with his own thoughts. The boy has a flair for intellectual pursuits but is often overtly aggressive."

Patrick's tongue was acrid, and his fists often got him into trouble. When they caught him fighting his childhood enemy, Ray Steel, it took two Marist Brothers to drag him off the boy. After separating the boys, the brothers told them to sort their quarrel out fairly to Marquess of Queensberry Rules.[ix] They intended the boxing match to be an example of self-discipline for the rest of the school, so they set the match to begin at recess.

At the sound of the bell, the boys began their bout. Points had been scored in both corners when Patrick suddenly lost control. He struck out, hitting Ray below the belt and crippling him. As Ray fell down, Patrick jumped on top of him, pummeling him with all his might. The referee and two of the brothers pulled Patrick off the injured boy and dragged him into his corner.

Later, when the time came for apologies, Patrick felt no shame. "I didn't do anything," he whined. "I don't even remember fighting in a boxing match."

"You're a dirty fighter, Patrick O'Leary," Head Brother O'Malley decreed later in his office. "I have no alternative but to expel you for misconduct."

Patrick O'Leary was crushed. If he was expelled, his mother would never allow him to finish school, and he had counted on receiving his leaving certificate.

"But I want to be a scientist or detective," he shouted, breathing heavily and turning red in the face. Once again his temper flared, and the boy lost control. He didn't remember hitting the principal's desk or making the textbooks crash to the floor. Patrick had no recollection of the look of terror on the old brother's face as he was dragged from the room. Patrick couldn't see what the fuss was all about, as in his mind he had done nothing wrong. Grandma O'Leary took leave of Sydney and went to Narrabri. She found employment on a farm as a housekeeper, as she thought Patrick would benefit from the fresh country air.[x]

"Patrick," she said, "you have acquired an illness, a flaw in your disposition. You can settle yourself out here on the land, and we'll return to Sydney when you've convalesced."

My mother's childhood was vastly different from Patrick's. For the first six years of her life, Emma didn't really know her father because he was away at war.[xi] She lived a cosseted existence with substitute memories of her father's face presented in the form of photos and letters. She vaguely remembered her father coming home wounded from the Syrian battles when she was four,[xii] but as soon as he healed, he was whisked away to New Guinea.[xiii] Paddy O'Riordan loved his children and wife dearly. On his return to Australia, he rarely spoke about the war. Instead, he concentrated on his family.

Sophie, Emma's mother and my grandmother, called Mumma, idolized her husband. They both conveyed to the rest of the world that they had a fairy-tale marriage. My mother and her older brother, Spud, adjusted quickly to their father's return. At night, Paddy tap-danced on the table and played the harmonica to entertain them. He would also play the fiddle while Sophie played the piano.

Paddy worked as a statistician and paymaster for the government. He was glad of the job's stability, as it wasn't long before Sophie became pregnant again. In the next five years, the family of four would swell to a grand total of eight. Paddy, however, didn't mind the changes that were enforced by the arrival of young children. He believed that the family's destiny was in the hands of God and that his duty to his family was foremost in the teachings of his beloved Catholic religion.

When Emma was sixteen, Paddy forbade her to go out with boys. By this time, all the local boys knew her as Icicle. The name hurt my mother, but Paddy laughed it off.

"You're too young to be carrying on with boys," he'd say. "You'd best wait a year before you try any of that malarkey."

So Emma completed her leaving certificate and left school. She hoped to become a veterinary doctor, but with so many children in the family, money was scarce. She knew she had to get a job, so she decided upon dental assisting as her career. On the day she met Patrick O'Leary, she had her nose buried in a new Georgette Heyer novel.[xiv] Like most bookworms, she found the novel impossible to put down. With book in hand, she walked down the hill to her surgery, oblivious to all around her.

"Ouch!"

Emma's book flew from her hands as the young man bashed into her. She quickly bent down to pick it up, his words resounding in her ears.

"You stupid idiot! Why don't you look where you're going?"

"Sorry," she mumbled, retrieving her precious novel and trying to move out of the young man's way.

"Hey! Not so fast." He was very sure of himself. "I want you to go out with me on Saturday night."

Emma stared at the man, shocked at his forward approach. "But I don't even know you…"

"Patrick O'Leary," the man introduced himself. "Well?"

"I'm not allowed out with boys." Emma's final words pushed him aside. "I have to get back to work."

Patrick O'Leary watched her go and laughed to himself. "This one is going to be harder than I thought."

As the day forged on, she forgot about Patrick, but when she went to go home, there he was.

"Well?" he asked her again, blocking the path.

"'Well' what?" Emma replied.

"I told you, I want to take you out."

"Where to?" In spite of Patrick's rudeness, she was fascinated. Emma had never been on a date before.

"A twenty-first birthday party," Patrick said. "What's your answer?"

Emma looked at him, shrugged her shoulders, and said, "I'll have to ask my mother." She heard his laughter as she walked away.

"Have to ask your mother," he mocked, shouting to her retreating frame. "You do that, Miss High and Mighty. Ask your mother!"

After much debate, her parents decided she could go to the party. They knew the boy who was having the birthday, and as long as Emma was home by midnight, they wouldn't worry. Patrick was waiting for her the next day outside the dental surgery, and Emma gave him the answer he was hoping for. Now he could tell Jimmy Jones he had won the bet. Emma the Icicle was going out with him, and the ten pounds were his.

Paddy gave Emma strict warnings about the dangers of alcohol and monitored the parties Patrick took her to. Emma told him that Patrick had proposed to her on their first date, and he laughed it off with the words "Fiddle-faddle."

He hoped she would eventually tire of the impertinent young man and seek out the company of other men. But to Emma, Patrick seemed "brilliantly informed about all subjects." He had an answer for everything, and he could be exceedingly romantic when he felt in the mood. He often charmed Emma with witty words and bravado, and as he was twenty-one and she was barely seventeen, Patrick seemed worldly and mature.

"I love you and want to look after you," he told her continually, and she began to believe him. They had been going out for approximately six months when the passenger door on Patrick's pickup truck suddenly stopped opening.

"It's jammed," he told Emma as she crawled across from the driver's seat to the passenger side. "I'll fix it later." They were on their way to a local ball, and Emma, who loved to dance, was very excited. All night long she whirled and twirled, while Patrick brought her lime drinks to quench her thirst. Suddenly she felt very strange. Her head felt giddy, and her knees kept buckling.

"I'd better take you home," said Patrick as he pushed her up into the car.

Emma crawled over to the passenger seat and then promptly fell asleep. When she awoke, she was being dragged out of the truck at Patrick's house.

"Why am I here?" she asked groggily, her eyes finding it difficult to focus.

Patrick ignored her question and carried her toward the front door.

"My mother's away for three weeks," he told her. "We've got the whole place to ourselves."

Patrick dumped Emma on the couch. She was aware of him tearing at her clothes as she drifted in and out of consciousness. Then he climbed on top of her and told her not to resist him. Emma was in a stupor. She couldn't think straight, and her head was throbbing. She let out a cry of pain when he entered her and then started to cry hysterically.

"Don't be so half-witted," he said, rolling off her to the floor. "What did you think was happening?"

Emma was crying. "I feel so awful…"

Patrick suddenly became nervous and laughed at her confused state. "You're drunk, you idiot!"

Emma didn't understand. "But I don't drink; I'm not allowed to…"

"You are so foolish," he crowed. "I gave you something to relax you in your lime juice."

Emma cringed with remorse and guilt. "What will I tell my parents?" she thought, struggling to come to grips with her situation and trying to stand up. She had trusted Patrick, and in turn, he had used her.

After they were married, my parents lived with Grandma O'Leary in her old weatherboard house, called the Muse. Grandma O'Leary tried to be considerate to the young couple, but her strict upbringing and former de facto relationship had left her emotionally scarred. To my mother, she seemed an unnaturally cold person, and her strict and unrelenting attitude to housework bordered on obsession. Emma's pregnant and ballooning figure made it difficult for her to walk. She longed for the days when Grandma would leave to visit her grown children or get housekeeping jobs that took her out of town. At these times, she felt more relaxed.

Emma finished her studies as a dental assistant, and on the night of her graduation, she gave birth to my brother, Michael. The new baby kept her busy, and she dedicated herself to home duties. Grandma kept a boarder, and it was Emma's job to cook his meals. She also had to tend to the goats, the chickens, and the vegetable garden. She missed her mother, but Patrick had limited her visits to her family to once a week. It occurred to Emma that while Patrick saw his mother every day, she was seeing her family less and less.

"Why don't you grow up?" he would say to her mockingly. "I'm your life now, not your bloody mother."

When Great-Grandmother Amy died, my parents moved into her house. Then, after a couple of months passed, Mumma, Grandfather, and Mum's four younger siblings also moved in. Mum helped with her brothers and sisters and took care of my brother and me. Her brother, Benjamin, was two and a half, and Michael was eighteen months old. The boys were always together.

"It's as though they're joined at the hip," Paddy would say, and everyone would laugh.

Paddy never fought with Mumma, and Emma secretly wished her marriage could be like her parents'. But Patrick thrived on arguments and sarcasm. He would insinuate that Emma was a failure; then he'd try to make things up to her by being witty and funny. In the past, Emma had never felt clumsy or stupid, and now, her feelings of inadequacy were on the way to becoming an everyday occurrence.

Soon after I was born, my mother became pregnant again. When she told my father, he became very agitated.

"You'll have to do something," he shouted.

"What can I do?" she asked lamely.

"This!" shouted Dad as he punched her in the stomach. Patrick didn't like babies. In his eyes, they required too much attention. They were small, weak, insipid creatures who did little else but cry and sleep. Emma was well aware of her lot in life, as she was constantly reminded of it.

"Look after the children. They should be seen and not heard," Grandma O'Leary told her. "It's your job to clean and keep your husband happy." The lectures were always forthcoming, but no one offered to help with the chores.

"That's women's work," Dad would shout angrily if a job wasn't completed. "You're such a lousy housekeeper."

The last thing Patrick wanted was another baby. A third child would be another burden, and he already resented the division of my mother's time among him, Michael, and me. As my mother doubled over in pain, my father waited for his horrific action to bring about the desired result. However, Emma didn't miscarry. Instead, she carried the baby to full term.

During the pregnancy, Dad decided it was time they built their own house, and he set about borrowing some money from the banks. Each bank refused the loan application and sent my parents away, their hopes dashed because they had no money and no credit rating. Soon after, Mum heard about a new style of bank called a credit union. She immediately applied to borrow £6,500 so they could purchase some cheap land and start to build a house of their own. The credit union accepted her application, and with the money they bought five acres of bushland.

Wild fauna and birds were abundant, and kilometers of untamed bush rambled over gullies and gorges. There were no shopping facilities, and the land was virtually uninhabited, except for the occasional hobo and a few uneducated families in shacks. There were no tarred access roads, and water and electricity had yet to be connected. Dad decided to build the house of weatherboard because it was all he could afford. He decided to build three rooms first—two bedrooms and a bathroom/kitchen area with a hallway to join them together.

Our family stayed at my grandparents' house until the new one was ready. On May 5, 1961, my mother went into labor with her third child. She was milking the goats when the contractions started, and she knew subconsciously that something was wrong. She called to my father to come and help her.

"I have to go to the hospital." Unable to stand, she was kneeling and clutching her stomach in the throes of labor.

"I can't take you yet," replied my father as he helped her up and kissed her. "I've got other things to do."

"But you have to...I..."

My mother tried to push him away, but he was too strong for her. "Go away," she shouted as he kept trying to kiss her.

Another contraction came and knocked her to the ground.

"Later," my father said, unbuckling his pants. "I said I've got other things to do."

My mother's pain during her third labor far outweighed her humiliating rape. She prayed for him to finish so she could get to the hospital, his act of violence upon her and her unborn child stamped deep into her heart. Afterward, as she lay in the hospital, she heard my father's voice.

"Please don't let him in here," she begged the nurse. Severe complications had left her heavily drugged, physically exhausted, and semiconscious. The voice continued shouting in the hospital corridor.

"I want to see my son." Dad's voice got louder, and the sister in charge became agitated.

"You'll have to keep your voice down, sir. This is a hospital."

But he wouldn't listen. "Go to hell," he slurred drunkenly, and Emma heard the sounds of a scuffle. After a lot of swearing and shouting, security was called. Then the police escorted my father out of the hospital. He was under strict instructions that he was not to visit my mother until she was ready to return home with her new baby, Liam.

CHAPTER 3

1961

When my mother came home from the hospital, we moved out into the crown land bush. Mum insisted that Dad build a wire enclosure the length of the house for us to play in. She feared we'd wander off into the bush because we were all so young. The wire enclosure was a lot bigger and safer than a playpen because it was fixed to the ground. I was quite content to sit inside it and fill old talcum-powder tins with sand while Michael built roads. As there wasn't any money for toys, we played with rocks, sand, water, and old pieces of wood and dirt. Natural materials became our toys.

As we grew older, my brothers and I climbed trees and ran barefoot through the bush collecting wildflowers and rocks in the scrub. We mixed flour and water to make glue and spent hours making bizarre bush landscapes out of paperbark, butcher paper, and Masonite. Our learning was experimental, tactile, and fun, and it gave us a sense of skill and practical achievement, as tiny hands could make many wonderful and exciting creations. When we first moved in, the house only had three rooms; it was virtually an empty shell. The floorboards were bare, and the walls weren't insulated or even lined. This made the building excessively hot in summer and cold in winter. My parents slept in the front bedroom, and we kids all shared the second bedroom. We put up a thin partition of Masonite to separate the two areas. My parents didn't have the money to buy a utility pole to connect the power to the house, so for the first three months, Mum cooked dinner outside on an open fire and lit candles at night so we could see.

As Liam was a newborn, Mumma gave Mum the present of a six-month nappy service because she didn't have enough water to wash his nappies in. We had a five-hundred-gallon rainwater tank, which allowed us to cope in winter, but in summer, supplies were always rationed. In the hot months, bushfires raged through the national parks, and water was our only form of protection. Once, when I was four years old, we had to buy extra supplies of water. A man came to the house with forty-four large drums of water and siphoned it through hoses into our tank. Later, when I was older, my parents bought a two-thousand-gallon water tank, but supplies in summer still managed to dwindle away in the sweltering heat.

We conserved all water. My mother was always on the lookout for rain, as this was her signal to wash a pile of clothes. It was important to hang the washing out in time for the rain to rinse the soapsuds off the clothes; then they would dry soft and wouldn't feel stiff like cardboard when we wore them. At first, we had only cold water, and washing clothes was both tedious and exhausting. We all bathed in the old washing tub, and afterward, Mum would hand-wash all the clothes in the bathwater and feed them through an old-fashioned wringer. We then scooped up the soapy, leftover water in buckets and poured it over any plants that managed to survive in the summer heat.

My family strung the clothesline between two gum trees and put a forked pole in the middle to stop it sagging. Sometimes when a wind blew up, the clothesline would collapse, and the clothes would become all muddy and caked with dirt. When I was four, Mumma surprised Mum with a Hills Hoist for Christmas. When you stepped out the back door, there it stood. It seemed eternally filled with washing, especially nappies. Mum would stand outside with a pump hose to wash them down on the clothesline because it was a lot easier than the tub. We were told never to swing on the clothesline because it was "a precious gift" and "as good as gold," but, like all children, we thought swinging on the clothesline was one of life's secret pleasures.

The toilet was an old bush dunny in the backyard. A wrought-iron lean-to was assembled around a can with a seat on it. Spiders and maggots often hid within it, and it smelled of kerosene, phenol, and rotting excrement. When the waste became unbearable, Dad would take it down into the bush and bury it. I hated the toilet. Maggots and blowflies congregated inside it, and the rotting fumes were overpowering in summer.

The kitchen, which doubled as the bathroom, had plastic blue curtains hung across wooden shelving on bricks to simulate cupboards. These glamorous curtains were made from old cement bags and sandbags that my father had used when building the house's foundations. Crooked pieces of laminate had been glued on the tops of these shelves to resemble makeshift cupboard benches. A white, scratched bath stood on the other side of the kitchen, but it wasn't plumbed in. It had a piece of plastic hung up in front of it as a curtain for privacy. My father's shaving mirror hung on a nail on the wall, and except for an old calendar, that was the kitchen's only decoration.

On May 2, 1962, my youngest brother, Jamie, was born. Soon afterward, my mother borrowed a further £6,000 to finish the house. This meant the walls could be lined and a living room with a separate kitchen area could be added. My father decided to build the extensions himself. This proved to be a long and burdensome task, one that took over twelve years to complete. One wall in our bedroom was lined with Masonite, and Mum decorated it with wallpaper. It had pictures of Popeye and Olive Oyl set on a bright-pink background, and it made the room much more cheerful. The wallpaper gave Jamie something to look at from his cot. Sometimes he'd press his face up to the wall and dribble all over the characters, kissing them and muttering in baby talk. This resulted in the paper peeling off in odd patches.

Going to bed was a feat in itself. The room was tiny, and we ended up pushing all the beds together. Jamie would bang on the sides of his cot with his bottle, and the rest of us would scramble over three single beds. Liam, who was two, slept on a camp bed, and if anyone accidentally walked on the middle of it, the bed would snap up and collapse in a heap on the floor.

Our backyard comprised five acres of bushland, but this seemed to continue on and on, as the area behind our lot was crown land and national park. My parents cleared the foliage around the house because of the ever-present bushfire danger. They built a goat shed, a feed shed, and a chicken coop. Our house stood on a rock platform with a sandstone belt running under the ground toward the back left area of the yard. This meant that for about half an acre, only thin, wiry grass would grow, meters high and burned yellow from the heat.

One of my greatest fears was sprinting through this grass to the tree house at the bottom of the yard. It was a haven for sun-baking reptiles. Female brown and black snakes laid their eggs in the "snake grass," and when it was hot, writhing nests of serpents hatched and made their home in the grass until they were old enough to slither off into the bush.

The heat of summer was upon us. The bush smelled dry and heavy with the scent of wildflowers. My mother hung the washing out and hummed to herself. We were happily playing cars in the sand, and Jamie was asleep in his pram. Blowflies buzzed past our heads, and dragonflies dive-bombed over the snake grass.

"I'll have to cut that soon," Mum thought out loud. "The weather is too dry, and it's a fire risk." She stepped back toward the washing basket and heard a movement behind her. Worried, she scanned the area but couldn't see anything. As she reached into the basket, she heard the noise again—a rustling sound and the cracking of dry, bladed grass. When she saw where the sound was coming from, her hands froze in midair.

"Michael, Shannon, and Liam," she called, and we looked up from where we were playing. "I want you to go inside the house."

"Why, Mummy?" Michael complained. "I'm playing police."

"Do as you're told." Mum raised her voice, and we knew she was serious. We quickly grabbed our toys and ran toward the house. When we were safely indoors, my mother turned and faced the red-bellied black snake. It was huge. My mother stared it in the eyes, took three steps backward, and willed it not to follow her. Her fear of snakes compelled her to run, but she resisted.

"Be calm," she told herself. "Don't do anything stupid." My mother knew very little about snakes, but she realized that black and brown snakes were extremely dangerous. A sigh of relief escaped her lips as she shut the back door behind her. Three little upturned faces greeted her, and Michael demanded to know what was going on.

"There's a giant black snake outside, and we'll have to wait till it goes back to the bush before we can go outside."

"What about Jamie?"

Mum gave a cry of dismay. Out under the washing line was the pram with the sleeping baby in it. Mum sprinted across the backyard and scooped the child up in her arms just as the snake slid toward the pram. With her heart pounding, she made it through the back door just in time to see the serpent coil itself around the pram wheels over the undercarriage.

Suddenly, we heard a loud squawking. With a flap and a hop, our great black rooster, Cuthbert, made his way toward the offending reptile. Feathers flying, he pecked wildly, his rattling coxcomb filled with anger at the snake's intrusion. The giant snake reared up and tried to strike, but Cuthbert was too fast. He pecked at it and ran off, his spindly chicken legs striding rapidly while the snake pursued.

"Watch out, Cuthbert; he's about to strike again," we called, but it was too late. Recoiling like a spring and pitching toward the rooster, the snake narrowly missed and received a claw on the back of his head. Two beautiful, black wings spread and lifted Cuthbert into the air, and we all gave a sigh of relief. Up on the chook yard roof and safe from the venomous biting creature, Cuthbert crowed, feathers ruffled in proud bravado. The snake was beaten. Reptile skin glistening, it slithered to the snake grass and back into the bush.

Mum didn't finish hanging the washing that day. She left it out in the basket to dry. Although common sense told her the snake wasn't really interested in causing a major catastrophe, the experience had shaken her.

"Thank God for Cuthbert," she said, and upon reflection she added, "We can learn a lesson from that rooster. Snakes don't like noise or chickens. From now on I want you all to carry a big stick when you walk through the bush."

"Why?" we all chorused.

"Bang the stick on the ground, and the snakes will feel the vibrations through the ground. This way, they'll know you are coming and run away." It sounded like the perfect solution. We were all scared of snakes, and none of us felt like reenacting Jamie and Cuthbert's adventure. My mother taught us how to make a tourniquet by ripping up an old shirt.

"You wrap it around very tightly and keep the limb still," she said. "Then get someone to run for help."

But we didn't want to think about being bitten by snakes, realizing the best way to solve the problem was to keep well away from them.

When my father came home from work, Michael would run to meet him. Sometimes Dad would throw him, screaming with laughter, up in the air and catch him, tickling him like a puppy. It looked like fun, and one time I thought I'd try it too.

"Daddy!" I called as I ran toward him, just as Michael had. There was tickling and laughing, but I felt a bit frightened. He was throwing me too high. Michael never went this high. Up and down, up and down.

"Put me down, Daddy," I cried.

Up into the air, higher and higher until…

As I came down, I saw his hands were by his sides. The floor jumped up to greet me with a whack. I lay there, stunned, wailing, and aching, while he laughed. "Stupid girl!"

After this experience, I decided I didn't like Michael's game, and I never asked my father to play it again.

During November 1963, I became ill. I was heavy with all the symptoms of the flu, and my temperature soared at an alarmingly high rate. Mum ran to the neighbor's house to see if someone could drive me to the doctor. By the time I got into town, the pleurisy and pneumonia were well advanced, and I was near death. The doctor immediately ordered x-rays.

"These are to keep you still," the radiographer explained as she placed some large blocks beside me. I didn't dare move, as the metal x-ray unit looked big enough to crush me.

There was no one to look after my younger brothers, so my mother called my grandfather and asked him to drive me to Camperdown Children's Hospital. My head ached from the temperature, and I was too dizzy to stand. When I arrived at the hospital, a trolley bed was waiting at emergency, and I was taken straight into a ward and transferred into a cot.

"I'm too big for a cot," I told the doctor feebly, but my grandfather convinced me it was for the best.

"It's just for a while," he said.

Hospital life was lonely. My mother visited me every day, but the austere appearance of the nurses and the loud, clanking sounds in the middle of the night frightened me. Echoing laughter filled the wards in the early morning hours, and sometimes the nursing staff and doctors would panic, racing into the ward and pulling the curtains around the bed of the little boy next to me.

My hospital sojourn seemed to last an eternity, and to make the time go faster, I began to count. I counted the sickly yellow tiles on the bathroom wall; I counted the medicine bottles on the nurse's trolley; I counted the beds in the wards, the nurses, the patients, and so on, until everyone told me to "shut up and stop counting." When I was released, it was three weeks until Christmas and four weeks until my third birthday.

After I settled back in at home, two-year-old Liam became ill. He kept complaining about a tummy ache, so Mum put him in her bed to rest. An hour went by, and she asked me to check if he was awake. I went into the bedroom and was amazed at what I saw. My brother's fingernails were glowing in the dark.

"Mummy," I called, "Liam's got shining lights in his nails."

"Oh my God," she gasped, and she immediately sent me to fetch Mrs. Peters, the neighbor. Mrs. Peters lived farther down the road and owned a car. She listened to my garbled message and came to my brother's rescue. As soon as she saw the sick toddler, she offered to drive us into town. Within the hour Liam was in the hospital having his stomach pumped. The verdict was unanimous. The boy was poisoned, but the doctors were baffled by the fact that they had found no residue in the child's stomach. Hornsby Hospital called the police, and officers went to search family property.[xv] They confiscated all items that could result in poisoning.

My mother was distraught. Her little boy was dying in the hospital, and she was being treated as a criminal. My father was nowhere to be found, so Mumma and Grandfather took us to their house and looked after us while Mum stayed at the hospital with Liam. Meanwhile, the police tried to contact my father. Liam became weaker and weaker, slipping in and out of consciousness while the puzzled doctors searched for answers. They tried antidote after antidote until finally one seemed to activate a positive response in the boy. The police went to the house to search the feed shed and came across a new brand of flea powder for cats. At that time, there was a flea plague, and Mum remembered she had used the powder on the cats on the same morning that Liam had taken ill. The police immediately sent the flea powder for tests, and the results indicated phosphorus poisoning. This was the information the doctors needed to save my brother. The clinical evidence showed that Liam had not swallowed the powder, and everyone wondered how he had absorbed the poison.

"Maybe it was through his wrists," the doctors argued, but their words were inconclusive, and my brother's poisoning remained a mystery.

My father had left for work at approximately nine o'clock that morning, soon after my mother treated the cats with the powder. During the poisoning crisis, no one could locate him; it was as though he had disappeared. At six the following evening, the police finally found him drinking at a local pub. They brought him to the hospital where Mum was waiting with all of us, and we were all told to go home and hope for a full recovery. The doctor's main concern was that Liam could sustain neurological damage, which might present as a nervous disorder later in life.

"Poison affects the central nervous system," the doctors explained to my mother. "You will have to monitor this child's health very closely for the next few years."

CHAPTER 4

1964

From the age of fifteen, my mother had been a registered animal breeder, so goats, kittens, and puppies played a very important role in our life. Animals were a great source of fun to us, but they were also revenue. Money wasn't plentiful, as Dad's work wasn't consistent, and he liked to drink and play the pokies.[xvi] He didn't want my mother to work, but she had four hungry mouths to feed. She took a job selling party-plan Tupperware in the hope that she could either sell from home or get other interested parties to encourage friends to buy from her.[xvii] My father tried to stop the venture by refusing to lend her the car, but somehow she persevered. She made very little money, but when she combined it with the cash she made from selling goat's milk and breeding kittens, she managed to keep food on the table. For years our diet consisted of potatoes and different combinations of mince. We ate shepherd's pie, mince on toast, peas and mince, or just plain old mince and potatoes in a bowl. Occasionally, we'd have sausages, and when this occurred, it felt like Christmas.

Every animal we owned had a name and personality. Sunshine Fresco was our first goat. She came from a great line of prizewinning Saanen goats.[xviii] Sunshine's mother belonged to a family in Turramurra and eventually became the Australian champion dairy goat five times in a row. With the help of Auntie Marge's bucks, we bred kids every year. By the time I was five, our little herd consisted of Rissole, the buck; Binki, the one-year-old; Kisty, the young doe and excellent milker; and two little twin kids called Samson and

Sally. My mother talked to the goats as if they were children. Whenever she would tend to them, she'd give a running commentary on what she was doing. She would clarify why she was giving the goats one kind of feed and the chickens the other or why she had to clip Rissole's hooves. She would tell me which animals needed special attention and explain how she would treat them if they became ill. Like many people on the land, Mum had the skills of a bush vet, self-trained and brilliant in the areas of natural therapies and emergency animal care. She had bottles of medicines, potions, and poultices because she was a breeder, and medical supplies were freely available for the animals.

Each morning, at the crack of dawn, we would awaken to the rooster's crow. My baby brothers would demand their breakfast, and then the goats had to be milked. Sometimes if a rooster was old, Dad would kill it for dinner by chopping off its head. He assured my mother that he would kill the chickens quickly, and it was Mum's job to do the rest. She would pluck and dress the chicken, feeling sick and unhappy, preparing it for dinner. On these occasions she didn't eat. I didn't eat either; the thought of the live chicken was always too fresh in my mind.

As children, we never went anywhere without dogs trailing behind us. They were protective and intelligent Labradors that sensed our youthful exuberance. To this day, I cannot remember falling down a crevice or over a rock without looking up into the big brown eyes of a barking canine.

My mother's day was filled with chores. She was a tiny woman with an athletic build due to all the laboring she did around the property. She always seemed to be carrying buckets, and, needless to say, she had great biceps. There were buckets for milking, buckets of feed, buckets of water to be poured in the old bath used as a drinking trough, and buckets for washing clothes.

Sometimes we'd go on bushwalks with my mother, and the goats would walk unleashed through the bush with us. When these walks occurred, I was in seventh heaven because I identified this behavior with my favorite book, *Heidi*.[xix] Michael usually led the way, and the dogs, Conrad and Sheba, followed him. They would bark at snakes and blue-tongued lizards along the way, and Mum would walk at the rear with my little brothers. We all carried sticks, even baby Jamie. His experience with the black snake near his pram had left a lasting impression on us all. On our walks, Mum would stop and collect dried wildflowers and seedpods.

"We can make pictures and wall hangings out of them."

We would stuff our pockets with pebbles, leaves, and other special treasures we'd find in the bush. With my mother, everything was a learning experience. She encouraged us to behave like children, reining us in like bedraggled puppies when we needed to be reprimanded and playing with us when she had the time. Mum encouraged us to get our hands dirty and taught us to respect nature. When she walked through the bush with us, it was similar to being on a science field excursion because she would tell us the names of different plants and fauna. The goats would hop from rock to rock, and we would imitate them.

"If you learn to climb like the goats," Mum would tell us, "you'll never fall or hurt yourself. See how they test the rock before they step on it? That stops them from falling off. Goats hop from rock to rock because the surface is safer than the ground. Have a careful look, and you'll see the rocks are smoother than the old bush track."

We all felt the rocks with our hands.

"If you tread in a pothole, you can twist your ankle and be stranded. So if you can, always walk along the rock formations." And that was what we did. We traveled along the ridges and around the gullies, exploring and naming rock formations as we went. We made Berowra National Park our endless backyard.

Often, I would watch as Rissole, the father of the goat herd, jumped down the cliff face with ease. To me, he seemed enormous, his long shaggy coat resembling those of the mountain goats in Peru. Rissole had an off-white coat and two giant, curled horns that were gnarled and notched in a half circle. Like most male goats, he smelled musky and rank, so my mother would wash him with dog shampoo. After his bath, she'd rub citronella between his horns so that he would smell like lemons. Once she had done this, Rissole was a pleasure to be around. We would quickly hurry to the feed shed and take out an old oat sack to use for a saddle. When we attached rope to his horns, he became the ultimate pony replacement. He would never gallop but only gently walk up and down with all of us on his back. Mum would sometimes pretend she was a bullfighter and charge at him, using her hands as make-believe horns. When she did this, Rissole would rear up into the air on his hind legs and charge toward her. It was quite frightening to watch when both of them charged hell-bent toward each other, set on a major collision path. How they both knew exactly when to stop no one knew; inches away from each other, they would suddenly come to a halt. Then Mum would throw back her head and laugh and give Rissole a big hug. It was an amazing show of animal trust.

When I was five, Taronga Zoo[xx] asked if they could adopt Rissole to sire goats for their mountain goat display. We were sad to see him leave, but Mum said it was for the best.

"He'll have a large enclosure and lots of girlfriends," she told us. But things weren't the same without our evening ride. We all vowed to visit him, but the wait seemed like an eternity. Finally, we all made the trip to the zoo.

When we spotted Rissole, he was a sight to behold. The old goat had never looked happier! We all called out to him, and he tossed his head in recognition. Then he clambered high up onto the rock shelf. Higher and higher Rissole climbed, until he was perched up on the tallest peak of rock.

"What's he doing, Mum?" Michael asked.

"He's showing us he's happy," Mum answered.

Then, as if to validate what she had said, Rissole called to six little female goats to come and join him. He was the king of his castle, a scrambling, hiking emperor with his magnificent doe harem.

My brother Michael was four and a half when he started school. Our area didn't have a bus service, so Mum drove him to a Catholic school in the Lower North Shore. Sometimes, Dad would refuse to lend Mum the car, and we would have to walk to the bus stop. It was two miles away, and to our little legs, the walk seemed like an Olympic marathon. Mum petitioned the local council to get a bus stop at the end of the road, and the council agreed. They let the bus travel to an old tin lean-to that doubled as a bus stop half a mile away from our house, and Michael began traveling to school by himself.

He was a receptive student, but he was very shy and reserved with strangers. People often commented that he "takes life too seriously" and that he was "very intelligent." While other children filled their lives with comics and water bombs, his interest lay in road maps. He also had a passion for road-building. After exploring the gullies and creek beds down in the gorge, he'd spend hours in the bush making tracks with an old miniature shovel.

Michael could be the worst tormenter in the world, but when he started school, I missed his company. My mother came to the rescue when she decided to teach me to read. Soon I was completing home readers, performing writing exercises, and, of course, drawing pictures. When Michael did his homework, I was encouraged to join in his learning activities. By the time I was three, my vocabulary and reading skills were advanced for my age. When she had time, Mum would volunteer her services at Michael's school teaching remedial students, and through watching her teach, I inherited her love of books.

It was a beautiful day. I didn't like visiting my paternal grandmother's house, but my father insisted I go with him and wait while he worked on some plumbing for his mother. Grandma O'Leary was a wiry little woman with a strong Somerset accent, a proud woman who rarely hugged us or smiled. She wore tiny glasses and reminded me of the witch from "Hansel and Gretel."[xxi] Sometimes if we were good, she'd offer us a Milk Arrowroot biscuit with pink icing. She always allowed Liam to take two biscuits because he was her favorite.

On this particular day, Grandma O'Leary wasn't in her house; in fact, no one was home. My grandmother kept lots of toys in a cupboard at the back of the house, and occasionally, if we were good, she would allow us to play with them. When we were older, these toys became the childish object of morbid fascination. We were told they had belonged to Dad's older brother Martin, who had died from meningitis when he was fifteen.

My favorite toy was an old wooden duck that had big green wheels; it trundled along when I pulled the frayed red string. I pushed and pulled it around the house until I finally ended up in the bathroom. The duck moved easily over the antiquated yellow tiles, rolling past the bath and behind the wood-chip heater. I squeezed myself under the green bath and felt around its huge enameled feet. The duck wasn't there, so I stretched out my arms to find my toy. It was lodged underneath the heater, so I crept forward on my stomach like a caterpillar, inching myself even farther under the bath.

While I was lying there, two big black boots walked past me. The boots had large treads like those on tires.

"They're tractor boots," I thought.

The boots traveled to the opposite side of the room, where the vanity basin and mirror were. I heard the sound of running water and wanted to see what was going on. There, in front of the mirror, was a grotesque figure. It was a large, curtain-clad frame topped with a curly gray wig. I didn't understand what I was seeing. I recognized the gold watch and the boots, but the face in the mirror, smeared with bright-pink lipstick, frightened me. The figure leaned forward and examined the face in the mirror. Smiling, it liked what it saw. Then as quickly as it had smiled, the face grimaced. A hand opened the medicine cabinet and pulled out a shaving mug and razor. After soaping the brush, the figure began to shave. The shaving soap caused the lipstick to bleed, and this created a pink foam effect. The figure really looked like a bizarre type of clown, and I began to laugh. The reaction was immediate. Down came a hand, pulling me from my hiding place. The laughter froze in my throat as I was heaved upward, toward the menacing face.

"Don't you tell anyone," the figure growled. "If you do, I'll cut you with my razor."

I felt the razor, a hair's breadth away from my face. My bottom lip trembled as I dropped to the floor. Then, sweeping out of the room like a grandiose diva, the figure retreated into another part of the house.

Water frightened me. I had seen baby chickens floating on top of the water buckets in the goat shed, their lifeless frames no longer fluffy and chirpy.

"They must have been thirsty. It's been so hot." My mother looked sad as she scooped them out of the water, wondering how such tiny creatures could make the giant leap, so high, up into the bucket.

Sometimes, after he had consumed several pints of beer, my father's voice would ring out, and everyone would jump to attention.

"Hurry up! We're going on a picnic!" Dad would demand that everyone pile into the truck, Mum in the front and the children in the tray. Then he'd drive fanatically into the bush. The road down to the bottom of the gorge was like a winding goat track. Unsealed and unevenly dotted with sandstone rocks that had fallen from the top of the gorge, it was unsafe after rain and always treacherous. The shire council had said that they would improve the road when more residents moved to the area, but for the time being, they saw it only as an access into the gully. The overgrown fire track was much too dangerous to drive on, and the council and fire brigade often would put up large red signs that read Danger! or Beware of Falling Rocks. However, these warning signs never deterred my father.

"What a load of rubbish," he'd shout at the signs as we went past. "They've got rocks in their head."

Faster and faster we'd speed, the Toyota's wheels spinning and the dust flying on the old bush track. We could hear my mother screaming for him to stop, but this only made him speed more. We'd all bump from side to side in the back while he slammed on his brakes to miss boulders or avoid sliding over the gully's edge. Holding on in the back of the truck was a real effort because there weren't any seats. We would bounce up and down on the tailgate bed, our little fingers clinging to the sides. We all knew that if the truck jerked in the wrong direction, we could fly off onto the track and be hurt.

Sometimes large rocks lay in the middle of the track, and Dad couldn't drive past them. On these occasions, he ordered everyone out of the truck and told us to move them. Our little hands would push and heave until the rocks loosened, and then we'd try to roll them away.

"Hurry up!" he'd shout, and we would claw our way over the backboard and back into the truck.

Mum hated the "picnic game," but Dad forced her to play along. On these occasions we never really had a picnic. There was never any food, just Dad, Mum, the truck, and four kids. We would travel downward, round and round, until we reached the river at the gorge's base. On hot days, Dad would give Michael and me swimming lessons. This meant he would throw us in the water, clothes and all, and watch us flounder. We would gasp for breath and swallow large mouthfuls of water. I was terrified of drowning. Once, too tired to continue struggling, I gave in to the river and went under. I opened my eyes and couldn't see the bottom, just murky-green water stinging my eyes. A hand came down and pulled me out, and I was thrown out onto the bank, gulping, breathless, and shocked.

"You are such a stupid girl," my father said with disgust. "Stupid and ugly."

On subsequent picnics, I'd run off with my brothers before my father could catch me. I'd pretend I couldn't hear him calling and go in search of jellyfish. Then Dad would get tired of calling me and go off with his rifle. Every now and then, I'd hear him taking potshots at wildlife and cursing if he missed. After he finished shooting, he'd scream at everyone to get back into the truck, and then he'd start the engine and drive off. We would all run after him, clambering over the truck's backboard and bracing ourselves for the long haul home.

One night, after we had eaten our dinner and prepared for bed, my father came home very excited. His eyes dashed around wildly as he grappled with words that seemed to fall too quickly from his mouth.

"I'm going out tonight," he told us.

"Where?"

"I'm going to catch a black snake that's been stealing chickens. Twenty of us are going. It will be like a posse! We're going to shoot it." In awe, we watched as my father gulped down his dinner, spilling it on his shirt and trousers. He swung out of his seat and left the room. Soon after, he returned with his rifle.

"A-hunting I will go, a-hunting I will go; I'll catch a fox and put him in a box and never let him go."

Dad laughed.

"Be careful," Mum said quietly, looking at the ground.

He turned to leave and shouted, "I'll be fine, but the snake won't be. I'm going to blow it to smithereens."

There was an awkward silence. It was always uncomfortable when he swung into one of his moods. We didn't like the rifle or how easily he could fire it. He loved to walk through the bush with it because it was his "right-hand man." We listened to the truck drive off, and my mother dismissed the issue with a change of subject.

"OK, kids, it's off to bed."

As I crawled underneath the covers, I gave a shiver. The wind had died down, and an eerie silence filled the bush. Whirlpooling questions raced in my mind.

"What if the gun backfires? What about the snake? Why do you need twenty people to catch one reptile? How will they know which snake it is when there are thousands out there in the bush?"

Suddenly, I heard a blood-curdling shout. It traveled through the bush and night from somewhere nearby.

"What the…" The male voice screamed and then stopped when the shot rang out. Thinking someone had been hurt, I sat up in bed, listening in the dark. Four gunshots followed, and then the bush was silent. I lay down again and pulled the bedcovers over my head. Then I put my fingers in my ears and tried to rock myself to sleep underneath the blankets.

When a southerly wind was blowing, the sound of gunfire could travel across the gorge. There was a rifle range about twenty miles away, on the other side of the ravine, and the sound of the hail of bullets could whip through the gullies like a carpet snake, weaving through the hollows until it finally reached our side of the gorge. The gunfire from the range would repeat, and we never heard it at night. We only heard it occasionally, on weekends and in the daylight. I never found out what happened that night, but I knew instinctively something was very wrong. The sound of gunfire had not come from the rifle range—it was too close for that—and I had heard voices before the silence. The panicked scream of someone taken by surprise and the rifle shots that followed still live with me today, making my heart stop and pound in my dreams.

My father's obsession with guns was both perplexing and unnerving. He had an old school suitcase filled with golden bullets of varying sizes hidden under the bed. We were told never to touch it, but occasionally Michael would drag it out as if it were forbidden treasure and look at it.

Sometimes Dad would tell us he was going hunting. He was worried about spies and Nazis, and he swore he'd make the world right. He'd then storm off into the bush taking random shots at invisible enemies until he'd tire of his game, come home again, and drink himself senseless.

Binki was screaming. I lay down on the bed, stuffing my fingers in my ears, but even the pillow couldn't muffle the sounds. The loud, guttural bellowing of an animal convulsed in pain cannoned in my eardrums.

"Oh dear, what can the matter be? Oh dear, what can the matter be? Oh dear, what can the matter be? Johnny's so long at the fair."

My words came between anguished sobs, marred by the goat's hysterical bleating. I heard my mother screaming, and more shots rang out.

"One—two—three—four—five." Five gunshots, and then everything seemed still. But the bush is never still!

I tried to concentrate on the noisy cicadas, but I could hear my mother sobbing and screaming, "You didn't have to do it like that. She died in agony."

Like most children, I played make-believe. I'd pretend I was a princess with long blond hair and walk around all day with a towel draped over my head. Sometimes I made up imaginary characters, and they joined in my games. Once I made up an imaginary friend.

"It is a six-foot-high green tree frog," I told my mother, not knowing how high that was but thinking it sounded impressive.

"What's his name?" Mum asked.

"He doesn't have one," I said. "He only knows me, so he doesn't need anyone else to call him."

My mother didn't have time to question me more. She needed to go shopping, so we all piled into the car, making sure my imaginary friend had a seat. The pretend game was fun, but I forgot it when the more serious task of shopping started. On the way home, I demanded that my mother go back to the shopping center.

"You've left my friend," I cried. Mum refused, and the battle began.

"Take me back," I yelled. "I want my friend frog."

After five minutes of hysterical wailing, my mother finally gave in. She turned the car around and drove all the way back to town. I stopped crying, and we retrieved my imaginary friend.

"This is never happening again," Mum muttered under her breath. "Tomorrow I will find you some *real* friends."

The next day, she tried to enroll me at the local Catholic school, but the nuns knew I was only three.

"But she can read," Mum argued with the principal.

"That makes no difference," she replied. "Besides, it wouldn't be fair to her brother."

The nun's answer didn't deter my mother. I was lonely, and Mum thought school would solve my problem. There was a public school up the road, and Mum wondered if she could get a place for me in the kindergarten class. Although I was three, my vocabulary skills were advanced. Mum told the school I was small for my age and filled in the enrollment form. In the age category she wrote that I was one year older. Luckily, no one asked to see my birth certificate. I took to learning like a duck to water. The patient kindergarten teacher encouraged children to learn at their own pace. My enthusiasm flourished, and Mum felt sure she had done the right thing by enrolling me.

She told my father, "When Christmas comes, I'll transfer her to the Catholic school so she can continue her education with her brother."

My ears immediately latched on to the word "Christmas." It was a time I anticipated with mixed emotions. Both fear and excitement presented themselves when I contemplated this holiday. An inward battle raged between the joys of Santa, the ritualistic visitations to church, and my father's relatives.

"Michael, please don't get up early," my mother would plead. "Santa will leave your stocking by your bed, and you can open it up straightaway." My mother's pleas never worked. At four in the morning, Michael would get up with his flashlight to see if Santa had come. He was so noisy Liam and Jamie would follow him. They'd creep out of the bedroom and into the lounge room, where the Christmas tree stood, carefully trying not to wake anyone. When the boys got to the tree, they would be confronted with an angry yell. It was as if my father were waiting for them. A belting always ensued.

Crying and howling, they'd run back to bed and lick their wounds. My father would then stamp through the house until he came to where I was hiding, under my bedcovers. I would then receive a belting like my brothers and spend Christmas morning confused and depressed. Every Christmas morning I'd recite the same prayer.

"Thank you, God, for dying and being born, so we could have Christmas Day." I'd say this childish prayer and then spend all day wondering if I was meant to cry on Christmas Day for penance.

Every year without fail, we each got a harmonica in our Christmas stocking. They were beautiful, all shiny and silver, wrapped up in tissue in a special box. The harmonicas were noisy but great to use as signals in the bush. On quiet days their sound carried across the gorge, right over to the other side. Once I received a doll, and I called her Maudie. She had bright-red cotton plaits with a smiling plastic face, and she wore a smart gingham dress over a straw body. I thought she was the most beautiful rag doll I'd ever seen.

My family divided Christmas Day between relatives. We spent the morning with Grandma O'Leary and the afternoon with my maternal grandparents. I loved Christmas afternoon at Mumma and Grandfather's house, as it was filled with fun. They had an enormous silver Christmas tree that touched the ceiling, and Grandfather let us eat chocolate Santas off the tree. Everyone sang carols, and Mumma cooked a traditional Christmas dinner. One year, Mum's youngest sister, Tara, received a beautiful metal cooking set from Grandfather and Mumma. She set it out beautifully in Benjamin's new Indian tent and demanded that no one touch it. Disappointed, I went off by myself to play with my new doll in the old green bathtub down in the bottom of the yard.

Suddenly I smelled smoke. Looking around, I saw smoke pouring out of the Indian tent. I dropped the doll immediately, clambered out of the bath, and screamed, "Fire!"

Inside the tent, a tiny campfire had been lit under the brand-new cooking set. A giant splash of water followed, and the flames went out. Rough hands grabbed and shook me while Tara screamed, "I told you not to touch it!"

Through the shaking, with chattering teeth, I tried to tell her I didn't do anything, but a resounding slap knocked me to the ground.

"Don't touch things that don't belong to you."

I looked up into my father's angry face. My tears continued, and an ugly whisper assailed my ears: "How would you like it if you were burned alive?"

Valentine's Day. Thursday, February 14, 1964.

The splash of kerosene was followed by a scream. The old man cowered when he saw the lighted match. He held his bottle close to him and tried to scramble backward. But there was nowhere to hide.

The tramp's back hit the rock face, and he fell to the ground, his screams muted by the engulfing flames.

The noise was deafening. It was four o'clock in the morning, and the crackling and hissing of burning bush had awakened us. Outside, the fire raged furiously, engulfing the treetops.[xxii] Only Liam remained asleep. Michael and I watched the firefighters from the bedroom window, while Jamie pointed a chubby finger at the red-and-gold flames and laughed. The bush burned with enormous ferocity, exploding eucalyptus gums and hopping from tree to tree. I looked at the six fire trucks parked strategically around the family home and wondered if the animals were safe. After assuring us that everything was under control, Mum worked tirelessly in the kitchen cooking rice custard and bread pudding for the exhausted firefighters.

As my father fought the fire with the other volunteers, he felt an overwhelming exhilaration. He hit the oat sacks on the ground with such force that sparks flew up, nearly blinding him.

"It's bigger than everyone," he shouted, but no one could hear him. He laughed when a gum tree exploded nearby, sending flares high up into the sky like firecrackers.

"You shall not be saved. You will atone for all your sins. I will burn you in the fire of hell, and you will suffer like all little sinners." The roaring bush drowned out the raving of the passionate madman as hysteria rose in his throat.

"It's an act of God," he proclaimed to the burning wildlife, "and it's purging this godforsaken earth."

Eventually Mother Nature quelled the fire. The wind changed and sent the fire leaping away from our house, and finally it rained. The newspaper reports read that there was a firebug on the loose, but the locals blamed an old tramp for spilling some kerosene on his campfire.[xxiii]

When the bushfire was extinguished, Michael was eager to inspect the damage, but we weren't allowed to play outside for a week.

"Just a little walk," he pleaded with Mum.

"You have to wait until it rains," she told him. "Otherwise the bush will melt your shoes. It's still smoldering." She was right.

When I sneaked outside and touched the blackened earth, the immense heat blistered my fingertips immediately. Pulling my hand back sharply, I saw the tendrils of white smoke rising from burned-out trees and wildlife. These were remnants of the fire's indiscriminate cruelty, a reminder of the savage night of firefighting. We waited impatiently until the weather broke. After the rain, we set out into the bush, armed with tiny shovels. To small children it was like a giant paint box, filled with charcoal and black bare rocks.

We drew everywhere, especially in caves. Some drawings denoted animals and cavemen, while others were carved with rock and then painted with clay from the creek bed. The fire had made new areas in the bush accessible to us, and we foraged through the debris, looking for hidden treasure. As we dug, we found bits of quartz and blue shale, red sandstone, and ochre yellow—rich earth colors for our creative artworks. We unleashed our imaginations and attempted to create our own prehistoric world, where dinosaurs ran wild and Australian animals mingled with the Aboriginal people in our schoolbooks.

The bus stop was empty.

"Michael!" Mum called the boy's name, but he was nowhere to be found. "Did he catch the bus?" she asked me.

"I didn't see him," I replied.

Mum immediately knew something was wrong. Michael was an extremely reliable child, but lately he had become more insular. He didn't talk as freely as he used to, and he often stayed in his room, refusing to come out. We all started to walk toward the school, all the while searching for Michael. Mum let out a cry of dismay when she saw him. His feet were dragging on the road, and he had been crying. He had a big pink bow on his head, and his shoulders slumped forward with embarrassment. Mum quickly pulled the car up beside him and jumped out. He had walked for miles because he was too scared to catch the bus with the bow in his hair.

"Who did this?" she cried, ripping off the bow.

"Sister Mary Immaculate," was the boy's hesitant reply. "I'm not allowed to take it off." Mum's anger was immediate.

"How dare she do this?" she asked the boy. "She has no right. I'll go up to the school tomorrow and sort this out." But the damage had been done. Michael had been humiliated, and he became even more withdrawn.

That year, August seemed hotter than usual, and we all got the measles.

"Mum, I don't want any more blankets; I'm too hot," I said.

"You have to stay warm because you have a temperature," she replied as she pulled my eiderdown up over my shoulders. She then proceeded to hang gray blankets up near the windows to make the room darker. My eyes hurt.

My head was blistering, and I ached everywhere. Red bumps covered my body, but I felt too tired to scratch them. German measles dampened my spirits. I didn't even feel like eating ice cream. My brothers had them too, but they weren't as sick. Every now and then, Mum would make me drink some water.

"You have to keep your temperature down," she kept saying. I didn't know what she meant, but the water felt cool and soothing on my sore throat.

"Sleep," my mother told me. But fitful meandering and monsters filled my dreams.

I tried to imagine I was at the bottom of the slope next to the goat shed. I loved that slope. Wild poppies grew there, straight and tall, like arrows pointing to the sky. Dad had brought the poppy seeds home one evening, and my mother had scattered them in the wind. Now they grew at random, mixing with the grass Mum grew to feed the goats. If I lay on the ground, the green lucerne stood high above my head, bouncing and swaying to nature's gentle rhythm. Wild yellow buttercups[xxiv] spotted the grass, and as I lay on the ground, the heavy scent of the wet, brown earth stung my nostrils. I liked the smell of the ground, especially after the rain. Everything seemed fresh, with the downpour washing away all previous activity. I couldn't smell the goat shed from the lucerne patch; instead, evening jasmine filled the air, enticing me, telling me to stay safe in my damp, green enclosure. Nearby, Christmas bells grew wild, and tiny yellow freesias bobbed to and fro. I liked freesias because they had a glorious perfume, a scent I wished I could bottle. The poppies splattered the field with random loveliness. I loved their wildness and didn't mind their strange smell. To me, their iridescence put them in the rainbow class.

By the time I recovered from the measles, it was the end of the year. I was asked to sing a solo in my class concert, and I was very excited. I knew the song backward because we had practiced it at school a thousand times. It was a Christmas carol about a doll. I knew it was a special event because my mother spent hours sewing me a new dress. My mother and brothers all came to watch me on the night of the concert. I was very nervous, and when it came time for me to sing, I thought I would choke on the words. My teacher smiled at me, a soft, gentle smile that filled me with instantaneous confidence. I liked my teacher. She was kind and never shouted, and she always answered me when I asked, "Why?" My scholastic progress at the public school had been excellent, but after the concert my father insisted I be transferred to the Catholic school Michael was attending.

"All the O'Learys are Catholic," he explained. "Besides, private schools are better than the public school system."

That Christmas, Santa left me a blue-and-white swing. It was love at first sight. The swing had a horse head at the front, with handlebars near the ears. It was the ultimate rocking horse. The higher I swung, the freer I felt. On the swing I'd make up songs. Music became a part of me as I experimented with tempo, pitch, and youthful musicality. Swinging on the horse and making up songs became my ultimate release. Some were nonsensical rhymes, while others were about the things I saw happening around me. No one could touch me on the swing as I climbed higher and higher, up into the clouds. I became shielded by the wind rushing past my face and the exertion of repetitive pushing. My feet drove me on from front to back, propelling me away from my everyday fears and into the realms of childhood fantasy.

CHAPTER 5

1965

Mumma brought Mum a Triumph Tourer so she could drive us to school. I was now four and had transferred to the Catholic school to continue my education.

"You must be brave," my mother told me when she saw me staring at a screaming child on a nun's lap. The child tried to tear herself away, and the nun loudly slapped her.

"What's wrong with her?" I asked.

"She doesn't want to go to school, because she's frightened," Mum answered.

I silently admitted I felt uneasy too. The nuns in their habits were different from the teachers at my old school. They were all black and white, their beads and crosses clicking loudly everywhere they walked. Because the nuns knew I was four years old, they put me in the kindergarten class again. Sister Mary Immaculate was my teacher. Michael had warned me that she was the "strict" nun, the one who you didn't talk to and the one you avoided at all costs.

It took me about thirty seconds to read the Dick and Jane[xxv] book placed on my desk. I remember Sister Mary staring open mouthed as I read the readers one by one until I came to the end of the reading curriculum box.

"How dare your mother teach you to read? Now you'll have nothing to do for the rest of the year."

For the rest of kindergarten, during reading time, I stood outside next to the water bubblers while everyone else in my class learned to read. I was told not to move, but in winter it became so cold, I had to hop from foot to foot to keep warm. My young brain pondered on what my mother had done. I knew she had done something really naughty by teaching me to read, but I didn't care. I loved reading, and I loved my mother. I didn't like Sister Mary Immaculate, and I vowed not to let her see that my exclusion from class upset me. I set my mind to hopping. To the left, to the right, and then higher and higher! I'd hop over school benches and on top of them and then dive for a second time around the bubblers. I hopped on every second cobblestone and on the cemented path near the gate. By the end of the school year, I was the best hopper in my class— a force to be reckoned with when entered in the three-legged race.

I put my hand in the newly aquired cardboard box and discovered a beading kit. My excitement blended with a new feeling. Guilt! My innermost thoughts were giving me butterflies. I looked at the big blue bear in the corner of my bedroom and sighed. It was covered in plastic, so clean and new, and so unlike anything I'd ever owned before. A thick pale-blue ribbon adorned its neck, and beaded eyes matched the black nose. The little girl who had owned the toys was dead, struck down with leukemia, and I had inherited two cardboard boxes filled with clothes and toys.

"Should I play with them?" I asked my mother. "Or should I be sorry she's dead?"

"You can do both," answered my diplomatic mother.

"I don't want to get you dirty," I told the bear after she had gone. "You look too good to play with."

The boxes held a few more items of clothes and toys, but none compared with the bear.

"I don't even have a name for you," I told him as I moved outside to play, "so I'll call you Bear." I sat with him on the back step, prattling on in an imaginary game until my mother called me inside.

I was gone only a few minutes, but when I returned the bear had disappeared.

"Be-ar!" I called. "Bear!" Over and over again, but it was gone.

"Maybe an Alsatian got it," my father volunteered, watching carefully for my reaction. "If you walk through the bush in that direction, you might find it."

I looked to where my father was pointing. I rarely walked in that direction. There was a house farther down in the bush, but no track connected the two homes. But my blue bear was lost, and I had to find him. I walked through the bush, twigs and rocks hurting my feet. Soon I came to a clearing. Bits of scattered blue lay everywhere. Torn fur and ripped-up cotton stuffing culminated in a shattered sob. I gulped and let my tears flow freely as I gathered pieces of bear in my skirt to carry back to my mother.

"Maybe an Alsatian did take him," she said. "There's no one else around."

It didn't seem fair! The object of my affection was gone. Tears still stung my eyes, but I was determined not to cry.

"Blue Bear is dead," I thought, "just like the little girl who owned him."

I was having nightmares. At night I'd crawl into bed and wait for my mother to kiss me good-night. My father had punched a hole in the bedroom wall, so I could see his shaving mirror hanging on a rusty nail in our makeshift bathroom. Every night before he went to the club, he'd come down the hall to shave, and I'd squeeze my eyes tight, hoping he wouldn't see me. Usually, he'd ignore me, but every so often, he would turn and wave the razor in my direction. With great swooping movements, he would slice up the air. Then he would drag the razor downward, as if he were carefully cutting something, not making a sound. Eyes transfixed, I would hold my breath until finally he'd break his stare and resume shaving.

I felt safer when my mother was around.

"Leave the light on, Mummy?" I'd ask, and she would leave it on for a while longer. I would stare at the exposed bulb until my eyes became watery and tired. Sometimes it felt as if my eyes were burning, the glare of the light bulb too bright for my weary attention. But it was the only way I could sleep.

The more I stared, the harder it became to keep my eyes open. It was a simplistic form of child hypnosis; I blocked out the pain by focusing on the light, and eventually, fitful sleep replaced my everyday thoughts.

Sometimes my father would take me out of school to visit Grandma O'Leary's house. If the creek was low, it was easy to catch tadpoles. I would slide down the embankment, cup my hands in the water, and laugh as the spawn wriggled across my palms. It was so much fun! On these occasions a grotesque figure would beckon me from the window. I would try to ignore him, but most times I couldn't break his stare.

As if hypnotized, I dropped the tadpoles back into the water and climbed up the muddy bank. The figure kept waving to me, and I kept walking—up the grassy slope, through the back door, and into the house. I walked slowly past the picture of *The Goose Girl*[xxvi] on the mantel and down the creaky corridor to the bathroom. The bath was filled with fiery hot water, and the steam hit my nostrils as my clothes were ripped off.

"It's too hot," I cried, struggling.

The figure looked at me disapprovingly. "Not as hot as it should be."

I stifled a scream as I was pushed into the bath. The mud on my legs began to disperse as my skin turned bright red with the heat. Then the voice began to berate me.

"You naughty little boy, you're covered in mud…dirty…dirty…dirty…"

I wanted to shout, "I'm a girl," but I couldn't. Feeling the scrubbing brush on my legs and arms, I curled myself up into a ball. I gripped my legs as the scrubbing continued, the sting of the water merging with the hard bristles on my back.

"Oh dear, what can the matter be? Oh dear, what can the matter be? Oh dear, what can the matter be?" I sang the words over and over again, never reaching the end of the rhyme.

The scrubbing stopped suddenly, and the figure waltzed out of the room. My hands wouldn't move; they stayed glued to my head, blocking out the yellow bathroom walls. I remained curled up in the bath until the water went cold and the deafening sound of the dripping faucet forced me to move.

The dripping tap annoyed me; it had no rhythm. It was unpredictable. Droplets of water escaped at indiscriminate moments. They seemed to be laughing at the pathetic little creature whose body was covered with red welts. I watched the leaking droplets burgeoning until they were too heavy to cling to the tap. My willpower was sapping away as each drop of water exploded into the bath below. It was as though I didn't have the tenacity to hold on. Finally, with a sweeping movement, I pushed the bathwater away from my body, freeing myself from the mental imagery of the dissipating droplets.

I thought of my horse swing rocking backward and forward in the back-yard. I had to get home. No one could hurt me on my swing. In my mind, I could kick my legs out at anyone who dared to come in front of me and push them to the ground. Besides, I was a lot taller on my swing, and I could swing above anyone's head. Higher and higher I'd climb, until I was flying. Escalating into the sky, my weightless body propelled like a feather. My words came out in songs and consoled me, an inner music forging my escape into fantasy. The more I rocked, the more secure I became in my insecurity.

The cranking of the old record player brought me back to where I was. Music from a scratched record played, prompting me to get out of the bath and walk toward the living room. The curtained figure was talking to some-one…someone I couldn't see. Smiling and tossing his head with flirtatious gaiety, he began to sing.

"Turn back the hands of time; turn back the hands of time. Turn back the hands of time. Let's live it over again."

He was out of time with the record, and I wanted to scream, "Stop it!"

From behind the door, I watched as he tripped over his imaginary high heels, stumbling and giggling like a schoolgirl. His words were slurred and his wig disheveled, but he didn't seem to care. He was captured by his mind's exhilaration—his psychosis—his reality as he busily entertained his guest.

My father hated cats and wattle. Cats made him angry, and wattle gave him allergies. The bush was awash with it. It grew wild everywhere, with big, gorgeous blooms, all soft and round like butterballs. Sometimes I'd collect wattle and put it in a cup on the table for Mum.

If my father saw the wattle, he'd transform into a wheezing, gasping creature that would tear at his shirt and shout, "You're trying to kill me. I can't breathe. It's your entire fault I'm sick because you want me to die." These comments would surprise me because my father didn't seem sick. He'd take one look at the pretty yellow flowers and explode. It was the same with lavender, wisteria, boronia, and roses. Dad would react by hitting the cup with his hand, knocking the flowers to the floor, and stamping on them.

He reacted similarly to cats. Mum bred British cream[xxvii] kittens in the hope of making extra money. In every litter we'd end up with some gray or apricot kittens and, if we were lucky, a pink British cream female. Mum could sell those because they were hard to come by.

Every time my father saw a cat, he'd try to kick it. When the mother cat had her kittens, Mum gave me a tiny gray mewling. I called him Timothy. I would dress him up and cuddle him as if he were my make-believe baby.

The voice crooned like Frank Sinatra, loud and sliding, as he felt the orchestra in his head.

"Three little kittens, they lost their mittens, and they began to cry. You naughty kittens, you awful kittens, I'll bake you in my pie."

The hot summer's day spelled trouble. The heat and dry wind gave rise to peculiar mood swings and short tempers. The heady scent of the boronia bushes told me they were in full bloom, and I felt comforted. I loved the boronia bushes because they were all prickly and spiky.

I could hear the meowing kittens, but I dared not look for them. They were only about four weeks old, and they were hungry. Louder and louder... frantically calling for their mother. I couldn't help myself; I had to follow their cries.

The old wooden crate was turned upside down, and I could see a tiny ginger paw trying to scratch its way out. Was anyone watching me? I shuddered and looked around. I felt the eyes burning on the back of my neck but couldn't see where they were hiding. The kittens sensed I was near them and began to panic, calling out even more. What was worse? Severe punishment or the prospect of the kittens' imminent starvation? Sick at the thought, I kicked the crate over so they could escape. Three relieved babies waddled off, one gray, another buff pink, and one ginger.

But there wasn't time to watch them. I quickly dove under a boronia bush to hide. The sandy base was large enough for my tiny frame to wrap around. As long as there weren't any ant nests, I could stay there in safety for hours, the bush's prickles protecting me from the outside world. I often got scratched, but I didn't care. Pain was a small price for solitude.

I watched the workman boots walk by me and kick the crate, sending it splintering in my direction. I froze and listened, not knowing when the figure would retreat.

"Three little kittens pie…Three little kittens pie…" the voice growled. "I'll bake you in my pie…"

"Run, Timothy," I prayed. "Run."

"Patrick." It was my mother's voice, calling. The tractor boots stomped over toward the house and disappeared.

Sister Mary Immaculate discovered I could sing and put me in the choir. She taught us "angelic" songs in three-part harmony. The hymns had very dramatic words printed in tiny red-and-gold Mass books. On holy days or at funerals, we were ushered into the church, where we sat upstairs near the organ, ready to sing. Sister Mary Immaculate said it was better upstairs because "it was nearer to God" and we were "God's little angels."

Each Mass seemed to last an eternity because I couldn't understand what the priest was saying in the Latin prayers.

"Pater noster, qui es in caelis, sanctificetur nomen tuum…"[xxviii]

Droning voices, clicking beads, kneeling, standing, thumping chests—we learned prayers in English in the classroom, but in church, Latin was "the language of God." Jesus understood Latin, and so did his Father and the Holy Spirit. I lived for the moment when the chanting voices would be replaced by songs.

At funerals, I would look down at the coffin and wonder about the person inside. I would shiver while people would cry and the priest would drone on and on. Stained glass windows filtered light onto the walls and offered some distraction, while gilded effigies stared at me with vacant, unseeing eyes. From the front row of the choristers' level, I could look down at the bereavement scene below.

"Someone has to polish that coffin," I'd think. It would gleam as if it were wet, the little silver crosses like mirrors, reflecting and channeling the light.

The tin cross could cut you if it hit you. It had razor-sharp edges with a nut and bolt in the center. It was God's cross, and God's work was never done. The silver cross flashed metallic in the sunlight. Raising it above his head, my father chanted in God's language.

Sister Mary Immaculate said, "God spoke to the pope in Latin. He whispered Christ's thoughts in dreams and prayers." So I decided that the devil spoke in Latin too, and that was how Lucifer knew what God was saying when he pushed him out of heaven.

Dad said he "knew the devil and God," and I realized that they had somehow gotten inside him, and they popped out when no one else was around. I didn't know how they had gotten inside him; I wondered if my father had eaten them at church.

"This is my body; this is my blood," they'd say at church, and people would eat the host. I hated that thought because I didn't like blood. I also thought that devils were evil! They lurked around the bush when no one was watching. Dad said he could sense where they were hiding, and I believed him. The tin cross protected him. It could seek out the devil and make him tell you what he was thinking. The devil was black…and red…and silver. My father, armed in wet-weather garb (his oilskin raincoat and rubber hat), would wait for the devil to make his move. His black tractor boots would stamp through the wet bush as he looked for the devil's clues. All he needed was a black cat.

When Jamie saw Leibchaun in the post office, he begged Mum to let him keep her. Cosseted and spoiled, the little kitten vied for everyone's attention. Leibchaun was emerald eyed and jet black. She possessed a beguiling personality, which everyone loved. When she was six months old, she suddenly went missing. We called her over and over again but didn't get a response.

As the day progressed, the weather became stifling. I went out to get a drink of water from the tank and heard a feeble meow. Mum climbed the ladder and crawled on top of the tank to rescue the cat, the tin burning her knees and hands. Leibchaun was crying, and so was my mother. The cat was up on the roof near the top of the tank, and it couldn't get down.

"You silly cat!" she cried. "Why didn't you come down where it's cool? It's far too hot up there."

When my mother reached the cat, Leibchaun was a pitiful sight. Her eyes rolled back in her head, and her breathing was labored. Droplets of foam salivated from her mouth. The little kitten was expiring. My mother became hysterical. She scooped the kitten up and ran the lengthy distance down the dirt road to the neighbor's house. Crying and pleading, she begged Mrs. Peters to drive her to the vet.

The diagnosis was sunstroke "combined with something poisonous she's eaten." The vet treated the little black cat and kept her under observation at his office for a few days.

Later, when Leibchaun came home, she seemed like her old self. Everyone breathed a sigh of relief and left her to rest on an old woolen jumper. The next morning, my mother found Leibchaun dead on my bed. White froth spewed down from the corners of her mouth, and her huge marbled eyes stared vacantly. My mother couldn't stop crying. I thought her heart was breaking, and I didn't know how to comfort her. We buried Leibchaun under a maidenhair fern near the sandstone plateau edge.

"She'll be happy here," said Mum. "It's cooler under the fern."

Sometimes I'd visit her grave and wonder if Leibchaun had gone to live with the angels.

"She is lucky," I thought. "I have to live with the devil."

I sniffed and rubbed my eyes the way most children do when they have the flu. My face was hot and my eyes swollen and sore. My mother took one look at me and said, "Go back to bed." I folded my arms and shivered, pulling the flannelette nightie closer to my body. Mum was juggling the boys' breakfasts, and I willingly bid a hasty retreat. After Michael caught the bus to school, Mum drove Liam to preschool. On returning home, I went back to bed, tired with the flu. I slept very soundly, and when I awoke, it was nearly midday, and my mother was in the kitchen, preparing my father's lunch.

"I promised I'd take your dad's lunch to him," she said, "but he doesn't know you're home from school." Mum looked worried. Her husband's jealousy often forced her to hide her devotion to her children. Jamie had just fallen asleep in his cot, so Mum put an extra bottle of milk near him and left him sleeping. He usually slept for over an hour, and she only planned to be gone for twenty minutes.[xxix] She put some sandwiches into a paper bag, picked up the thermos, and started toward the front door.

"Come on," she said. "You can hide in the back of the car, and he won't see you."

"It doesn't matter that I'm still in my nightdress," I thought. "I'm not getting out of the car." We were driving up the road toward the mouth of a fire track near Galston Gorge. The area was a sandstone clearing surrounded by thick bushland, and my mother used it as a lunch drop point while my father worked in Dural. At this time of year, wildflowers grew in the sandy soil, and boronia bushes were in full bloom. As I climbed into the Triumph

Tourer, Mum began to crank the engine. The car had been a present from her mother, and although it was antique, it was a reliable means of transport. The car spluttered a bit, and after an enormous cough, we started down the road.

The drive to Galston wasn't very far, but the Tourer was slower than a normal car, making the journey seem longer. When we got to the top of Somerville Road, the houses became more prevalent. We drove past the corner shop run by the Johns and went down the winding road toward the gorge. As we neared the clearing, Mum gestured to me to jump into the back of the car.

"Quick," she said. "Your father's raincoat is on the floor; put it over your head so he doesn't see you."

I picked up the coat and crawled under it. At the same time, I caught a glimpse of my father's truck driving down the road toward us. It swung in front of us and turned to go up the bush track to the clearing. I noticed some-one else was in the passenger seat, as I could see the top of his sandy-red hair over the dashboard. It was Michael.

"What's he doing here?" I thought. "He's supposed to be in school."

I pulled the raincoat over my head and settled on the floor between the back and front seats of the Tourer. My mother stopped the car, and I heard her pick up the lunch bag and thermos. The car door slammed, and I could hear my parents talking. At first they were talking softly, and then suddenly Dad's voice started to get very agitated. I was sitting in blackness, listening to him arguing.

"I'm going to kill you, bitch."

"Don't be silly, Patrick; put that thing away."

"Shut up and do what I say, or I'll blow your fucking head off."

I began to shake beneath the raincoat. I hated it when my father became aggressive, as trouble always followed. At that moment, I heard another car churning up the gravel track.

"Shit!" Dad shouted as he pushed Mum up against the car. "Shut up or I'll kill you." I peeped out from behind the rubber raincoat and knelt down next to the window just in time to see an old, brown station wagon drive up. In it were three people, two men and a woman. They seemed to be in their early twenties. The men both sat in the front of the car, while the woman was in the back. The lady had shoulder-length brunette hair, and the driver had sandy hair that just touched his shirt collar. The other male passenger had a medium complexion with straight, stringy hair.

"Maybe they are going exploring in the bush or stopping to collect wild-flowers," I thought. As the car came to a standstill, my father turned toward it. He dropped the rifle to his side and took Mum's wrist in his hand.

The young driver got out of his car. He must have sensed something was going on, because he yelled to Mum, "Hey, are you all right?"

My mother didn't answer, as Dad pushed her roughly against the car. She fell backward, and he reached for his gun.

He fired two shots. One whizzed off into space, while the other hit a sign-post on the other side of the trees, near the road.

"Holy shit!" the young man yelled. "He's got a gun." He ran to the station wagon and got in. He tried to start his car, but the engine failed him. Dad walked toward him and pointed the gun at the windshield. I heard an ear-splitting shattering of glass as the bullet hit the windshield and exploded in the young man's face. Screaming, yelling, and maniacal laughter in the bush followed this as the dead man's friend leaped out of the passenger seat and tried to run.

"Please don't kill me…please!" The man's pleas fell on deaf ears as the .303 rifle stamped Dad's answer in his skull. I could hear the girl's whimper-ing, but I couldn't see her. My father walked around the car to where she was crying on the floor in the back.

I saw this as my chance to move. Before, I had been glued to the window; now, I was ready to run. My mother was crouching behind the closed front passenger door of the Tourer, her face frozen and her eyes fixated on the ground before her. I slid between the seats into the front and gently pushed open the door, ever so slightly, just enough to slide down on the ground next to her. Mum was gulping for air like a fish out of water. Her hands were curled up, clawing at the dirt in front of her. I looked back at my father. The girl was screaming as Dad pulled her out of the station wagon by the hair. He brought the rifle butt down and smashed her in the face. She fell to the ground with a thump. The car door obscured her body, but I could see my father raising the rifle high into the air and pounding her with it, as if he were mashing potatoes.

I grabbed my mother's arm. Somehow, through her shell-shocked hysteria, she heard me utter the only word that escaped my lips: "Run!"

Mum grasped my outstretched hand, and we ran down the bush track to the road. We crossed it, climbed up the steep hill to a rock, and hid behind it. Bush surrounded us, but from our hiding place, we could look down onto the clearing below. The woman was no longer moving, and Dad was dragging her by the leg to the other side of the car. He went to his truck and rummaged in the back for his tools. Out came another black rubber raincoat like the one I had been hiding under. He put it on and reached for something else in the truck before making his way back to the girl's body. I watched in horror as he took a machete and began to viciously hack at the girl's neck. I heard a rasping sound next to me and turned to see my mother vomiting on the grass.

It was almost as if Dad had forgotten our very existence. He held the girl's head by the hair and rolled it in the dirt, patting it to mix the blood and dirt together. This formed a caked covering, like a muddy mask. With a blood-curdling yell, he took on a David-and-Goliath stance. Then he twirled the head high in the air and let it go. It flew through the air and landed with a thud. He kicked the head and then repeated the action, playing a macabre game of soccer.

Then, as if he were drawn like a magnet, he started toward us. Down the track and across the road, until he stood in front of the giant rock we were sheltering behind. Dad babbled the incoherent words of a madman. Mumbling gibberish, he stopped and looked up at the huge rock, swinging the head by the hair; and then he suddenly released his grasp. It was as if the whole world went into slow motion.

"Goal!" he shouted as the head hurtled through the air and hit the rock with sickening force. My father looked up at the rock and started walking toward us.

"Oh no! He's seen us," Mum whispered.

His gaze was upon us, but in his mind, he was seeing something else. With his head half-cocked, he turned and picked up the head. Seeming distressed, he mumbled to himself, half walking, half lurching back down the bush track toward the clearing.

"Run!" I cried desperately, clutching my mother's hand.

We ran stumbling and unseeing through the heavy bush. The spiky foliage whipped our legs and arms as we ran back in the direction of home. Both of us could hear footsteps following behind, and I began to panic.

"Is he following us?"

I heard the footsteps again. They were lighter than an adult's. They were more like a deer's or a child's. My mother and I kept running and stumbling through the undergrowth and over the ridges, while my brother Michael followed us home.

Marge Banning was clearing her land so she could build a proper shack on the property. Hearing a motor, she looked down the slope and watched as the brown station wagon drove slowly up the dirt track in the distance. The car had no windshield.

"It's probably being dumped," she thought, piling rocks and bushes into a heap. The car crept farther up the track and became obscured by trees.

"Damn litterers," she cried in annoyance, and kept working.

About fifteen minutes later, she saw him. A black vision was marching through the trees near the top of the gully. She folded her arms across her chest and watched from behind the wall of the wooden lean-to. In one hand he carried a machete, and in the other, a blackened swinging ball.

He was coming closer now, and she could see him more clearly. A deep-red film spattered his raincoat, and the ball was taking on grotesque human features. Auntie Marge crouched behind the wooden slats, shuddering. She dared not move. Through the holes in the slats, she could see the muddy tractor boots crunching past her in the undergrowth. His arm was outstretched, and the machete scraped the side of the lean-to in his stride. The figure was oblivious to Auntie Marge's cringing inside the makeshift shelter. Ensconced in his delirium, the stomping man muttered in inarticulate monosyllables. He waved what he was carrying in the air and made his way up the bush track, heading toward the main road.

Three frightened souls ran for what seemed an eternity. Blind terror rendered us mute and switched our homing mechanism to automatic pilot. We ran over the tops of the gorges, avoiding the gullies, until we finally arrived home. Exhausted, we went our separate ways. I crawled beneath a clump of boronia bushes to the left of the house. It was the perfect spot for a child who wanted to hide. I craved isolation, and when I curled up at the base of the bush, I felt safer. Time stood still for me as shock set in, and I fell asleep in exhaustion. Hours later, the sound of my father's truck woke me.

"He's home," I thought, feeling cold and shivery. My head ached, and my palms were sweating. I was frightened, but everything was hazy.

"Was it real?" I asked myself. "Or was it just a nightmare?" I could not know. I felt so groggy, so out of sync with everything. As I moved, my thoughts seemed to reverberate, sounding like hollow shouts in my head. I thought I'd move my arms and legs, but any bodily movement seemed to take an eternity. Everything was distorted. Night had fallen. I dragged myself out from under the bush and ventured back into the house.

I looked into the room where my family had gathered. My father and brothers were seated around the table for dinner. Liam and Jamie giggled together while Michael stared vacantly into space. He looked very strange, almost ghostlike. Mum's eyes were fixed and wide, like two giant black saucers in her face. She carried a plate of food to the table and placed it in front of my father. He immediately started to eat, tearing at the chicken on his plate like a hungry bear. Mum seemed to be in a trance. Too shocked to acknowledge anyone or the day's activities, she sat down at the table without eating anything. Instead, she got up again and started to clear the plates away. Trauma had taken its toll, and my mother moved around the room like a robot. She was staring blankly, absorbed in whatever she was thinking. I saw blue bruises on her arms, and her shaking hands made the cup dance around on the saucer when she carried it to the table. My father ground some white tablets into a sugary paste and added them to my mother's tea when she wasn't looking.[xxx]

"Drink your tea, woman." Mum did as she was told. "Now go to bed."

Mum was frightened. Her car had disappeared, and she had no phone, no escape, and four children in the house. As she went to bed, she knew she might not be alive in the morning. Paralyzed with fear, she lay down on the bed. For some reason, she could not stay awake. The room was spinning, and her body felt weightless. My mother was drifting far away, floating from the tablets' effect.

I slid off my chair and left the room with my brothers. I felt nauseated as I skulked off into my bedroom. I dragged my eiderdown off the bed and climbed into the cupboard. I sat in the dark, shivering and shaking, until I felt it was safe enough to fall asleep. Underneath my eiderdown, with my eyes closed tightly, I rocked from side to side, praying, willing the night to sweep the day's events from my memory with childish religious fervor.

Some hours later, I was dragged from my hiding place in the cupboard and made to stand at the end of my parents' bed. My mother, plagued with nightmares, awoke with a start. A dismembered head danced in the air at the end of the bed beside me.

The Devil croaked, "Get out of bed and shut up. If you make a noise, I'll kill you."

Her eyes widened in horror. Not a sound escaped her lips as she slid out of bed and onto the floor. The Devil grabbed her arm and pulled her to her feet, growling, "Get a move on, woman!"

The truck ride to Auntie Marge's property was short. I sat shivering in the back, pulling my nightie closely around me, trying to keep warm. Suddenly we stopped, and the Devil said, "Get out."

The moon was full and the bush night clear as we walked toward the end of the track. The brown station wagon was parked just at the end of the clearing. My mother stopped, but he propelled her toward the car.

"If you want to see your precious boys alive again, you'll do as you're told," he said, throwing her to the ground. He opened the car door and put it in neutral.

"Steer," he commanded.

I could smell kerosene—or was it petrol? The oily smell seemed to coat everything. The Devil pushed at the back of the station wagon with me while my mother guided the vehicle down the dirt track. Only the cracking of twigs and breaking of branches told of our presence, a deathly silence consuming the bush.

Closer to the cliff…

Closer and closer, until we reached the edge.

Suddenly the Devil spoke. "Get out of my way."

My mother and I huddled together while he struck a match and threw it into the front of the car. He ran to the back; screaming, he pushed again. The car went over the edge, shooting sparks into the bush and exploding when it hit the bottom of the gorge. The fire burst, throwing high, smoky tendrils into the air, illuminating the greenery that surrounded it.

On the cliff face, the figure in the black coat laughed hysterically. Chanting maniacally, waving his arms wildly in the air, he watched the light show. Ten thousand flames roared through the silent bush, mingling with his effervescent gibberish. As the strange, mangled words sprouted from his lips, he laughed again. The Devil came over to where we were cowering on the ground and began his sermon.

"Sinners," he ranted, "their blood is on your hands. You are the guilty, and your punishment is in my hands. All who have murdered will rot in hell, so you belong to me. Suffer, little sinners. Drown in your guilt until I take mercy on you and relieve you of your godforsaken lives."

The sermon went on and on, filled with words that had strange meanings or meant nothing. My mother kept falling asleep, and the Devil kept shaking her awake. Finally, it was over.

"Get in the truck," he said, and this time Mum sat in the back with me. I don't remember the ride home, but his laughter echoed on throughout my nights to come. It pealed out in anguish, knelling like ten thousand clanging bells in my dreams.

The Devil touched my soul with catatonic fear and totally controlled my mother. In the middle of the night, she sat bolt upright in bed and then fell back on the pillows, moaning like a zombie and then falling back into a restless sleep. I wondered, did she dream of skulls and faceless people? Were her nightmares like mine? Did one nightmare finish and another one start? Did she have dreams within the dream, and when she thought she was awake, was she still fast asleep? I knew she could hear the Devil whispering. Did he invade her sleep and claw his way deep into her dreams? I wondered. Was it the same for her as it was for me? I had heard his maniacal dirge. Did she hear it too? Resounding in my ear, alcoholic, hot, and heavy. He breathed those same words over and over again until they pummeled my subconscious into submission.

"Don't worry, my darling. I love you. You're having a terrible nightmare. It's just a bad dream."

The Devil's words would ring clear in my mind for many years to come.

When I was in my twenties, a psychiatrist friend told me we were suffering from posttraumatic stress syndrome, the kind that war veterans experience when they have experienced trauma.[xxxi]

The weight of shock, combined with the fact that my father was drugging my mother with barbiturates to subdue her, made our escape impossible. No one mentioned that day. It was as if it didn't exist. Every now and then, Michael would shiver as if he were trying to remember something and then shake his head like a dog with a flea in its ear. My mother was totally debilitated. She told me she didn't have the strength to stand, so she crawled around the kitchen trying to assemble the pots and pans for dinner. I was four years old and had no idea I was in a dysfunctional family. I tried to help her, but every time she stood up, her knees buckled, and she fell to the floor. In the end she'd give up and sit on the kitchen floor while I followed intermittent directions, my eyes transfixed by her white face and blank stare.

The burned machete made its way home again, and my father painted it with Pot Black and put it in front of the fire. It became the fire poker. It poked at the burning logs in winter, and my father dropped it heavily on the sandstone fire slab when he wanted to repress us. The effect was instantaneous. The machete could control us by casually pointing in our direction. It enforced a cruel reticence, silencing everyone's laughter with a single gesture. Years later, when I was nearly ten, I stretched out my hand and tried to touch the blackened piece of metal, but my fingers never made contact. They recoiled because I was overcome by a sudden wave of nausea.

During this time, Auntie Marge came to visit us. She told my mother she had seen Patrick running wildly, as if driven by an evil force, through the bush with the machete.[xxxii]

"You should leave here," she said in a hushed voice. "It's not safe. He'll kill you."

But my mother had become withdrawn and silent. It was almost as if she had left her soul in the ravaged bush. Michael was the same. Whenever he had the chance, he would run down into the gorge, disappearing for hours until he was called. I found solace in my cupboard. I would stay in it for hours. It was black inside, and I could disappear.

The kitten was newborn, its eyes still closed and its fur flat like a wet seal's. It hadn't taken long for my father to break the kitten's neck. Just a snap of his fingers, and it lay inert on the flat rock face.

"If you say anything to anyone, this will happen to your mother," he said as he began to cut. "Then, your brothers will be next."

The razor blade stopped in midair and waved above my toe. I tried to move my legs, but they were tied too tightly. Lingering above my feet, he began to chant, "This little piggy went to market; this little piggy stayed home…"

"Oh no, he's going to cut me." The razor blade chopped at the air above my feet, and the voice warbled on. "This little piggy had roast kitten; this little piggy had none…"

I shut my eyes, and nothing happened.

"Open your eyes, little kitten," he said in a singsong voice. I watched as he began to slice the little creature into mangled bits. The razor blade was covered in blood as he poked and hacked.

"I'll make you watch and hear them scream," he threatened. "Then you'll be next." I turned my face away. The animal didn't look like a kitten anymore. It looked like mulch sluiced up on the rock.

Slowly, as her daze passed, my mother seemed to return to normal. My father took us to visit Grandma O'Leary. My mother cornered Dad's eldest brother, Jack, in the hope he could help us.

"You've got to help us," she cried frantically.

"Nonsense," Jack answered. "You're not being logical."

"But he's violent, Jack. I'm frightened he will kill us."

"Don't be ridiculous; his mood changes are probably caused by the nervous breakdown he had when he was fifteen," he said.

"Why didn't anyone tell me about it?" Mum asked.

"It was none of your business, that's why."

Mum began to cry. "Jack, I don't think I can take it anymore…He can be so brutal…"

"You married him, didn't you? Surely you heard the priest when he said, 'Marriage is for better or for worse.'"

"I'm going through the worst," Mum sobbed. "I have to get out of this."

Uncle Jack was enraged. "How dare you think like that? You are his *wife*, and he owns you. No one will ever disgrace the O'Leary name with a divorce. That's a shame worse than death itself."

Jack's tone softened. "Go home to your husband, woman. It will work itself out."

Uncle Jack was very tall, and to me, he seemed like a giant. He was married to Auntie Cheryl, whom Dad forbade us to speak to.

"She's an idiotic woman who will fill your head with nonsense," he said.

Six months after Uncle Jack's conversation with my mother, Auntie Cheryl took her children and ran away. Uncle Jack and Grandma O'Leary were furious, and we were never allowed to mention her name again. When I was in my twenties, I ran into Auntie Cheryl in a coffee shop. She told me that she had been very lucky to get out of the marriage when she did.

"Why didn't you say good-bye?" I asked.

"I was in no fit state," she replied. "My parents broke into Grandma O'Leary's house and rescued me. I'd been chained to the bed for over a week and was unconscious."

I stared at the huge scar on her left cheek and hugged her. Auntie Cheryl sensed my concern and added, "Don't worry, dear; I have a lovely life now. I even have a gentleman friend who takes me ballroom dancing."

Sister Mary Immaculate asked the class what we wanted to be when we grew up, and everyone got a turn to answer. I said, "I'm not sure…maybe a vet or a doctor."

I felt at home with animals. My cat, Timothy, was beautiful. He had cute white paws and a furry chest. His trusting green eyes could fill with kittenish mischief, and then they'd close into slits. Sometimes, I'd dress Timothy up in doll clothes and push him around in Jamie's pram.

Sister Mary Immaculate wanted everyone to tell the class about their father's occupation. There were lots of different answers. "Butcher, baker, clerk, pig farmer…"

Then it was my turn.

"And what does your father do?" Sister Mary inquired.

I took a breath and blurted the words out. "My father kills people," I said, and all the children laughed.

Sister Mary Immaculate eyeballed me and through pursed lips hissed, "How dare you! You're always the actress, Shannon O'Leary, always trying to be funny." Her voice rose to a deafening pitch. "Class, Shannon O'Leary is a very naughty girl. She is a liar and has forgotten God's special rule: 'Honor thy father and thy mother.'"

When I went home after school, two police officers came to visit my mother. I was ecstatic. "Maybe they are here to help us," I thought.

But the two officers didn't take any notice of me. Instead, they went with my mother and surveyed the field of dancing flowers. My brilliant poppies swayed in the breeze, all pink, red, yellow, and orange, in my favorite grass patch.

"I'm sorry," said the officer, "but they will have to be removed."

My mother agreed with a nod of her head, and I began to cry. Bulb after bulb had their stalks and flowers ripped from the earth and placed in hessian sacks. I was devastated. They had been so beautiful dancing in the sun.

"Don't take my poppies," I shouted, but the two officers said they were illegal.

"Opium poppies,"[xxxiii] Mum told me later, "can make people very sick."

"How silly," I replied. "Only someone silly would eat a flower."

"They can make you sick because they're dangerous," Mum explained. "It's a bit like drinking medicine when you're not sick."

That explained it. I knew about the medicine shelf and that I was never to touch it. There were lots of different bottles on the shelf because as a registered breeder, my mother needed to mix medicines for sick animals. Bottles and tins all in a row. Caustic potash and ether for dehorning the male kids. Nembutal and Nembudine for pain relief when the does went into labor. Chloroform, liquid paraffin, ammonia, caustic soda, and ethanol. Chalk, spirit of salts, and Hibitane. Insecticides, flea powder, Gamma Wash, and an antiquated packet of Ratsak.[xxxiv] The top shelf also held two packets of strychnine that had belonged to my great-grandmother. My mother waxed the top of the chloroform and ether bottles because they seemed to evaporate more quickly than other chemicals. Despite her efforts, however, the bottles still emptied rapidly, much faster than she could ever use them.

I hated the shelf. Reaching hands would sometimes take the bottles down, break their seals, and pour the contents out. I hated men's handkerchiefs too, all folded up and waiting for the liquid from the bottles to soak into them. When I saw a handkerchief, I'd throw it away, hoping the Devil wouldn't find it and that the hanky wouldn't find me.

The police were about to leave with my poppies, when Mum spoke to them. "My husband…" she said in a faltering voice. "He's…he's very violent."

The policeman shook his head and said, "I'm sorry, Mrs. O'Leary, but we don't deal with domestic cases."

"But I'm frightened."

The policeman started his car and said, "I'm sorry, but there's nothing we can do now. Maybe you could call us if anything happens in the future?"

"I don't have a car anymore, and we don't have a phone," my mother answered. As their car drove off, my mother felt the door to freedom shut in front of her face. Her arms and legs were covered with bruises, but the police hadn't seemed to notice.

Lately, my mother had been becoming increasingly tense. When she was with us by herself, she tried to be patient and kind, but as the day drew closer to night, she was forever watching the clock. She'd look around nervously like a misplaced scarecrow. She bordered on being dangerously thin and was often jumpy and irritable. When my father came home, she fell silent, as if she were absorbed in her own thoughts.

"It's all your fault," Dad would yell. "I'm like this because you are so useless; you're a failure as a mother and a wife."

My brother Michael was also becoming increasingly withdrawn. He was top of his class when it came to any kind of theoretical knowledge, but his communication skills were halting and self-conscious. His teacher put his frightened nature down to shyness and embarrassment.

"He gets one hundred percent in his test results," she told my mother at his First Communion, "and that's all that matters in the long run." But Mum wasn't sure. When she was alone with the boy, he would voice his opinions, but when confronted by others, he stared at the ground and said nothing. My mother warned us to be quiet when our father was around, and Michael hid in his room, immersing himself in the set of encyclopedias. He knew the flag of every country and where the country was situated on the map of the world. Michael memorized all the street names near our school, and we all thought he was brilliant. My father, however, would tease him mercilessly.

"Speak up," he'd shout. "Act like a man."

I wondered if Michael was frightened of my father. I knew my mother was terrified of him, because her teeth would bite her lips when he was in a bad mood. Sometimes he'd grab her arm so tightly she'd whimper like an injured dog. Her arms were always covered in bruises. I used to amuse myself by counting them and watching them change color from red, to black, to blue, and then into a murky dark yellow.

"I'm not a very good example for Michael," Mum told Mumma when she came to visit. "I never speak when Patrick's around; it causes too many arguments. Besides, I'm stuck out here with no car and no phone. I really don't know what to do with Michael, other than take him to a doctor. You know, I think he's happier building roads in the bush than talking to people."

Mumma didn't know what to say. "Does he seem happy when he's playing?" she asked.

"Definitely," Mum replied.

"Well, let him be. It's probably a stage. Maybe he'll grow out of it."

The teachers at school also worried about me. I was overly sensitive and had developed a nervous stutter. I had trouble mixing with the children in my class, and according to the nun who taught me, I distanced myself from my own grade, preferring to play with the older children.

"She must learn to play with children her own age. After all, she is the youngest in her class, and she'll come to no good mixing with the upper primary children."

But I simply didn't comply. I hated playing chasing games, and I didn't want to play mother and father with the other children.

"I will never get married," I pledged. "Instead, I'll own an orphanage and have thousands of children who will talk to me."

I also liked the company of boys, and this alarmed the nuns. "She should learn to mix with the girls," they complained.

"She has three brothers," Mum ventured. "Maybe the girls frighten her."

The nuns knew this wasn't the case. I was fighting my own personal war, but no one could find out what was going on inside my head. I seemed passive to all on the outside but fiercely determined within. I was the odd child with my own opinions and unusual behavior. At recess, I would fight the boys gladiator-style on the playground, and I always won. Once, I climbed on top of the low concrete sewerage tank and challenged one and all to a duel of strength. I fought all the boys in my class pirate-style on top of the half-buried tank until I was the last one standing. There were no severe fistfights, just all of us pushing one another until I was left standing on top of the concrete tank. I was tiny and canny, and I knew how to make them unstable so they all fell off. It was great schoolyard fun until I refused to come to class. The nuns of course decided to put an end to my unladylike rebellion immediately.

"Any boy who plays with Shannon O'Leary will get the cane and detention." My classmates were hammered into submission, and I was totally devastated. Suddenly I was even more isolated. My stammer became worse until I stuttered like a tongue-tied lizard. I felt the cape of loneliness being thrust upon me because I could no longer play with boys and I didn't know how to communicate with girls.

Then Michael came to my rescue. To everyone's astonishment, he suddenly stopped speaking.[xxxv] He wouldn't utter a word, and in order to ward off any further introversion, the nuns decided that both of us should go to elocution classes. Terrified, I ran home and asked my mother what "electric-ution" classes meant, and Mum explained that it meant speech classes. The classes would take place at lunchtime. Michael and I arrived in the room and, to our surprise, found there were only five other children in the class. The teacher was a tall, thin woman with a large smile and grand, expressive hands. Every time she talked, she would wave her hands about and pull dramatic faces. I loved these classes because they kept me captivated. We'd recite wonderful poems in halting voices and act out characters from our favorite stories. Mrs. Evans would teach us the poem and then get us to recite it back to her.

"Enunciate!" she'd shout. "Enunciate!" But none of us knew what she meant. She would give us speech exercises to practice at home, and she told my mother that I should learn to sing.

"Singing always cures stuttering," she said. "The more you sing, the more control of your voice you'll have." And so I sang. I sang in the bush, in the car, in my bedroom...I would sing everywhere. Michael slowly started to speak again. Mum would sit with him for an hour every afternoon and talk to him. Sometimes he would answer her questions, and at other times he would remain silent, listening to her stories. Then Mum decided Michael needed something to look forward to, so she came up with the idea of us both sharing a birthday party. This was a unique notion because he was born in May and I in December. However, neither of us minded because we found the prospect of a pink cake for me and a chocolate cake for Michael very exciting. Mumma and Grandfather were bringing Mum's younger siblings, Benjamin, Leah, Jessica, and Tara, and Michael and I each invited two friends from school.

For the past year, Dad had been building an addition to the house, a bedroom for the boys and a kitchen area for Mum. The rooms weren't ready, and this new addition looked like a half-finished shed. It had three walls and a large unfilled area at the front, like a garage without the door. My father set up a trestle table in the half-finished building shell, and Mum put up balloons. Tara, Mum's younger sister, was in charge of the games. She was ten years old and a born athlete. Tara geared all the races to the fastest and strongest child, herself. Michael and I were not very sportsmanlike, and we began to sulk. We were glad when Grandfather took over the games and threw candies at random, making everyone giggle and trip over one another. Silly prizes and noisy whistles left us deliriously happy, and Mumma's cupcakes were made in heaven.

It was then decided that we should play blind man's bluff. I had a hatred of the game and refused to play, using the excuse that the day was hot and my five-year-old legs were tired. I went to my room to play by myself, but it was in an uproar. Mumma had a hairbrush, and she was chasing Leah around the room.

Leah was wailing at the top of her voice, "I didn't do it; I didn't."

Leah was a large girl, and she dodged my grandmother with ease, yowling and howling her protestations. While she was pregnant and carrying Leah, Mumma had contracted German measles,[xxxvi] and this had resulted in her daughter being born mentally challenged.

"Give it back to me," Mumma commanded. "Give it back at once."

"It's mine," Leah bawled. "You can't have it; it's mine."

Mum was standing in front of the bedroom door, snatching at the pound note as Leah tried to run outside. "Give it to Mumma," she said to her sister. "You know it's wrong to steal."

"I didn't steal it." The tantrum continued. "It was given to me. If you take it, you're stealing it off me." Leah's voice reached hysterical proportions, and then she began to sob like a two-year-old. Mumma gave up the chase and sat down on the bed.

"Tell us, then. Who gave it to you?"

"I can't tell you," she said, rubbing her eyes. "It's a secret." The tears poured down onto her chest, and she looked at me. "Tell them I didn't take it, Shannon," she pleaded. "Tell them."

This was the moment they had been waiting for. Mum grabbed the pound note and gave it to Mumma.

"You know you're not allowed money," she said. "Even if you didn't steal it, you mustn't accept money from strangers."

"It wasn't a stranger," the girl cried. "It's from my boyfriend."

Mumma was shocked. Leah was fifteen in physical age, but she had the mental age of a ten-year-old. She was never allowed out on her own; she was always chaperoned.

"What's his name?" asked Mum, hoping to catch her out.

"It's a secret," she replied.

"Secrets are dangerous," answered my mother, but Leah refused to talk to her.

Sometimes when we were alone, I'd get angry with Leah because she'd go on and on about my father.

"I love Patrick," she'd say passionately. "I'm his favorite; he told me so."

"Don't be silly, Leah," I'd say, eager to change the subject. "You're in love with John Wayne." Despite Leah's mental boundaries, she had an almost faultless memory when it came to facts about John Wayne. Leah knew every fact about the Hollywood cowboy. It was as though her brain had fixated on every aspect of his life and she had cemented it all in her memory.

"If only she could read and do arithmetic instead of listing facts about that cowboy movie star, I'd be a happy man," Paddy would say.

I silently agreed. Leah's talk and passion for my father made me uneasy. I knew he gave her money for telling tales on us. She was his "little secret agent," a spy paid to spout trivial information.

"What did Emma do today?" he'd ask if Leah and my mother went shopping.

"Who did she talk to, and where did you go?"

A few months after the birthday party, my father finished the new external walls of the house. The lounge room had two glass doors that led outside to a big flat rocky area.

"Later," my father said, "I'll build a sandstone BBQ area."

Joined to the lounge room was a small dining room with a hole in the wall that connected to the kitchen area. A slab of laminated Masonite would eventually transform this area into a small breakfast bar. There was also a tiny laundry area with a washing machine and wringer connected to the tank outside, but the bathroom was still in the old kitchen area.

None of the new walls were lined and the floors were bare, but everyone was glad to have more room in the house. The boys moved into their new room on the other side of the house, and I stayed in the original children's bedroom, next to the bathroom and my parents' bedroom. When I was a small child, the place seemed enormous, but it was really a small three-bedroom weatherboard house.

My mother longed for the time when we could connect the phone, as our home's isolation was becoming her main concern. Emergencies always popped up. One day my brothers found me hanging from their window, spluttering and trying to free my neck from the rope that was tied to an exposed beam.

"Quickly, Mummy!" Michael shouted. "Shannon's turning blue."

After racing to the scene, my mother dragged me inside the window and released the rope, saving me from strangulation.

"I didn't do it," Michael cried when he received a belting for his lifesaving effort.

"She wanted to fly," my father told my mother. "Boys will be boys, and they pushed her out of the window."

The rope burns on my neck eventually disappeared, but the terror of not being able to breathe became a persistent nightmare. I tried to conquer my fear by holding my breath. At night I'd practice trying not to breathe, counting the moments of stillness before I went to sleep. Often during the night, I'd awake to the clamor of the Devil.

"Sha-nn-on," the voice would call in my ear, and I'd pull the covers over my head, pretending not to hear.

"Sha-nn-on," the singsong voice would call again, but I'd push it away, too tired to open my eyes.

I would be relieved when sleep came, and then suddenly I would awake again, thinking, "I need to go to the toilet." The thought would spur my body into action. Heavy with sleep, I'd stumble through the dark house and into the dark backyard.

"No moon tonight," I thought on one occasion. Everything was bush black and quiet. The toilet door was propped open with a brick, so I waved my hands in front of me, feeling for cobwebs.

"Good…no spiders."

Bang! I happened upon movement and a confrontation. Fear glowed bright in large pink eyes and small gnashing teeth.

"It's only a possum." I was filled with relief. After going to the toilet, I made my way inside again. "If only it wasn't so dark."

My heart was beating too loudly for coherent thought when he struck. The Devil's hands, all rough and leathery, covered my mouth and eyes. He had waited, poised like a giant snake, behind my door where no one could see him. The hands pushed me down on the bed while I grappled and writhed, whimpering.

"Shut up," he growled. He warned me that if I made a noise, the beast would devour me with his backlash. The Devil would kill my mother and brothers; he would kill everyone. His hands left my mouth, and I knew what was coming. I took a breath and brought my hands up to my nose. They formed a cup of air as the pillow bore down on my face.

"I must keep my hands up," I thought. "I can't let them collapse on my nose."

The Devil pressed down hard, but I could still squeeze in some air around my fingers. Just when I thought I couldn't breathe anymore, the pillow bounced up again. Footsteps! I could hear the Devil retreating in the dark as he traveled down the hall away from my room. Panic set in.

"He might come back," I thought. I made a mental note to remember to sleep with my hands cupped around my nose as I carefully slid down between the wall and the bed. Once I reached the floor, I could inch my way toward the cupboard. The Devil couldn't fit in there; he was too big.

Some people call it animal instinct, and some, gut feelings. Others call it being psychic or being able to read a situation from visual clues. With me, it was just something that happened. My mother always knew when my father was on his way home, because I'd disappear. I'd run and hide under the house, feeling his impending arrival before I could hear the sound of his truck hitting the gravel on the road outside. The area under the house was cramped, an inviting combination of cool and dark, which I had to double over to reach. A labyrinth of foundations and dirt and a haven for spiders, it was the perfect place for a child to hide. I felt invisible under the house, so I often retreated there with my dogs, Sheba and Conrad. I'd lie flat on the ground with the gold and black Labradors and pass the time by drawing in the dirt.

One day, Sheba went missing.

"Something is wrong," Mum told me. "Sheba is about to have puppies. She wouldn't disappear."

The golden Labrador stayed away all night.

"Sheba," my mother's call rang out through the scrub. "Sheba." Her frantic tone made me feel uncomfortable.

I crawled under the house and found Sheba sleeping. An enormous lump rose from her head, distended and bruised. She looked so sick. Emptying my brown paper lunch bag, I offered her some scraps to eat. But the dog didn't seem interested; instead, she whined and drifted back to sleep.

When I was five, my favorite book depicted a little girl who looked after her baby brother because he had a cold. In the story, the girl gave her brother hot soup and toast and kept him company. I think the influence of this book propelled me into the nurse role for Sheba.

"Have you got a headache, girl?" I asked. "I'll get you some water." I found an old dish and checked to make sure no one was around. "You'll like this," I said, placing the water beside her. The tank water was cool and inviting, and the dog was thirsty. She drank as much as she could and then licked my hand. She knew I was trying to help her.

A week went by, and everyone thought Sheba was dead. My mother couldn't believe her eyes when she saw the dog slowly walking toward her. Sheba was a pitiful sight of skin and bone, her head rolling from side to side when she walked. Her tail dragged between her legs, and she was in whelp. As soon as Mum saw her, she knew the dog was hurt.

"What happened, girl?" she asked while examining the lump on the dog's head. "Who hit you?" But the dog couldn't answer. "Where are your puppies, girl?"

My mother took the malnourished dog to the vet.

"Looks like she's been hit on the head with a bottle," he said. "There has been quite a lot of bleeding, and she may have a blood clot."

"I don't understand it," Mum answered. "Who in their right mind would want to harm such a beautiful dog?"

Within the week, Sheba died of a brain hemorrhage.

It was a cool, gray day in May, and my father had taken me out of school for an appointment.

"What appointment?" I thought as I reluctantly got inside the truck. I balked suddenly, smelling the strange odor before it hit me. Then, everything went black.

When I awoke I was in my nightdress and I was bound to a chair. It was still daylight, and I was in Grandma O'Leary's kitchen. It was a mess. There was a huge pile of dirt in the center of the large kitchen table in front on me, and my father's tools were scattered across the table. I stared at the odd character pouring water on the dirt. He was all too familiar.

"If only I could break free," I thought. I struggled in vain to loosen the rope, but my hands were tied firmly behind my back. A rope had been looped through the rungs of the chair, so if I struggled too hard, it would topple over.

"I'm making you a chocolate cake," the figure told me in a singsong voice. "You're going to love it."

I wanted to shout, "I hate chocolate cake," but the gag around my mouth was too tight. My ankles were tied together with shoelaces, and when I kicked my feet, they dug into my skin. The person laughed.

"Now don't be silly, dear; Grandma O'Leary will get you a nice cup of milk to wash the cake down."

I watched as he pushed the lid of a tin off with a screwdriver and scooped up two large tablespoons of white powder. He mixed it with water in a glass and pushed it toward my face. I shook my head in vain.

"Oh, you poor dear," he said as he untied the gag. "That's better."

I looked directly into his grim blue eyes. They drilled into me, scrutinizing my reaction with an iciness that sent a shudder down my spine. The gray curly wig hadn't been combed properly, and it sat precariously, perched sideways on his head. Bright-pink lipstick was smeared across his face, smudged into strange splotches. He had tied a muddy, worn curtain across his overalls, and it ballooned out when he walked and cascaded limply inward when he was stationary.

He pushed the glass toward me again, and I clamped my mouth together tightly.

"Do as you're told," he shouted.

I knew I couldn't drink whatever he was holding. It was all too ominous, as it had come from his toolbox.

"Drink it now," the voice ordered, and I shook my head.

I saw him raise the glass. As he threw the contents in my face, I closed my eyes. A splash of caustic soda hit me in the corner of the eye, and I screamed. My cry seemed to break his concentration, and he changed instantaneously.

Suddenly he was my father again, picking me up and throwing my head under the tap to wash the powder off. This heightened the burning sensation, and my cries became more intense. I was still attached to the chair when Dad dropped me to the floor. He untied my hands and ran outside, leaving me to fend for myself.

I groped for the tea towel hanging near the sink and rubbed my face furiously. I tried to open my eyes but couldn't. I felt the shoelaces on my feet and untied the bow; then, still crying, I felt for the sink, reached up, and tried to mop more water onto the tea towel.

"Oh no!" Soft, rubber-heeled footsteps came through the door. "You'll be all right, dear." The voice was trying to comfort me. I felt someone pick me up and take the towel from my hands. "You'll be better in no time."

The real Grandma O'Leary bathed my eyes and took off my wet nightie. After wrapping me in a towel, she started to clean up the mess on the table.

"What have you done?" she kept muttering to herself over and over again as she scrubbed the table clean. I lay down on the carpet and closed my eyes. It felt as if I had two fire pits in my head. I pressed my hands against them and began rocking and praying that I could go home to my mother. Waiting seemed an endless and exhausting process. When my father finally returned, Grandma O'Leary spoke to him in a hushed voice in the next room. After they finished, he picked me up in his arms and drove me home to our property in the bush.

Mum took one look at me and pleaded for Dad to give her the car keys.

"She has to see a doctor," she cried.

The doctor diagnosed chronic conjunctivitis and advised my mother to put antibiotics into my inflamed and burning eyes. "You'll have to be careful because the condition is very advanced." My mother was confused and worried about permanent eye damage, as she knew my eyes had been perfectly normal that morning.

"Is it possible for this to flare up so quickly?" she asked the doctor disbelievingly. "Maybe it's something else?"

"I'm sure my diagnosis is correct," the doctor assured her. "Just take the girl home; she needs to rest in a dark room." He handed my mother the prescriptions. "I've also included some medicine to stop the itching and to help her sleep."

The next day I woke up feeling awful. There was tightness in my chest, and I was having difficulty breathing. My eyes were swollen and still searing in my head. Through blurred vision I watched as my mother burst into tears.

"Let's get you straight to the doctor. He'll fix you up in no time."

My temperature was also dangerously high. I could barely stand, so she carried me to the car. After dropping Liam and Jamie at Mumma's house, she drove me to the doctor. After he examined me, he sent me to have some x-rays of my lungs and advised my mother to return home to wait for the test results. I slept fitfully for most of the day until the doctor knocked on our front door and woke me.

"You'll have to get her to the hospital immediately," he informed my mother. "She has a spot on her lung, and we have to treat it immediately. With her allergies to penicillin-based drugs, we have very little time to see if we can control the infection."

When my father returned home, I was put in the back of the car, and we sped toward Camperdown Children's Hospital. In no time, a police siren screamed behind us, and the car pulled over to the side of the road.

"I've got a sick child who needs to go to the hospital," my father said as the officer peered at me through the back window.

"I'll radio it through for you," said the policeman. "Stay with me, and I'll give you an escort."

The policeman took off with my father in pursuit. I felt too groggy to sit up, my head throbbed, and the siren was screaming again. Through damaged eye slits, I watched the red flashing light reflect on the car's roof as we sped toward the city. When I arrived at the hospital, I was put on a trolley and wheeled inside. I was then subjected to a series of physical examinations that I found very unsettling.

"It's my lungs that are sick," I thought as the doctor examined the lower regions of my body. I thought the medical staff's interest was unwarranted, and I tried to get up, but they told me in no uncertain terms to lie down and behave myself. I was very upset, and through this attention I became aware that I could now feel pain. Usually I controlled my aches and soreness. I'd concentrate on something I liked until I didn't feel anything, just numbness. At the end of the examination, the nurse dowsed my private parts with antiseptic and became outraged.

"It's disgusting," she said. "Someone should be held responsible."

I didn't know the implications of what she was saying, and because her tone was so angry, I misconstrued what she said. In essence, I felt that I was responsible for my body being "disgusting." Hence, I was filled with embarrassment, and I never told my mother about the examinations or the nurse's words.

Over the years, different people have commented that my mother should have realized what was happening to me, but I was stony, silent, and unyielding. I also knew that she was fighting her own battle to stay alive.[xxxvii] The people who censure my mother probably have never experienced the immobilizing terror of constant trauma. Before they criticize, they should experience what she went through—the mental torture, drugging, beating, and rape—and see where this kind of degradation leads them. Would it empower or cripple them? I wonder! The faultfinders should look at the nonexistent family services and protection laws that were around in the 1960s and realize that families in trouble had no access to help.[xxxviii]

When I was seven, I wrote a poem that I feel explained our silence:

> *Cry tears…hurt,*
> > *cry sound…wounded,*
> > > *cry nothing…tortured.*

The teacher who read the poem ripped it out of my book and threw it in the bin, muttering, "Morbid little creature." In truth, I feel that many people had their suspicions, and some even knew what was going on in our home. Still, nobody did anything.

My mother visited me in the hospital every day. The sulfa-based drugs the doctors prescribed worked and eventually brought the pleurisy and bronchial pneumonia under control. Mumma and Grandfather looked after the boys, as

I wasn't allowed visitors, but on one occasion Liam and Jamie came to the hospital. The two little boys were left outside in the toy room to play while Mum read to me. Suddenly, we heard a loud commotion. We turned toward the door and were amazed to see Liam and Jamie tearing through the hospital ward on a tricycle. Liam was peddling furiously, and Jamie was screaming, "Stop! Stop!" Three nurses in starched white caps ran after the boys, but it was too late.

Crash!

The tricycle and the little boys collided with an enormous gas heater in the middle of the room. Black smoke poured everywhere, and startled nurses tried to prevent a fire hazard. All the children in the ward started to laugh and giggle as Mum ran toward the boys and scooped them up into her arms. The head sister charged toward them and demanded that the boys be removed from the ward immediately. We said some very hurried good-byes, and my mother quickly made her way out of the hospital.

I was left to recuperate, and from that day on my stay at the hospital was more enjoyable. Nurses let me ride on the medicine trolley while they administered medicines to the healthier patients, carefully telling me they would avoid heaters at all costs.

My visits to the hospital continued throughout the summer and into January 1966.

"The black spots smell like a hospital," I thought as I lay in bed waiting to get my tonsils out. I had been in and out of Hornsby Hospital eight times in the past few months, and each time my temperature had been too severe for them to operate. Eventually, on the ninth visit, the dreaded tonsils were ready to be removed. Before the operation, I became so frightened I hid in the toilet, standing up on the seat so no one could see I was in the cubicle.

I had practiced this game before. Sometimes when my father came to school during recess, I would hide in the toilets so nobody could find me. He'd give up waiting for me and go home. I hoped the doctors would do the same thing and forget about my dreaded tonsils. Eventually they called my mother to the hospital, and she knew exactly where to find me.

"Come out here at once," she commanded. "I'm not bringing you back for the tenth time." When the nurses wheeled me into the operating theater,

I could smell an odor that reminded me of the hanky. I woozily tried to run away, my preoperation sedative paralyzing my motor coordination skills. Fear pitted me against the medical staff, and I became hysterical.

Hospitals frightened me, and so did the black spots that flooded my mind when it was subjected to the anesthetic. An orderly held me down and pushed the mask over my nose.

"Just count to ten," the voice said. There was the smell of gas and then black.

CHAPTER 6

1966

The Peterses lived in a pink fibro house on the opposite side of the street, farther down the road. Their house, which resembled a broken-down farmhouse, had old trucks and bits of machinery in the front yard because Bob Peters, Martha's husband, restored vintage cars for a hobby. Sometimes he'd give me sixpence for polishing his tools. Bob kept his shed in immaculate order, and he would whistle and listen to me sing as I worked. One by one, I'd arrange the spanners from smallest to largest on an old oilcloth in his shed.

Mrs. Peters often visited my mother. Martha Peters, mother of four kids, had a heart of gold buried beneath her twenty-two-stone frame. She was an enormous woman with a prolapsed hernia in her lower abdomen. Martha had developed the hernia by carrying her youngest child, who was bedridden. The distended part of her body shook uncomfortably as she walked. When Martha Peters moved, it seemed as if the whole world rumbled along with her. In summer, Bob Peters would let me pick apples and oranges from his orchard. On weekdays, he rode his bicycle into town to catch the train to work. I'd often stand at our makeshift gate and wave to him as he rode by, making sure to keep well clear of his overprotective blue heeler, Bluey. One day while I was waving, I slipped and knocked out my front tooth on the fence. Bob didn't see what happened; he just kept on riding.

Debbie Peters was seventeen and very grown up. She was tall and pretty, with thick blond hair that stuck out in a bob; she looked like the models on billboards. I liked the way her hair scooped up at the ends, never moving, stuck together with gluggy hair spray. Occasionally she came to babysit us. Afterward, if Dad offered her a lift home, she'd always run off with a hurried "No, thank you." She told me my dad was creepy and said, "I don't like him one little bit." My father told Debbie and her brother that he was a detective who worked for the Secret Service, and they believed him.

"It explains a multitude of things!" she said. "Especially why he snoops around in the middle of the bush."

Rosalie Peters was Bob's youngest child. She personified encouragement to all who felt that life had shortchanged them. Totally bedridden, she saw no one except her family and her doctor. That is, until she met me. I had no one in the vicinity to play with other than my brothers, so Rosalie became my best friend.

When I walked into the Peterses' house, the first thing that hit me was the overpowering smell of kerosene and stale urine. They used the kerosene for cooking and heating the four-room house, and the urine smell came from Rosalie. She had no control over her bodily functions, as she was suffering from hydrocephalus, water on the brain.[xxxix] The shunt system for brain drainage had not been invented yet, and the doctors had thought Rosalie would only live until the age of three. Little did they realize that with her mother's courage and devotion, this child would surprise them and live until she was fourteen. Rosalie's head was enlarged to such severe proportions that her hair was balding, and it stood out in fine tufts where it had rubbed against the bedsheets. Blue veins strained under the skin, and I could see her blood pulsating through her temples. Her teeth were underdeveloped and half-rotted because her tongue thrust forward compulsively.

Her enormous head was as large as her small, wasted body. Sometimes with a great effort, Rosalie would thrash her arms about using her upper arms and elbows, but on most days, her hands fell limply to the sides of her brutally atrophied body. She suffered from relentless migraines caused by the excess fluid and pressure in her head. You could tell when Rosalie had a headache, because her eyes would roll back in her head and she would groan loudly.

When Rosalie was in pain, her moaning raised alarming activity. Martha Peters would tell me to hold Rosalie's hand while she raced around collecting clean nappies. In no time, these nappies became towels, dampened by tank water and placed on Rosalie's huge forehead.

Mrs. Peters would soothe her daughter by saying, "Hush-a-bye, my love." Then she would tell me, "She's not well enough for stories today, dear. You'd better go home."

After I got over the initial shock of meeting Rosalie, I would sit with her for hours. I would chatter to her, never doubting that she understood what I was saying. Rosalie's vocabulary was limited to a few words, but I did most of the talking. When I paused for breath, Rosalie would put in an appropriate "eh" or "whaa" as an answer. Her bulging blue eyes would follow me around the room when I moved, and she'd chortle and "gaa" at all my jokes. I needed a friend to talk to, and I knew that Rosalie could never disclose my secrets. She was trapped inside her body, unable to move, captive to my incessant prattle. Rosalie was my friend, and beneath her hideous exterior was a child fighting to get out.

One day I discovered Rosalie could rip things up. I asked her mother for some old telephone books and let her rip the pages out. While she did this, I found the pages that were still whole and made paper airplanes. To my delight, Rosalie began to laugh as I threw them around the room. After a while, I carefully placed one in Rosalie's hand. Sometimes, Rosalie would manage to throw it. Her aim was terrible, but to continue the game I needed only the encouragement of the sheer pleasure of watching her follow the plane with her eyes. I felt safe playing games with Rosalie because there was never a winner.

At home and at odd hours, the "Games Man" would come and visit me in my room. He was a strange-looking creature with a black woolen face made from a beanie hat. His white cardboard eyes and mouth were stuck on with sticky tape, and they sometimes fell off onto the floor. This was the only part of his games that ever amused me, because I'd imagine stamping on the pieces when they hit the ground. The Games Man had a strange laugh, and he carried a rolled-up newspaper, which he would hit me with if I made a mistake. He said he knew everything and that he was "in charge of the rules."

"Rules are made, and rules are broken," he'd squeak, and then he'd dissolve into peals of laughter. "Don't break the rules, because I have eyes in the back of my head."

The Games Man loved to play blind man's bluff. He'd stand with newspaper in hand and command me to walk past him when he turned his back. I'd try to carefully creep past him, but the newspaper would come down hard, smack on my head. I didn't understand that his real eyes were staring through the woolen beanie and the cardboard eyes were stuck on the back, making them look like he was staring at the wall. The Games Man taught me to be impassive. I quickly learned that if I showed pain, the game would drag on and on. However, if I demonstrated no feeling at all, the game would be shorter because he would become bored.

This became my defense against so many of his warped scenarios. For self-amusement, he'd invent all types of situations. Some were just silly cruelties, while others became more dangerous. When I'd see the cigarette coming toward me, I'd try not to react at all. I'd try not to wince, move, or cry out, and in the wake of my emotionless state, the Games Man would finally lose interest and leave me alone.

"How does he know where I am?" I'd think when the paper came crashing down on my head. "He hits me every time."

Then as if to answer my question, the Games Man would say, "Remember, there can only be one winner in the game, and that will *always* be me."

Michael and I entered a Time Life book competition, and each of us won a copy of Time Life's *Australasia*.[xl] We were reading the books when Michael had his brilliant idea. He lined the Paddle Pop sticks up in a row, and Liam asked in awe, "How did you eat all those ice creams?"

"I didn't eat them," he answered. "I found the sticks at school."

Michael had a plan to make some money. He wanted something to sell to the children at school and had come up with an idea.

"Most kids bring money for the tuck-shop," he said. "We will make Aboriginal paint brushes and sell them."

"But do Aboriginals use paint brushes?"

None of us were sure. In the past we had done cave painting down in the gorge with bits of stick, leaves, clay, and charcoal. We'd never used a paintbrush on rock before.

We stood waiting to put Michael's innovative moneymaking scheme into action.

"You make them like this," he said, scraping the Paddle Pop stick on a rock. "They have to be nice and pointed."

We all copied.

"Then you get the other end and strip it into little bits like a brush."

"Easy!" I thought, trying not to snap the wood.

"What now?" asked Liam after he had finished.

"We have to get some brown and black paint to color them in. Then when kids put them in water, the color will run out on the paper." Liam and Jamie ran off to find some paint.

"How much will we make?"

"I reckon I can get two cents a brush at school."

"But what if they don't believe they're Aboriginal paint brushes?"

"I'll think of something else."

After school the next day, Michael came home with nearly a dollar. In our minds he was a genius.

"We'll make more," we said, but he decided against it.

"We have to make something different because they won't buy the same thing twice." He thought for a while and then snapped his fingers.

"I know. We will make genuine Japanese ducks out of paper, and the kids can do Donald Duck impersonations." We spent the hour making origami ducks. The next afternoon Michael came home with even more money, but there was also a note from his teacher.

"No more moneymaking schemes will be tolerated at school." Michael's career as an entrepreneur had been cut short, but he still had one more idea.

My brothers and I named every land in the bush we deemed to be ours. We had Conrad's Caves, named after the dog because he found them; Caveman's Cave, because it had a window and looked like a house; Picnic Rock, which was my mother's favorite picnic spot; and Waterfall Rock, because the sandstone colors looked like water falling over a cliff. We had lots of names for different areas of the bush, so we could meet at places and never get lost. They were children's names, given to suit the landscape, or Aboriginal names from a pocket-sized dictionary my mother insisted we carry. Mum had a great respect for the bush and for the people who could survive in it.

"The bush is a wild creature, and it cannot be tamed," she'd say, describing the foliage. "Yet the Aboriginal people can find food and make medicines because of their inherent knowledge. We should try to do the same."

Michael had built fire tracks all through the bush with his little shovel. Sometimes he'd get Grandfather's stopwatch and time us as we ran barefoot through the gullies. If we couldn't make the run from point A to point B in the required amount of time, we'd be in "big trouble." We were never sure what the "big trouble" was, but the thought was foreboding enough to keep us running, sore feet and all. One day he took our Time Life books and the Aboriginal Dictionary to Caveman's Cave.

"We can use them as a reference," he said, holding up a pointed stick. "We'll draw with this."

We chipped away at the base of the rock opposite, collecting pieces of blue shale, and then we found some white-and-orange clay farther down at the gully. The cave soon became a decorated artwork as we copied the Aboriginal drawings with childhood precision. But Michael said, "It isn't good enough. If we want to be famous, we have to do rock carvings as well," he added, turning the book's pages until he found a photograph. "This one will do."

Three eager faces clambered to look, and Jamie started to laugh.

"Those men have three legs," he exclaimed, not realizing the fertility significance of the male genitalia.

Michael and I found a rocky expanse on the left-hand side of the gorge, and we started carving and chipping our way into history. Four sweaty children had a sandy vision. Many years later I went back to our special carving place and admired the brass plate firmly attached to the rock's surface. My brothers and I had chipped our way into history, as our rock had been classified as an Aboriginal site.

Sometimes while I was walking in the bush during the heat of summer, I would chance upon snake nests. Once I saw a pile of them under a rock, all writhing like fat whitish-brown string. There were about six of them squirming like thick worms.

"Don't touch them," Mum warned. "It's a baby snake nest." My hands flew back to my sides. I hated snakes. They struck a chord of terror in my soul. I hated seeing them draped like lazy lengths of black rope, baking on the rock shelves in the sun. Sometimes they were up to five feet long, enormous slithering creatures that would slide away when they heard us coming. They dominated the untamed bush of my backyard, hiding in winter and posing a silent threat in summer.

The Games Man loved snakes. He had a special place on Marge Banning's land where he'd dug a shallow trench between two butts of earth. Over the top he'd put a heavy, rusty plate of metal that had formerly served as the back door of a truck. The door still had a huge iron bolt on it, and it made an awful grating sound when the Games Man pushed it to one side. I always thought the Games Man could lock the door, but as an adult I realized that there was nothing for it to hold on to, just two bits of earth.

The trench was just big enough for me to lie in, my arms pinned to my sides, until I somehow managed to bend them half upright. The metal door was warm in summer, and I would get itchy with the heat. The air in the hole always smelled rusty and dank. I learned how to breathe shallowly, and I never screamed for help. I had learned long before that screaming only made the situation worse. Screaming always resulted in me being gagged or having tape put over my mouth. Instead, I'd place my palms flat on the metal door and push. Little bits of dirt would fall into the hole, and the door often groaned, but it never lifted, as it was too heavy.

Sometimes when I was lying in this makeshift grave with the huge metal door above me, I'd feel things crawling on me. They were usually bugs or cockroaches. Once, the Games Man became very excited because he said he had some baby snakes.

"You've dug your grave," he'd say to me before pulling the door over the top of me, "now lie in it."

He let the creatures fall onto my body, and they wriggled and squiggled across my chest. I don't know if they really were snakes. He may have been playing a trick on me because in reality the baby snakes that fell on me were not much bigger than large earthworms. I closed my eyes and tried not to look, too frightened to cry out or move. I squeezed my body tight and tried to breathe shallowly, totally repressed by paralytic panic.

I hated snakes. If I saw them in the bush, I'd keep my distance, holding tightly to my dogs' collars. The dogs loved snakes. They'd run around them barking and force them to rear up in anger. Then the dogs would catch the reptiles in their mouths and jump around, throwing them to the ground and breaking their backs. I was sure that the dogs' luck would run out one day and they would be bitten and die. So I held on to their collars, seeing every stick's movement and every blade of shuddering grass as an impending snake.

"Come and play with the snake."

The figure was sitting on the crocheted bedspread in Grandma O'Leary's bedroom. The empty wig box was on the floor, and her cupboard was wide open and in disarray. I didn't want to play. I wanted to go home to my mother.

"Hurry up now. Be a good girl. Grandma O'Leary is waiting."

"That's not right," I thought. "Grandma O'Leary's in the hospital."

"Here, snake," the wigged figure called, "come and play with this *darling* child."

But I didn't want to play, and I should have been at school.

"Hurry up, you stupid girl." It was an agitated voice. "Don't you *dare* keep me waiting!"

I knew what the voice meant. When he dressed as Grandma O'Leary, he was angry, and anger always resulted in punishment. I had been playing the snake game since the age of three, yet every time it came time to play, my legs would refuse to move. It was a punishment I found difficult to handle and one I blocked out of my mind as soon as it was over. The figure would lunge forward and pull my hair, dragging me down to the floor in front of the bed.

"Down on your knees, and beg the snake's forgiveness," it would command. "Go down to hell where all bad children go."

I never needed to reply. Immersed in material, the snake would eventually find my face. Rubbing and throbbing, pulsating its way to an explosion. I hated the snake, its poison smeared all over my face.

In July 1966, the real Grandma O'Leary suffered a stroke and refused to die. Michael and I were taken to the hospital to visit her.

"I don't want to go," I told my mother under my breath.

"Your father wants you to do this."

"Why?"

"You two are the eldest, and you have to visit her," Mum told us in a hushed voice.

The Manor Convalescent Home looked like a giant green-and-white country house. It had grand, old-fashioned verandas with opening french doors that led out to leafy trees in the garden. Wisteria grew over the walkways in the garden, and the purple flowers emitted a fragrance that reminded me of my grandmother's house. Neither Michael nor I spoke, as we had been warned not to make any noise. Our relatives on the veranda were unnaturally quiet as we filed past them into her room.

There she was…like a doll propped up in bed. Massive pillows supported her head, and blankets had been neatly folded across her tiny body. Her hands were all purple and blotchy from her years of detergent use as a cleaner. They lay aged and withered on the covers by her side. I looked at the woman on the bed, her white nightdress reflecting her sunken, dull-gray features. She looked as if she were asleep. Suddenly an eye opened, and she was watching us. She couldn't move or speak; she just stared. I stared back, noticing that two stringy gray plaits fell down from her head over her shoulders, nearly reaching her waist. I shook my head in disbelief.

"It's time to go now," said my mother, ushering us from the room.

I waited until we were outside the room before I asked, "How did Grandma O'Leary grow her hair so quickly?"

My mother looked at me as if I were crazy. "Don't be silly, Shannon; you know she's always had hair that length."

Still I persisted. "No, she doesn't! She has short hair. Short, curly hair, and she's grown it long overnight." My mother looked exasperated; she must have thought my visit to the hospital had upset me.

"Stop it," she warned as my brother started to laugh. "You'll end up getting us all into trouble." She turned to my father as he walked across the veranda.

"She looks better," he said. "Go home; I'll see you later." He handed my mother the car keys. My mother quickly turned to get in the car, and we followed. Grandma O'Leary didn't look better to me. To me she looked totally different.

Two days after our visit, on July 30, 1966, Grandma O'Leary died. The family whispered that someone had slipped her brandy to bring on her final stroke, but I wasn't supposed to know that because I was just a child. Everyone said it was an act of God because the poor woman couldn't move her limbs. Grandma could only manage to move her eyes. They followed people around the room without anyone knowing what she wanted to say. She just stared and stared.

Ethel May Curtis took many of her secrets to the grave. Before her stroke, she had confessed to her eldest child, Liam, that John O'Leary was not his father, but she hadn't revealed the fact she had never married him. Her death certificate listed cerebral thrombosis and arteriosclerosis[xli] as the cause of death and stated that her age was seventy-six. Grandma O'Leary's real age, however, was sixty-eight; the extra eight years were added to cover up her first child's conception at such a young age. Born into the Anglican Church, Ethel had pretended to be a devout Catholic for all her adult life.

After Grandma O'Leary's funeral, my father went missing. He was gone for two days, and no one could find him. When he finally came home, he was dirty and disheveled. Everyone asked where he had been, but he said he couldn't remember. He said, "I didn't even know two days had passed." He still thought it was the day of his mother's funeral.

Jamie wanted to be either an elephant or a chook man when he grew up. After a while he realized he could never change into an elephant, so he decided that the life of a chicken carrier was for him. He had seen the red trucks with crates of live chickens driving down the road, and he thought it would make a worthy occupation.

"All I have to do is drive my truck all day and feed the chickens when they get hungry," he said. "Chook men have the best job."

Michael wanted to be like Professor Julius Sumner Miller on the ABC show *Why Is It So?*[xlii] This desire changed as Michael grew older and new information shows aired on the various networks available in Australia at the time. In 1968 he wanted to go on *It's Academic* and win a truckload of money.[xliii] In his mind, he was as smart as Albert Einstein. Every day he'd ask me questions, and I never knew the correct answer. He'd ask, "What's the capital of Germany?" or "How many people live in Peru?" Everyone used to tell me Michael was a real "brain."

Liam wanted to be a superhero. He was always running around the yard yahooing and pretending he was invincible. Sometimes when we were in the car, he would want my mother to stop driving so he could get out and play by the creek on the way into town. My mother would refuse to stop, and Liam would trick her by throwing pieces of Jamie's clothing out the car window. My mother would have to stop to retrieve the items, and while she was doing this, Liam and Michael would run off and catch tadpoles. Mum soon realized that clothes always flew out of the window at the same place, and she began to avoid driving past the little creek with the willow trees that always looked so inviting. My brothers loved to climb trees, swing on ropes, wrestle one another, and goad one another into walking near bull joe nests. The big black ants,[xliv] which were common where we lived, could cause a nasty bite, one that left us with "blue bag" antiseptic painted all over our toes and legs.

The tree house in the big gum down in the backyard was Michael's special domain. It had a wooden ladder leading up to a platform where Michael could sit and contemplate the world. Sometimes he would sit there for hours just watching the bush. I never knew what he was looking for, and he said he was "just keeping guard."

"This is the boys' tree house," he told me over and over again. "No girls allowed, so keep away."

Ever since I can remember, I have been frightened of heights. I don't know why, but I am terrified of falling. To this day, I still dream that I'm falling off ledges into chasms below or tripping up flights of never-ending steps. I place my foot on the stair and miss it completely, falling down and waking up with a start. The shock of slipping is so great my heart pumps wildly and I find it difficult to sleep again. Sometimes as a child, I would also dream I was flying, arms outstretched like Wonder Woman, through the skies. I'd career high above the bush, crisscrossing above the trees and jagged rock faces until I'd land safe and secure at my destination. I loved this dream. It was so wonderful I could have stayed in it forever. This dream, however, had no bearing on reality. In real life my fear of altitude knew no boundaries, and I avoided heights wherever possible.

Michael's tree house wasn't my favorite playing area, so I was surprised when I heard him call, "Come up here, Shannon."

"No!" My reply was definite.

"What's wrong? Are you chicken?"

"No." I didn't like being called chicken. I knew it meant that I was a coward.

"Shannon's a chicken; Shannon's a chicken." Michael shouted it loudly from the treetops. Tears stung my eyes.

"I am not chicken," I said, and to prove him wrong, I climbed up the ladder to the platform. A hand grabbed me by the shirt and hurled me up into the air. I sailed over the platform, down past the tree, until I hit the ground. A smirking adult face snickered at my predicament as I doubled over an injured ankle.

"That will teach her," my father jeered.

Michael, thinking it was a fabulous game, joined in with the words, "I told you; I warned you. This tree house is for boys only."

From then on, I kept away from the tree house, but I didn't keep away from trees. I discovered everyone knew I was afraid of heights, and this made trees an invaluable hiding place. No one searched for me high above the ground; they always looked under things. My new aim in life was to become invisible so I could confuse the predator. I would pick my hiding places at random in order to avoid being found. I'd hide up a tree or under the house; I'd hide in the boronia bushes or in the burned-out tree stump down in the gully. Inside my cupboard and under the bed became my nightly hiding places, while during the day, I practiced jumping out the window to see how quickly I could escape from my room. A crown-of-thorns bush grew underneath my window, so my first few attempts at jumping resulted in scratches and bruising. But this didn't deter me. Eventually I could jump out the window, clear the thorn bush, land on my feet, and keep running until I could find somewhere to hide.

My brothers were also expert tree climbers. Often, they would play Tarzan or Superman. We didn't have a television, but everyone at school loved superheroes.

Once when Benjamin, Mum's younger brother, was visiting, all the boys started to show off. Liam was climbing as high as Benjamin, and the older boy was urging him on.

"Can you do this?" he shouted, and Liam copied. Up into the tree they went, until they seemed as high as a two-story building.

"Hey, look at me," Benjamin shouted, jumping from one branch to another.

"I can do that," cried Liam, and he jumped too. I closed my eyes. I didn't like the way the game was heading.

"Bet you can't do this." Benjamin jumped neatly from one gum tree to another. The smaller boy's eyes widened.

"Can too!" he shouted, and he jumped. His feet barely scraped the other tree's branch. He sailed toward the ground, turning a somersault as he fell, and landed on his back. He didn't move, his head inches away from a tooth-edged tree stump.

I bolted up to the house, screaming, "Mum! Liam's fallen out of the tree." Michael followed, calling, "He's dead. He's not moving. Help!" Mum and Dad both came out of the house and ran to where Liam was lying.

My father picked him up, and Liam opened his eyes.

"Are you all right?"

Then, in his most pronounced melodramatic style, Liam replied, "Where am I?"

Liam was shocked and bruised, but miraculously he had remained unhurt. Relief and laughter followed, and Liam milked the reaction from his audience. An actor had been born.

In retrospect we were all trained actors, my mother included. My father's behavior would go from tolerable to tyrannical in the blink of an eye. This taught my brothers and me to be multifaceted and skilled in controlling emotion. I constantly had to read his character before he expressed which mood was consuming him. He demanded that his reality become mine, and because I could not see what his psychosis revealed to him, I was forced to pretend. I was thrust into the roles he created, and I tragically knew that if I failed to present him with a perfect performance, I would never survive.

"Always the actress," he'd laughingly tell people in conversation while squeezing my arm above the elbow until it bruised.

The people would laugh, and I'd smile, all the while wanting to scream, "If only you knew!"

My father's world was filled with deadly games, but through active participation, I learned to read people around me. I was so accustomed to reading my father's emotions and characters, I became noticeably in tune with all that was going on around me. I had the hearing of a bat, sharp and clear from constant practice, and I could tell at a glance if someone was distressed, happy, or miles away in thought. This was a rare quality for one so young, and people started to tell my mother, "She's old beyond her years." People would tell her I was "filled with wisdom" and had "a rare gift." Mumma said I was fey, while Grandfather said he "loved the Irish in me." The children at school began to call me a witch, while one old priest called me "the devil's advocate."

Sometimes, words would just pop into my head, and I'd say them out loud. One day this happened at a school assembly.

Our local parish priest walked past me, and I said without thinking, "His mother's going to die tonight." All the girls and boys gasped in horror. I gulped, taken aback by my own words.

"Was it blasphemous?" I thought. "Will I be struck down dead?" I waited all day, but nothing happened. The next day, the principal, Sister Monica, told the school that the priest's mother had passed away in her sleep.

"You killed her," said one little girl as she walked into class. "You must have put a curse on her." Her words launched my mind into a state of frightened confusion. My father said he knew God and the devil, and as a result, I didn't know whether I was to blame for the woman's death or not. What if the devil had tricked me into thinking he was God? My father had warned about this kind of thing,

Maybe instead of being "an instrument of his peace," I had become "an instrument of destruction," I thought. My mind was in a quandary. Was I was guilty or innocent? There seemed only one alternative. "I'll have to do penance," I decided. "Penance" was a new word I had learned in class. It meant I would have to be sorry and ask for God's forgiveness. My main concern was how God measured the crime. The more I pondered the question, the more confused I became. Childish riddles invaded my head.

"Are ten Hail Marys worth one Lord's Prayer, or was the rosary invented because Mary needed more prayers than Jesus?" I never worked out the answers, dancing round in circles until the questions became bantering conundrums inside my head.

I spent a lot of time in church. Every Sunday morning my father took us all to Mass. During lunch break at school, I often sat in the church and talked to the statues. The austerity and silence of the church fascinated me. The stained glass window's color enthralled me, yet its violence repulsed me. Father Ignatius, the priest, recited his Sunday sermon in English. At church, all the women covered their heads with mantillas or hats, and I wore a furry white bonnet with pompoms. It was obvious to me my father had told him many secrets in confession, because no matter where my family sat in the church, the old priest would always end up directing his speeches to us. My mother and I would squirm uneasily in our seats while my father would meet the priest's stare squarely, with a half smile on his face.

"If a man tells his priest he has committed murder, the priest must take the secret to his grave. It is a communication between the man and God, as the priest is a go-between, a mere vessel used for Christ's interpretation."

These speeches made me fidgety and nervous, and I ended up twisting the pompoms of my hat. I wanted to know how saying "I'm sorry, God" could wash an enormous sin like murder away.

"What about the people who are dead?" I asked Sister Mary.

"Their poor souls will go to heaven, and they will have eternal happiness," she retorted, and I was impressed. Eternal happiness had a fairy-tale ring to it, and I thought it would be wonderful to be happy forever.

During the 1960s the church was slowly changing the words of the Mass from Latin to English.[xlv] I was pleased because I couldn't understand Latin, but my father wasn't at all impressed. He said, "The devil got into the church and stole the Mass."

"Misereatur tui omnipotens Deus, et dimissis peccatis tuis,"[xlvi] he'd mumble. "We will all be burned in hell's fires."

I didn't like hell's fires, because once they were lit, it took forever to put them out. The Devil lit fires around my home, and the bush would explode into a tinderbox of flame.

In religion, Sister Mary Immaculate told my class, "The sun will fall on the earth if man keeps on with his evil ways. It will burn us all, and we will not be saved until the final resurrection." I was terrified.

"We've already had two world wars," she would lecture. "If there is a Third World War, God will send the sun down to burn us all." I worried continuously, dreading the impending final hours, not old enough to believe any different. I lived in fear of the world burning, and I wondered how long it would take everyone to die.

"Would the sun fall quickly, or would it take years to reach the earth? Would everyone slowly melt, or would the sun crush us to death?" I thought.

"Please, God, don't let there be a war," I added to my prayers at night. "I don't want the sun to burn me. The sun is so much bigger than a cigarette."

Heat like the burning sun only inches away from my nose. The torchlight would glare, blinding me as I tried to hold up my hands to shield my eyes.

"What's that?" I'd panic. "Something heavy on my hands." I couldn't move my arms. Terror kept my eyes open, the light blazing and making them water. The weight was bearing down on me, and I felt my arms could snap.

"What's wrong with my mouth?" I thought. "Why can't I scream?" I tried to make a noise, but the hand was too tight across my mouth. The torch pressed on my forehead. It was too bright, searing, so I closed my eyes. The weight shifted, forcing something into my mouth. In and out, in and out, until I choked and gagged.

"Where's some air? Get off my arms," I tried to say. It was no use, as it was too heavy. My brain was screaming as the weight shifted the hand back over my mouth. I made a gulping sound as I choked and tried to fight the overwhelming nausea. Thrashing my head from side to side, I attempted to fend off the sticky stuff that covered my face, sickeningly warm and salty. The torch dropped away from my eyes. Everything should have been black again, but it never was. Instead, the world was a shiny gray, dotted from the glare of the torchlight that had scorched my eyes. The weight eventually left me. It walked away, but I would lie frozen in my bed. I dared not move for fear it would return.

CHAPTER 7

1967

My mother had entered the goats into the Hawkesbury show, but Dad wouldn't drive her to the showground.

"I'm sure Kisty would have won a prize," Mum said to Auntie Marge. "She's such a good milker."

"Why don't you go anyway?" Auntie Marge asked. "You don't need him to take you; catch a train."

Mum laughed. "What, with four children and two goats? You've got to be joking."

But Auntie Marge wasn't joking. "There's a train station near the showground. Just buy tickets for yourself and the children and put the goats on their leads."

"Do I buy tickets for the goats as well?" She laughed. The question seemed ridiculous.

"Yes!" We stared open mouthed at Auntie Marge, who went on to explain the Dog and Goat Act.[xlvii]

"You buy tickets for the goats, and the Railway Authority can't stop you because they've never changed the law. Your goats are classed as real passengers. They can even sit on the seats if they like."

So, there we were. Two goats, four children, and my mother heading for the Hawkesbury show on the train. We put down hessian bags for the goats to lie on, and they were quite content. Passengers laughed when they saw us, but on the way home we didn't care. We were all too proud. Kisty was wearing her championship milking ribbon, as she had won first place in the show.

"Who are you?" I'd always asked the question slowly, hoping to get an even-tempered reaction. I thought I knew who it was, but I always had to be sure. Sometimes my six-year-old brain made a mistake, and I would call him by the wrong name. When this happened, I'd receive a belt across the ear for being discourteous.

"Whaa!"

I had my answer. It was the Baby. The slobbering infant didn't visit me often; in fact, in the course of ten years, I only ever saw it five or six times. I didn't like this caricature. It was a travesty, a demanding, spoiled baby that always got its own way. As I pretended to make baby food in a cup, loud bursts of anger hit my ears. The Baby was crying. It was time to comfort him and give him solace.

"Good Baby," I'd say, patting him on the head.

Goo-gaas and baby talk followed. I understood some of it, while the rest was incomprehensible. I would be standing upright while the Baby sat down, yet it was as tall as I was. Sometimes he'd sit huddled in a corner, all red faced and bloated, the stubble on his face black and spiky against his saliva-covered chin. The white towel was a make-believe nappy.

"Sing," the Baby would order, so I'd put my arms around the pretend child and begin to sing.

"Rock-a-bye, baby, in the treetop. When the wind blows, the cradle will rock." The Baby would wobble when I tried to make it sway by pushing its shoulders to and fro. It was too heavy for me. It was a spitting, burdensome baby.

"When the bough breaks, the cradle will fall, and down will come baby, cradle and all."

"Whaa!" the Baby would scream. He hated the last line, but I relished it. I wanted the cradle to fall, to smash the baby so I wouldn't have to see him again.

"Whaa! Whaa!" the Baby would continue.

"Shut up, you stupid baby," I'd think. "Shut up and go away."

Sister Luke was new at my school, and she had taught my mother and her sisters when they were little. Sister Luke was an intelligent and artistic teacher who loved her students and tried her best to understand them. She didn't understand me, but she liked my spirit. One day while walking up the stairs at school, she asked me how things were at home.

"Not good," I replied all too trustingly, "but hopefully my parents will get a divorce." The impact was immediate.

"You have no right to say such things, young lady. Divorce is a sin, and by wishing your parents to do such an evil thing, you are sinning too." I was shocked. I didn't expect this reaction. Sister Luke always said she wanted to help.

"But they are fighting all the time," I mumbled, "and Dad hits Mum."

"You should stand in the room with them," she replied. "Then they'll stop fighting."

I laughed, and she glared at me.

"My father would punch me through the wall," I muttered under my breath, and I went into class. Any confidence I had entertained in Sister Luke was shattered. Lately, an all-consuming tiredness had overwhelmed me during school hours. I'd get dizzy and need to lie down. My face was often irritated and itchy, and my eyes hurt when I had to keep them open during the day. At night, nocturnal noises played havoc with my sleep. The Devil visited me, bringing with him the black spots. The black spots formed when I smelled the overwhelming fumes hidden in the hanky. They were dizzy, deep black spots, and they burned my nostrils and mouth. Sometimes, after the hanky had overpowered me and I had woken up again, I'd be too frightened to sleep. I'd hide under my blankets with my fingers in my ears, waiting for the shouting in the next room to stop.

Eventually the house would take on an eerie silence, but I'd will myself not to sleep. The one-sided arguments were becoming more frequent. My father shouted and hit things while my mother occasionally whimpered. I was too frightened to get out of bed anymore. I began to wet the bed because I was too frightened to walk outside to the toilet. The Devil always slunk around in the night, hidden in the shadows, a huge black figure, ready to pounce on me and shake me until my teeth rattled.

"I'd rather wet the bed," I thought, "than face him. I'll sleep on the floor."

"You're too old to wet the bed," my mother would reason with me.

"I know," I'd mumble, remaking the bed and lining it with newspaper. I felt ashamed and guilty, but my fear kept me trapped in bed.

Sometimes the tables would turn, and instead of lying awake, I'd be too tired to rouse myself from sleep. Instead I'd be trapped, the black spots making me dizzy. I would feel as if I were falling…falling in and out of sleep at an all-too-confusing and alarming rate. When I'd finally lie awake again, I'd try to remember bits and pieces, frightening realities mixed in with little black holes. If my body hurt, I tried not to notice; instead, I tried to concentrate on remembering.

"I will remember," I'd vow. "I won't forget."

Then the headaches started. Small throbbing ones at first, and later, the type that tell you to lie still with your fists clamped over your eyes. At school, Sister Luke would let me lie down on the sickbed outside the classroom, wondering what was wrong with me. Sister Luke took our class for religion, and every day before lunch, she would call me up to her desk.

"Is everything all right at home?" she'd ask, genuinely worried about my health.

I'd answer, "No." When she tried to probe deeper, I'd stand looking at her, not answering. Occasionally I'd tell her it wasn't anybody's business what went on in our family, and she'd stop the questions, not knowing which tack to try. Stubborn, I resolved to protect those around me. No one could separate my metal jaws. I was like a closed steel trap that had rusted in the rain.

"Only a fool would talk," the Devil had told me, and I knew he was right. Sister Luke could never outsmart the Devil, even if she had God on her side.

My mother stood with her hands on her hips and watched the goanna.[xlviii]

"What's he doing?" I asked.

"He's waiting for us to leave so he can eat the eggs."

I looked at the chook yard. It seemed fairly secure to me. "How will he get in?"

"Like this!" My mother picked up a rock and threw it over toward the giant reptile. It landed with a thump, and the startled goanna raced up the closest gum tree.

"See his claws?" Mum continued. "He can easily climb or dig under the fence."

The goanna's beady eyes watched us, blinking occasionally, staring us out.

"He looks dead," I said. "Like a statue."

"Come on." Mum laughed. "I haven't got time to watch him all day."

A few days later, the goanna came back. Broken eggshells and flurried chicken feathers told us of his invasion. The goanna had moved from his tree house into the chicken coop, but Mum said we didn't have to move him out.

"He'll only eat what he needs," she said.

"How do I love thee? Let me count the ways…"

The counting began.

"One, two, three, four, five…"

And on and on!

"Sixty-five, sixty-six, sixty-seven, sixty-eight…"

The rope wasn't tight, but I couldn't move.

"Ninety-nine, one hundred, one hundred one, one hundred two…"

No tears or screaming, only silent shivering, yet the kitchen was filled with noise.

Goldie was squawking, her brilliant feathers flying, as he held her above the boiling pot of water. The bird's feet were tied together, and with sadistic pleasure he lowered her, inch by inch, into the water. I shut my eyes and tried to block out the bird's pain. The screeching stopped when she hit the water. The smell of wet feathers and hot chicken flesh overpowered my nostrils, and I fought to stop the rising vomit from spewing all over my father. He put the lid on the pot and held it in place.

Fear had kept me immobilized, and Goldie's death left me overcome with powerless guilt. When my father turned his back, I knelt down and freed myself. The rope around my ankles wasn't very tight, and I ran out of the kitchen, never looking back. Past the chickens and the goat shed, through the bush and down into the gully where no one could find me. Goldie was dead, and I blamed myself for not saving her. When I eventually returned home, feathers were scattered outside the goat shed and in the chicken coop. The frantic search had begun. Two small bantams were missing, and so was the goanna.

"When we find him, he'll have to go," Mum said. "We can't have him killing our chickens."

It was feeding time, and as my mother poured out oats for the goats, I made my way toward the goat shed. It was a hive of activity. Two little kids kicked up their heels, bleating and skipping from side to side. I pulled the warm bottle out from behind my back, and they bolted forward, trying to push each other away in their hurry to get the milk.

"Hurry up, Mum," I called. "Sally's hungry, and Samson won't let her near the bottle." Samson pushed his sister aside and greedily sucked at the teat. Sally, my favorite, bleated and trotted around in a circle. Mum came over to the fence and gave me her bottle.

"I'll feed Sally," I said as the kid clambered over her brother. Slurping and spilling some milk on the ground, the baby goats finished their meal in a flash.

"Greedy boy," Mum reprimanded as she stroked Samson. "Settle down."

Splash!

A bucket of water tipped over and hit the feed bin. I heard a huge bang and a clatter as the goanna scrambled out from underneath the chaff bags in the corner. He ran out of the shed as fast as his fat legs would carry him, clambering over the fence and up the nearest gum tree.

Mum ran outside after him shouting, "Go away and leave my goats alone."

"Could the goanna kill one of the goats?" she asked my father later.

"It eats chickens," he said, "and your father says it wouldn't be hard for it to rip a goat's throat out."

My mother felt there was only one alternative. When we left for school, she went to find Dad's rifle. After she fired the first shot, she was surprised to find herself sitting on the ground. The gun's kickback was stronger than she expected. She tried again, clumsily reloading. Shot after shot. Up in the air! Down into the bush! Everywhere except at the poor goanna. My mother's shots even missed the tree. The baker found her sitting crying under the tree when he dropped in to make a delivery. He looked at the exhausted, sobbing woman and took the rifle. It took him one clean shot to kill the large reptile. The goanna fell from the tree and lay still on the grass in forty-degree heat until we came home from school.

When we heard the story, Michael was ecstatic. "I can take it to school for science."

Mum agreed, and she wrapped the goanna in newspaper and put it in the refrigerator. Michael was very proud as he carried the newspaper parcel to the bus stop. Everyone wanted to see the dead goanna, but he wouldn't let them. Instead, he put it under the bus stop seat for safekeeping. Half an hour went by before the bus finally arrived, and we all went to school. That is, everyone except for the goanna. It lay forgotten under the seat.

We were in forty-degree heat, and it had been over twelve hours since the goanna had been shot.

"Phew! That really stinks," said Liam, pulling a face when Michael retrieved the parcel after school. "Leave it here."

But tenacious Michael carried the parcel out at arm's length, bringing it home to my mother. Mum took one look at the ant-ridden newspaper and yelled for Michael to get it out of the house. She sprayed it with insecticide and told us to keep away from it. This wasn't difficult, as the dead goanna stank. The next morning we left for school. Michael managed to get the goanna on the bus, but no one would sit near him.

"Don't forget your stinky friend," my little brothers laughed when Michael prepared to get off the bus.

"How could I?" replied the unimpressed miniature biologist. The goanna was becoming an embarrassment. Michael stuffed the parcel under a train seat and sat farther away. All the kids on the train wanted to know what the stink was, and he pretended he didn't know. The train pulled up at his stop, and Michael quickly jumped out. He turned toward the ticket gate and remembered his precious parcel.

"Oh no!" He watched as the train made its way from the platform.

"Too late," he thought. "There goes my goanna!"

The next day we heard a funny snippet of news. It was broadcast on the radio that a train had been evacuated in Melbourne because of a "bomb-like" device. The newspapered apparatus had been unwrapped, revealing a stinking reptile.

"Some vandals will do anything," said the voice on the radio. "The whole carriage had to be fumigated." My little brothers and I were very impressed with the news, so proud because, in our eyes, Michael was famous.

Mrs. Davies ran the Brownie troop. Every Monday afternoon we would learn to tie knots, play games, sing campfire songs, and try to earn badges. I didn't mind being in the Brownie troop because they sang lots of songs. At night, Mrs. Davies would take me home to her place and wait for my mother to collect me. I would sit and smell the dinner cooking, wishing that one day they'd invite me to eat with them. They seemed such a happy family.

Tuesday was ballet class. Everyone called the teacher Auntie Jane. She was tall and blond, and she wanted desperately to dance. Her husband wouldn't hear of it, however, and she was destined to teach. Auntie Jane taught the lessons in her lounge room. Near the TV was a brilliant-orange oil lamp, and if we were good, she would turn it on so we could watch the oil travel up and down the glass tube. Auntie Jane said I was "a real little character," and I was surprised when her husband, Ernie, said he liked me. Ernie had an austere nature that made children wary of him, but he didn't scare me. When he turned his back to ignore me, I kept on talking and asking questions until he would become so frustrated, he'd ask, "Where do you get all those questions from?"

I'd answer him with childish logic: "They just pop into my head, and I have to ask them."

Auntie Jane and Uncle Ernie had given up all hope of having children, and they asked me out on special occasions. Once I even stayed over at their house.

"There's been some trouble at home," Jane explained to Ernie as she showed me to the spare room. I gasped in amazement as I entered a room filled with frills and frothy décor. My own room at home was bare and forlorn in comparison.

It was sitting on the spare bed, and my heart thumped strangely as I met its fixed stare. The clown had bright-yellow hair with large black crosses for eyes; its broad red mouth laughed and leaped out at you, its colorful jumpsuit paling in insignificance to its brightly painted face.

"It's beautiful," I cried. "Please, can I sleep with it?"

"You can have it," Uncle Ernie said, and Jane beamed her approval.

Noises! Scratching sounds under the bed. I dared not look, but they were getting louder. I felt a tug at my blankets and pulled them tightly around me. It was no use. The blanket whipped away and hid under the bed.

"It's so cold. I really need my blanket."

More scratching, and then it stopped. I eased myself over the side of the bed and felt for the blanket.

"There it is." Pulling it up, I lay back in bed and covered up. "I must cover my feet," I thought. "Otherwise someone will come in the middle of the night and chop them off." I was obsessive about this, never sleeping until covered from head to toe.

"If your feet don't fit in, they have to be cut off. Everything has to be tidy." The words rang out in my head. "There are no vampires, just the man who chops off your feet."

The scratching had stopped.

"It must have been a cricket outside my window," I thought, and then I relaxed.

Too late! The clown was on top of me, hitting and punching me. Its furry yellow hair got in my mouth and up my nose. I wanted to scream but couldn't; a hand covered my mouth. Touching hands…I hated those hands and the very bad breath. The weight was on me again.

"Get it off," I tried to scream, but nothing came out.

Anger and fear all rolled into one, and all thoughts of the clown disappeared. There was jerking and grunting, and things brushed against my face. Then sticky stuff, all over my nightdress. The weight moved, and the clown returned. He spit in my face and laughed in a high-pitched, squeaky voice, half-whispered but deafening against my ear.

"I hate the clown," I thought. "I hate it with all my heart."

The church was changing. Little by little, the Latin Mass had been replaced by English. Everyone in my class was preparing for the First Communion. It was a very serious occasion because once we made our Holy Communion, we welcomed God into our hearts. As we sat in the church pew, we all recited our prayers, trying to remember the words by heart. This was our practice run-through, and everything had to go perfectly. As the group leader, I was very proud and full of responsibility.

Sister Luke called us forward to take our practice host.

"This is my body; this is my blood," she said as she placed it on my tongue. Her face turned to anger when she saw me gagging.

"I can't swallow it," I said, trying not to bite it.

"Don't be disrespectful," she scolded in a quiet, controlled voice. "Remember, you are in front of the Lord." I panicked. I didn't want to bite God's arms or legs off, and now he was stuck to the roof of my mouth.

"Just settle down," Sister Luke said when she saw the tears streaming from my eyes. "The host will dissolve in a few minutes."

It seemed like an eternity. The religious experience was totally overwrought by an anxiety attack.

"I hope you'll be more sensible on Sunday," she reproved later.

Sunday came, and I was determined not to disgrace myself. Mum had made me a veil and borrowed a pretty white dress. I had to wear a special scapular near my heart and a shiny Communion medal.

"Please let me be good," I prayed. "I have to be excellent, or they won't let me go to the party afterward." The church was filled with the relatives of the children receiving their First Communion. My mother sat down in the back with my brothers, and I couldn't see my father anywhere. I managed to get through the Mass without a hitch. No one knew I didn't swallow the host. It dissolved in my mouth while I bowed my head in sublime reverence. At last the Mass ended, and I began to relax. The organ played the final hymn, and I rose to lead everyone out of the church. Filled with pride, I led the procession of newly blessed children down the aisle. Walking slowly with newfound holiness, I made my way toward the hefty church doors, trying to keep my head bowed in reverent prayer.

I saw the foot as it kicked out in front of me and connected with my shin. As I toppled over, there was a hushed "ooh," and I was submerged by a wave of mortified humiliation. I picked myself up, and there he was, sitting in the pew. The Devil's eyes laughed and burned a hole in my back as I hurriedly picked myself up and made a hasty retreat from the church.

Later that day, my Communion medallion disappeared; only my scapular remained. I wore it next to my heart for a week. It wasn't the first time things had disappeared. By the time my Communion certificate and my medal had vanished, I knew my scapular would be next. Reaching into the darkness, I hid it in the farthest corner of my cupboard, half in a hole near the corner of the uneven floorboards.

The noise pierced my eardrums, and I shivered. If only the fuzziness would leave my brain and the headache would stop. The Devil's hands were shaking me. Groggy, I opened my eyes in time to see my precious cat flying through the air over his head. Timothy, yowling and trussed up like a chicken. I closed my eyes and tried not to listen, but the noise pierced my brain like a soldier's lance.

"Shut up, cat," he said as he threw him on the floor and secured him with his foot.

Poor Timothy's head was bleeding, his frightened eyes dazed pools.

"Cats taste like chicken," my father said as the axe came down on his paw.

Timothy howled and there was a crack, his neck broken under my father's foot. The paw came close to me, and blood dripped on my head.

"This is my blood!" the voice hissed.

My hands were tied behind my back and my feet crossed over and tied, in imitation of Jesus.

"Jesus died on a cross," he sometimes said, "but little children have to suffer first."

I turned my head from side to side, trying to avoid the cat's paw. If I moved too much, I wouldn't be able to keep my balance. The voice raved on, drilling into my being.

"When I decide you have suffered enough, then you can die, not before… understand, I make the rules…you die when I say…" There was blood on my face, all warm and sticky. There was blood on my lips, but I wouldn't taste it.

"If you tell on me, I'll do this to your mother," he threatened, and I believed him. I mustn't talk; I mustn't scream. I must be silent. Movement would only anger him, so I breathed shallowly, trying to stiffen my body against his attack. I had learned in the past that if I didn't cry, he often became bored.

"Enough of this game."

The searing smell of the handkerchief burned my nose and mouth. Then, everything went black.

I woke to find someone dragging me by my feet. It was the Games Man, his woolen hat askew and devoid of cardboard features. I could not close my eyes properly. The tape was so tight that it fixed my eyes in a slanted, elongated position. Everything was distorted, and I had a throbbing pain in my head.

"Please, God, don't let me throw up," I prayed, resisting the bile as it came up into my mouth.

My eyes began to water, and I wanted to wipe the tears away. But I couldn't. A sheet fastened both my hands to my sides. I was all wrapped up, like an Egyptian mummy. He caught the sheet by the knot tied above my stomach and carried me to the bathroom. Then, as if I were the kitten, he lifted me up and proceeded to dunk me in and out of the cold bathwater. In and out, in and out…the action repeated itself over and over again.

"Ding dong dell, pussy's in the well. Who put her in? Little Tommy Finn. What a naughty boy was that to drown poor pussy cat…"

If I tried to wriggle free, I would swallow water, and that would cause me to gasp and cough for air. Instead, I tried to concentrate on breathing every time he lifted me out of the bath, taking a large gulp of air and holding on to it while I was submerged. There was no escape, so I tried to focus on staying alive, my fear strengthening my resolve not to drown. Eventually the dunking stopped. Was it the Devil or the Games Man? I wasn't sure which person he was. Both characters seemed to intermingle, switching and changing in a torrent of impulses, a minefield of explosive mental inclinations. The character dumped me on the floor. I clawed my way out of the wet cotton sheet, and I ran,

and ran,

and ran…

The school assembly gave me an opportunity to sort out my thoughts. Notes about what we should and shouldn't do were not of much interest to me; instead, my eyes wandered up to the second-story roof, and I immersed myself in morbidity.

"How would I get up there?" I wondered. "Maybe I could climb up the drainpipe." I imagined myself shimmying up the pipe and onto the roof. Then I'd walk along the gutter's edge as if I were on a tightrope and look down at the children below.

"Everyone is at assembly. No…it's too busy there," I thought.

My mind traveled across the roof and drifted toward the other side of the building. Looking down in my imagination, I could see that the workers had prepared the ground for the new church. Graders had turned over brown earth to clear the area, and big granite blocks had been collected for the foundations. No children were allowed to play on that side of the school until the building was finished.

I felt safe.

"This is better," I thought. "No one is around."

In my mind, I took a deep breath and jumped. I fell spread-eagled through the air until I welcomed the soft dirt on the ground. And there I would stay, dead, until school ended and someone eventually found me.

My fantasy eventually came to a halt when the student lines started to move back to class.

"I can't kill myself." The depressing reality gnawed at my soul. "If I kill myself, what will my mother think? My father will turn on her because I'm not there." The soul-depleting thought sucked all energy out of my bones, and I tried to concentrate on what was happening at school. However, classroom activities only ever served as a diversion; the fantasy kept coming back. It haunted me, and I craved a mind-numbing solution to all the turmoil and fear around me.

Then thoughts of Rosalie flashed through my mind.

"If I jump off the building, I mightn't die. I might only hurt myself," my conscience warned me. I imagined being enslaved to a bed for the rest of my life, paralyzed and unable to fend off the predator. I bit my lip so I'd feel the pain, doing everything in my power to stop my need to end it all. At the age of six, death to me was a bitter reality. Having seen and smelled death, I was endowed with an adult recognition of mortality. To me, death meant the end. It meant the end to all afflictions, a never-waking blackness that stilled the mind and defeated the body.

When I was seven, I told my classmates, "It only takes three days to die, and if you're lucky, the pain is so great you slip in and out of consciousness and you don't suffer as much." They retorted that I was weird, and, with a falling heart, I agreed. I knew I thought differently from the other children. They never spoke about death, or devils, or frightening nights.

I had a reputation for being "the child who makes up stories for attention." Once, I turned up at school without any underwear, just my tunic. Everybody thought it was a great joke except for Sister Mary.

"How did this happen?" she screamed two inches from my face. I racked my brain trying to remember, scanning the morning's events until they stopped abruptly in a black spot. No memory, just an awful-smelling hanky and then black.

"I don't know," I whispered. "I can't remember."

"Liar," the old nun hissed as she ushered me to the corner. "Maybe this will help your memory." One stroke, two…it never mattered how much anyone hit me. I didn't feel the pain anymore. I had taught my brain to switch off, to slowly become anesthetized to the cruelty around me.

Luckily for my physical well-being, I had the Ten Commandments and the Catholic religion to grapple with.

"It's a mortal sin if you kill yourself," I thought in trepidation, trying to remember whether a person who committed suicide went straight to hell or stopped in purgatory first. There was only one solution to my dilemma. I would have to run away. When I arrived home after school, I scribbled a note on a crumpled piece of butcher paper.

> *Dear Mummy,*
> *I am going away. Please do not worry about me.*
> *I love you very much.*
> *Lots of love,*
> *Shannon. XXXXX*

I got ready to leave and packed my brown schoolbag with some clothes and an apple. I wished I had some money, but there was only the sixpence under the Sunshine milk can. My mother left it there for emergencies. She had told me, "Go down the road until you come to a telephone box, and ring the police if your father kills me." I knew I couldn't take the sixpence with me; it was far too important. Without money, running away seemed a pointless exercise, so I stuffed the note under my mattress and decided to rethink my plan.

I began to think about digging in the backyard. I had a recurring dream where my hands were dirty and blackened. In the dream, the day was stifling hot, and I could almost taste the dirt on my lips as I anxiously scooped up the ground. My heart pounded heavily, as if I'd been in a race. Then my fingers felt something cold and metallic. It was a treasure trove. Shiny silver coins lay everywhere. I felt so excited; there were lots of coins…one…two…three. Shillings and pennies…sixpences and three-penny bits. As if in slow motion, a coin floated down in front of my face and landed *plop* onto the earth. Then another one fell...and another. I couldn't dig them up fast enough. Then all was disclosed as my eyes focused in front of me. In childish dismay, they fixated on the pair of black tractor boots. The boots stood next to the hole, close to my hands, at the edge of the cavity. I looked up to see him laughing at me. His bellow rang in my ears as he opened his hand and revealed the coins. I wanted to shout "No!" as his fingers uncurled and more gleaming coins slipped to earth. My heart sank. There never was a treasure; it was just the Games Man's trick.

"Pennies from heaven," he sang, and I started to cry. Dry, wretched sobs that never managed to escape my lips.

"It's only a dream," my mind raged, but I could not wake up. "Please let me wake up so I know it's not real."

I shuddered at the dream's memory and clasped my brown suitcase.

"Now's my chance," I thought. "I can leave it all behind."

Thoughts of how my mother's face would look when she read the note floated through my mind. I knew she would cry, and it wrenched at my heart. I hated it when my mother cried. Sometimes when she was milking the goats, I saw tears streaming down her face, her eyes gray-blue whirlpools of despair. I knew my father would turn on her if I wasn't around. My mother reminded me of a wiry cat he liked to kick. Her despondency and worry crippled me and squashed my thoughts of escape. I couldn't go through with it, so once again I crumpled the note up in my hand and stuffed it under my mattress.

"I'll wait a bit longer," I thought. "Maybe Mummy will run away with me."

CHAPTER 8

1968

It sat on the bench, a polished green plastic icon of communication. Mum said it was a lifesaver, and Jamie thought it was magic. Every time the new phone rang, he'd jump into the air with Liam and break up into childish giggles.

Jamie was a very vocal child, and his small, angelic appearance belied his strong opinions. He liked to be called Jumbo because he loved elephants, but sometimes we called him Bullfrog because his big, booming voice seemed to come out of nowhere.

Jamie had started school, and he was an open, forthright child. News day was always the most exciting day for his kindergarten class, as every child got to speak to the classroom. Eager children who could barely suppress their enthusiasm told tidbits from home and holidays. It was finally Jamie's turn to talk to the class.

About eleven o'clock, the new green phone rang at home.

"We are terribly sorry," a voice said.

"Sorry for what?" replied my mother.

"We were sorry to hear about your husband's death."

My mother knew something was wrong. "Is this some kind of joke?"

"We are ringing to offer our condolences," the voice continued.

"But he's not dead," she replied. "He's here at home."

There was a commotion on the other end of the phone. My mother heard muffled talking, with the hands on the other end covering the receiver so she couldn't hear properly.

"Hello," she said impatiently. "What's going on?"

There was a pause.

"We are sorry, but it would be of great assistance if you could come up to the school immediately. We have a problem."

My mother got into our old Hillman and started the car with a screwdriver because the keys had disappeared. She then drove to school, where Jamie was sitting dejectedly in the corner.

"What's wrong?" my mother demanded. "What's going on?"

"You'd best go inside, Mrs. O'Leary," answered the flustered secretary, directing Mum into the principal's office. After a long conversation, Mum came out and gave Jamie a long, extended hug.

"You've got the day off," she told the unhappy boy. "You can come home with me."

"I won't say I'm sorry," boomed his bullfrog voice. "I'm telling the truth! *I don't have a father...My father is dead!*"

Mumma was worried about Grandfather. His blood pressure was very high, and the doctors advised him to avoid stress at all costs. My grandmother wanted to get away from the city, up to the Central Coast so Paddy could relax. They rented a large house in Blue Bay and invited my parents and my brothers and me to holiday with them. Blue Bay seemed like a magical place. The sky was a great expanse of aqua, and the sea was an untamed green. The beach was so white and warm I wanted to stay there all day, breathing in the salt air and letting the sand run through my fingers.

Every morning, Mumma placed an enormous bowl in the middle of the table, and I'd wake up to find it filled to the brim with fresh fruit. She also cooked sausages and put them in a large yellow billycan. They made the perfect picnic lunch on slabs of white bread and butter. Mumma was very beautiful. She had a long swan neck, alabaster skin, large blue eyes, and curly blond hair. When she sat on the beach, she looked like a radiant cover girl from the *Woman's Weekly*. Mumma always went to the beach fully clothed down to her knees. Consequently, she became known as Sexy Knees. She wore the clothes because her legs had been burned in a fire. When she was courting Grandfather, the chip heater in her bathroom had exploded, and he had rescued her from the flames. Mumma had been terrified of fire ever since, and she remained in awe of Paddy's heroic deed. She idolized my grandfather, and I idolized her.

After our holiday in Blue Bay, it was decided that Mumma and Grandfather would move up to the Central Coast. They were making plans for the move when Grandfather had his first heart attack. Everyone was shocked because Grandfather never got sick. We all thought he was invincible. He loved working hard, and he took on extra work as a bookmaker's clerk on weekends. Grandfather knew every horse, its lineage, and its potential for becoming a champion. However, the weekend work, combined with the stress of his weekly job, caused him to collapse at the races.

When we visited him in Sydney Hospital, he was in a public ward. All the walls were painted mustard yellow, and they seemed to reflect the gray and red tones of men convalescing in their beds. Grandfather had tubes up his nose, and he could barely stay awake.

"Sing a song for me, Gracie," he mumbled, knowing I'd sing a Gracie Fields tune for him. From the time I could speak, Grandfather had taught me the songs closest to his heart.

"You've got a true Irish voice," he'd tell me, "all haunting and perfect in its pitch."

He had two nicknames for me: Lady Daa and Little Gracie, after Gracie Fields. Grandfather had met her at a war recital, and he thought she was the funniest and most beautiful entertainer in the world. Years later, when I was a teenager, I'd write letters to the star, and she'd write back, flattered to be remembered by a thirteen-year-old in Australia. By that time, she was in her seventies. She'd write and ask me to visit her with my mother, but we couldn't afford the journey. So I made a shell necklace and sent it to Capri, telling her that we were extremely busy, and when we had time for a holiday, we'd fly over and meet her. When I finally went to Capri in my twenties, Gracie was dead, but through her old records and correspondence, she'd taught me to see the funny side of life. I wrote and received reassurance through her letters. She was a great star, yet she took the time to correspond with me, encouraging me to aspire to my dreams through song.

When Grandfather asked me to sing that day in the hospital, I became overcome with shyness.

"You wouldn't want to let your grandfather down," he said, trying to smile and bringing forth my realization of just how ill he was. I warbled "The Gypsy Rover," and his eyes filled with tears. All the men in the ward clapped and cheered, and someone said I'd made his day. I felt humbled.

"No!" I thought. "Their smiling faces have made my day." Suddenly, I felt I was worth something.

When Grandfather finally came out of the hospital, Mum's sister, Jessica, went missing. It was the worst thing that could have happened, because Jessica was Grandfather's favorite daughter. She was his "blond and blue-eyed bombshell," his vivacious daughter with the peaches-and-cream complexion and million-dollar smile.

"Where would she go?" Paddy cried. "At thirteen years of age, she's got nowhere to hide." Grandfather walked the streets of Sydney asking strangers and searching for any place his daughter could be hiding. He finally located her at the Wesley Centre.[xlix] Poor Jessica had fallen pregnant; she had run away in the hope of getting an abortion. After bringing her home, Mumma took her on a holiday, where she had the baby and put it up for adoption. That devastated Grandfather. His daughter's shame and distress and his inability to protect her broke his gentlemanly demeanor.

After the baby was born, Jessica never really recovered from the pain of being parted from her firstborn. Her young life spiraled onward, as she was a tumultuous teenager suffering from sexual exploitation. Jessica had no counseling, so she struggled ahead on her own, journeying into adulthood. She forged her own course, often falling back on her innate ability to try to make things right by striking out at others. Jessica craved love and was often unwittingly noticed by others because she exuded an aura of unbridled sexuality. Her personality was compelling and bright and her nature erratic and whimsical. She ploughed through her teenage years looking for stability and unsettling those around her.

Mumma and Grandfather decided to move out of the city. With his hypertension and bad heart, the Central Coast seemed an ideal place for him to retire. However, Grandfather still had a few years left before he could retire, so instead of traveling every day to work, he stayed at our place during the week. He'd stay overnight on weekdays and travel home by train on weekends. My father was always on his best behavior when Grandfather stayed with us. He seemed kinder to my mother and acted like a gentleman around Paddy. The Devil in him refused to show his face when Grandfather was in the house, because he was afraid of him. Grandfather had been an altar boy, and he had visited the Holy City, Jerusalem, during the war. His cousins were priests and nuns, and one of them had even met the pope. The Devil was no match for Grandfather. Even if he threatened to rear his ugly head, he would wither away and hide when Grandfather glanced in his direction.

Grandfather's gentle presence made my mother and me feel more at ease. He helped with the chores and never complained about Mum's cooking, because he always cooked for himself.

"A man is best to make his own cup of tea," Paddy would joke with my mother. "It's better than taking the risk of being poisoned by a female who can't boil water."

The car was swerving all over the road. Grandfather fumbled in his pocket for his pills. Two frightened boys rolled from side to side in the backseat.

"I think he's drunk," Michael whispered to Benjamin.

"My father doesn't drink," he replied angrily. The car nearly hit a post.

"Well, something is wrong!" Michael was scared. The lovely day out to the races with his grandfather was being ruined by the car ride home.

"Slow down, Grandfather."

But Grandfather didn't hear them. The pain in his chest gripped tighter and tighter, making it difficult to breathe.

Benjamin tried to smooth things out with Michael. "Stop worrying. The road straightens out in a minute."

Grandfather managed to take control of the wheel. Eventually the car turned in to my grandparents' driveway.

"Home at last," shouted Benjamin as he jumped out of the car.

"How was it?" Mum asked as the boys rushed through the door.

"I'm never going out with him again," said Michael. "Grandfather can't drive properly."

On the evening of April 29, 1968, the phone rang.

"Hello." My mother's voice lowered, and her face went white. "Yes, I know," she said. "My father is dead." I stood and watched her from the doorway as she called the club, trying to contact my father. "Go and get some warm clothes," she called to us. "We're going to your grandmother's house."

Grandfather had been found dead on a train between Lindfield and Central Stations. Always in control, he panicked during an angina attack. Frightened and too embarrassed to cause alarm, he had hidden behind his newspaper, placed the tablets under his tongue, and tried to appear normal. The people next to him didn't realize what was going on when his newspaper dropped to his lap. Everyone on the train thought he had fallen asleep.

Later, when a conductor found Grandfather dead, he still had six undissolved heart tablets under his tongue. Coronary thrombosis and arteriosclerosis caused his death.[1] Today, heart surgery would have saved his life.

For our family it was an immeasurable loss. Grandfather had been a firm foundation in the lives of his wife and six children, and the news of his death devastated all. Jessica blamed herself for his death, while Leah howled endlessly. His youngest child, Benjamin, was only eleven, and Tara was twelve. Later she became so distraught she tried to jump into the grave with her father's coffin.

My mother organized the funeral arrangements, and she said I was too young to attend.

"Grandfather is dead, and the funeral's on Thursday," I told Sister Luke.

"Are you all right?" she asked me, and I shook my head.

"I can't cry!"

"That's all right, dear," she said philosophically. "Some children are not close to their grandparents." I cringed and watched her retreating, rosary beads clicking loudly, heels hitting the concrete walkway.

"I loved him," I wanted to shout. "Don't you understand? I want to cry, but the tears won't come out." My loss had weighted my tongue, and I couldn't talk. My tears wouldn't flow, and in their place I felt only numbness and grief. Grandfather had protected me. His presence in the house had influenced my father's personalities and made them behave. I had lost a genteel spirit and a dear and valuable friend.

Sometimes I felt I knew what it was like to be dead. When I lay in the cold, damp grave with the rusty metal door above me, I could almost feel the arms of death reaching out to grab me. I'd lie there in silence, listening, hoping to hear the footsteps of release yet fearing the insanity they would bring with them. Sometimes I pushed my palms against the door above me, scratching at the metal. I hated the sound but sought to anesthetize myself against anything I feared. Entrapment encouraged my mind to play bizarre survival games. If I was lying on my stomach, I'd think, "Dead bodies become overwhelmed by dirt and decay." Then I'd try to beat death at its own game. I taught myself to taste the earth, filling my mouth with soil. It tasted horrible, but through my bizarre rebellion, I experienced a small victory. It was almost as if through tasting the earth, I conquered my fear of lying in it.

All the landholders in the area were asked if they wanted to sell their land to Lend Lease. The Peters decided to hold out until they could get a better sale price, and we did the same. The Valdermere family, five acres away, decided to exchange their broken-down shack for a modern two-bedroom flat on the Lower North Shore. When they moved out, I watched them from behind a tree. Mr. Valdermere wore baggy brown trousers pulled in at the waist with a bit of old rope. He had rolled his yellow-white shirt up at the sleeves, and he was smoking. The black-rimmed glasses perched on his hooked nose looked too big for his thin face.

"He looks like a skinny rubber man," I thought, balancing myself between the tree and the fence. I carefully placed my hand between the barbs on the wire and peeked out for another look.

Mrs. Valdermere came out of the house carrying a cardboard box. Her teenage son and daughter followed, and they loaded bits and pieces into their battered station wagon. Mr. Valdermere's gray hair looked almost white in the sunshine. Flies buzzed past him, and he waved them away, muttering under his breath in a different language.

He stamped the cigarette butt out in the dirt and shouted, "Is zat it?" in his thick Slavic accent.

His family nodded.

"We'll be orf, zen…"

The Valdermere family drove away. As soon as they left, my brothers automatically claimed their five acres of bushland and added it to ours. Miles of crown land and national park surrounded our properties, so our backyard seemed endless. After all, the land developers wouldn't be moving in for years, and as youthful pioneers, my brothers felt the gorge should be explored to its fullest capacity. At this time, my father was refusing to work, so my mother decided to sell Avon and Stanhome products to pay the mortgage. This required her to drive to people's homes and sell products in a party-plan style. Sometimes my brothers and I would wait in the car while Mum smuggled us out chocolate cake. Once Jamie crept into a client's backyard and hid under their outside table. After about half an hour, he returned with an enormous sponge cake decorated with lashings of cream and strawberries. Jamie had the face of an angel, and he was clever as a fox.

"They just left it on the table," he said innocently as our hands all delved into the cake.

My father hated the thought of my mother leaving the house, and it wasn't uncommon for us to find the car wouldn't work. The mechanic would come out to fix the vehicle and complain that parts of the engine were missing. He'd replace the parts, and then they'd disappear again. Strangely enough, the car always started for my father.

"You are going to stop work," he told my mother repeatedly. "You've got no right to work. I'm the man in the family, and your place is in the home."

Mum would try to explain that they needed the money, but Dad's drunken rages continued.

"You'll give up your job, or I'll break your bloody neck."

It was useless arguing with him when he made up his mind. If customers rang my mother, he would answer the phone rudely and hang up on them. If people rang him for work, his attitude was the same. He'd stay unshaven and angry until his humor changed. When that happened, he'd transform into a happy, elated man. His moods made no sense, and I was glad when he went to the club at night. Many times I'd hear him shouting at my mother in the middle of the night. Aggressive and then sullen and often loud and belligerent, he'd continue ranting on until the early daylight hours. My father believed "the devil moves in mysterious ways," and I fearfully wondered if he was trying to move in with us.

My grandfather's death changed my grandmother's way of life. In September 1968, Mumma got her driving license and purchased a new station wagon. Grandfather had wanted to travel, so Mumma decided to spend the small amount of money left in his will on a family holiday in Lightning Ridge.

"It's a good way for me to practice my driving," she said. She would drive Leah, Tara, and Benjamin in her new station wagon, while my mother would drive my brothers and me in the old Hillman.

The thought of a holiday made my heart sink because it brought back memories of the last time my family traveled together. The trip had been a disaster. About two years before Grandfather's death, my cousin Gemma, who was on my father's side of the family, invited us all to her wedding. Dad decided to make the journey in his new green Toyota truck. It was in the middle of winter, and Michael, Liam, and I had to ride in the back with a tarpaulin stretched over our heads. Ropes attached the tarp to the backboard of the driving cabin and the sides of the truck, which were about eighteen inches high. We all lay down on a thin horsehair mattress with our pillows and eiderdowns over our heads while he took off at a breakneck speed to Victoria. Once he was behind the wheel, my father was a man possessed. He sped down the highway and refused to stop until he was forced to buy petrol. Consequently, there were no toilet or food stops. My brothers were lucky, because when they got the urge, they could just urinate over the side of the truck, while my mother and I had to wait uncomfortably until he stopped.

At first, Jamie was lucky, because he sat in the front with my parents, but when Mum asked Dad to slow down, he slammed his foot on the accelerator and went even faster. My brothers and I were buffeted from one side of the truck to the other, and we lay for hours with our fingers in our ears trying to dull the deafening sound of the tarpaulin flapping in the wind. Jamie became terrified when my father began shouting, and he started to bellow. This resulted in my father slamming his foot on the brake and throwing the screaming two-year-old in the back with us. Jamie refused to lie down, and Michael and I became terrified he would bounce off the back of the truck. There was an extra piece of rope hanging from the backboard of the driving cabin, so I tied it around his middle. When we went around corners, Jamie's feet lifted off the ground, and he swung for about twelve inches. He thought it was a great game until he bumped his head, and after he tired of it, we released him, wrapped ourselves in the eiderdowns, and fell asleep.

We arrived in Victoria the day before the wedding. It was to be a country wedding, as Gemma's parents ran an enormous apple orchard at the base of the Dandenong Mountains. Mum, Dad, and Jamie planned to stay in a caravan near the farmhouse, while Michael, Liam, and I would sleep in the truck. When we arrived, Gemma's younger brothers invited Michael and me to go bushwalking in the hills on the edge of the farm. My legs tired easily, so I trailed behind them, stepping over rocks and trying to keep up. Half an hour went by, and I realized someone was following us. I could hear footsteps but couldn't see anyone. Michael refused to look, saying he didn't care, while my cousin got quite excited.

"There he is!" he shouted. "Look! Behind that tree!"

I immediately recognized the figure in the flannelette shirt. A woolen hat obscured the Games Man's face. As he followed us, he laughed—never speaking, just chuckling. As we ventured higher up the bushy mountain, we came to a large rock formation. I quickly hopped from one large ledge to another in order to leave him on the other side of the rock face.

"Ouch!"

A stone hit me on the back—and then another and another. Suddenly I was overcome with anger. With shaking hands, I picked up two large rocks and took aim. I threw them as hard as I could at the laughing figure. One bounced off the rock near his foot, while the other hit the rock face behind him.

"Go away!" I shouted. "Keep away from me. I don't want to play."

The figure grimaced and put up his arms in mock horror. He kept stalking us but didn't attempt to stop us. Instead, he took delight in picking up muddy stones and throwing them at me, watching me jump from rock to rock to avoid being hurt.

The Lightning Ridge holiday proved to be totally different because my father refused to go with us.

"I have work to do," he told my mother, although we all knew he hadn't been to work for quite some time. We didn't know where my father went in his truck; we were just thankful when it disappeared.

The whole week away without my father would be my mother's first taste of freedom in years. Throughout my childhood years, she lived on the adrenaline of a phobic—distressed and anxious on a day-to-day basis. Nerves had caused her weight to plummet to forty kilos because she couldn't keep food down, and she had become irrational and impatient. The slightest sound of my father's truck would put her into a panic, and she'd tell us to disappear and keep out of his way.

Occasionally Dad would remain drunk for days at a time. He would come home late at night, intoxicated and incomprehensible, refusing to wash and rarely eating. He wore the same clothes day in and day out, drinking bottles of beer and stinking because he never bathed. At night I'd listen through the wall as he waited for my mother to fall asleep and then changed characters. The Devil would appear and wake my mother up again, shouting while punching the wall and forcing himself upon her. Eventually, my father would succumb to drunken exhaustion, and the house's silence would be pocketed by intermittent screams from my brothers' nightmares. Sometimes my father was so inebriated he'd urinate in the bed, unable to rouse himself from his alcoholic stupor. The days and nights became cyclic, a chain of events that repeated when he woke each day.

A couple of days before the holiday to Lightning Ridge, my father exploded in a fit of rage. With the derision of a madman, he shouted wildly, "You have to choose between me and your stupid holiday." Then he shook her as he threatened, "I'll kill you, you bitch! You're a failure as a wife and mother, you stupid slut." His hand connected with her face. "Who are you having an affair with? What's your boyfriend's name?"

He released her suddenly and marched toward the bench. Both hands grasped the telephone cable and ripped it from the socket. The green phone flew through the air and smashed against the wall with a crash.

"It's my phone," he screamed at her. "Your friends can't help you now." He laughed as my mother picked up the broken phone and he walked outside.

Mum could hear his truck driving away in the distance as she searched for five cents. She ran down the road to the phone box so she could ring the doctor.

"You've got to help me," she pleaded. "Please come quickly."

The doctor promised he'd pick her up from the phone box as soon as he could. When she got home, she smelled the fire immediately. Dad had driven up the road, changed his mind, and then driven home again. Upon coming home and seeing the empty house, he had begun to vent his fury on the furniture. He had grabbed a newspaper and screwed it up into balls, throwing them onto the double bed.

"One match, two match, three match—you've met your match," he garbled on and on. The newspaper burst into flames, and the bedclothes began to smolder. Soon there was a small fire. He reveled in the flames and was laughing maniacally when my mother and the doctor arrived.

"I burned all the junk that was in it," he shouted, motioning to the bed when she walked into the room. "What's he doing here?"

The doctor tried to calm him down by counseling him, and my mother raced around filling buckets with water to throw over the bed. We were all running with cups of water, trying at the same time not to slop the fluid on the floor.

Dad told the doctor, "Mind your own fucking business," and he went on dancing around the bed.

"Sixteen men on a dead man's chest, yo ho ho and a bottle of rum…"

Water hit the flames, which gave a hiss and went out. Michael and Mum carried in more buckets of water, and the rest of us carried cups. There was lots of commotion, him singing deliriously and us shouting.

"Sixteen men on a dead man's chest, yo ho ho and a bottle of rum."

The water went everywhere.

"Patrick," the doctor ventured, "you should see a…"

Smash! My father's fist punched a hole in the wall.

The fire was gone, and so were we.

"Get out!" he screamed, and we all scattered.

The doctor stayed with my father while my mother whimpered in the corner.

After two hours of negotiating, it was decided they should see a marriage guidance counselor. My distressed mother wanted desperately to have my father committed, but the doctor wouldn't hear of it. He said he was concerned for our safety.

"Your husband has a multiple personality disorder. If I commit him, he will prove he is sane, and when he is released, he will kill you and the children. Let's try and subdue him with some form of therapy first." He gave my mother the number for Lifeline and told her to seek some help. She didn't know how counseling could help, but desperation led her to try anything she could to improve her disastrous situation. Hours later, after the situation had calmed down, the doctor left, and once again, we were left to fend for ourselves.

Just before we left on our holiday to Lightning Ridge, the Games Man visited me. He said he didn't want me to go away because he'd have no one to play with. Lately, he had invented some new games. My brothers called one of these Hogan's Heroes, after the TV series. The boys would wear painted cardboard Nazi symbols on their sleeves and run through the bush yelling,

"Heil Hitler." The Games Man would set up a course through the bush and time us with a stopwatch. I never wore the cardboard symbol, as it was my role to run barefoot through the gully to designated areas in the bush. Sometimes I would be chased, while at other times I would reach the end of the course and find that the Games Man had become bored and moved on to some other diversion. Twice, I had to run the course in a zigzag pattern to avoid the potshots taken by the Games Man's rifle. As an adult, I know he could easily have hit me, but he found more pleasure in watching me fall hysterically, dodging bullets as I scrambled over rocks.

Before we went away, the Games Man came to see me, and he wasn't wearing his woolen mask. Disorientated eyes stared glassily, his mouth ripped into an ugly fixed smile. In his hand he carried a hamburger and a hammer, and he seemed filled with agitation. The Games Man walked over to where I was drawing in the dirt and put the hamburger down on an old bit of discarded wood. The hammer went up into the air and came down with a resounding smash on the hamburger.

Splat!

He didn't get the effect he wanted, so he picked the burger up and started to rip it apart. The Games Man threw it in the air, and I watched in silence while pieces of food flew everywhere. I stood very still, hoping he wouldn't remember I was there, but he lurched toward me, grabbing my hand and forcing it onto the piece of wood where the hamburger had been. I saw the hammer rise into the air again. I tried to wrench my hand away, but the hammer caught the side of my thumb, and I screamed in pain. Blood oozed from my finger as I ran toward the house sobbing, meeting my mother at the door.

"What happened?" she shouted.

Before I could answer, a voice said, "She caught it in the car door."

It was always the same. He spoke, and I said nothing, never lying but also never letting anyone know the truth. My father's gaze drifted away and stopped at the very tall gum tree on the left side of the yard. I shuddered. It was hard to see, but on the third fork of the tree's massive trunk, a rusty deep-sea spear gun had been set up. My father said this was his new invention—his way, he said, "to keep out unwanted trespassers."

The holiday to Lightning Ridge went ahead as planned and proved to be an excellent break for everyone. For the whole week, my mother ate properly and her mood lightened. I played in the caravan park on the swings, and my brothers met up with some of the local children. Everything was going smoothly until my brothers invented a new game.

"You've got stinky-itis." The cries rang out through the caravan park, and all the kids ran for cover. It was a silly bit of fun, but Lightning Ridge wasn't ready for our childish games. In the 1960s, the small town was a mishmash of people, some of whom were educated while others were not. The game of tag had been a great success with the children, but now some adults believed the disease was real.

"You can't play it anymore," Mumma told us. "Some of the people don't understand there's no such thing as stinky-itis."

"Well, they must be stupid," Michael and I said.

"They've never been to school, and they think you've all got hepatitis," replied the ever-patient Mumma. "Please stop playing the game." But it was too late. All the kids who had played with us were complaining of terrible aches and pains. The smart parents told their kids to "come off it!" while the others dragged their offspring to bed, dosing them with castor oil and prescribing them a week off school.

The next day the park was empty, and I had all the swings to myself. It was a glorious day, and the clear-blue sky stretched cloudlessly on forever. Elation came with solitude. I pushed my feet back and forth, straining so every fiber in my being propelled me into the radiant Australian atmosphere. In my mind I was flying, higher and higher…climbing beyond all that was worrisome and earthbound.

We were all enjoying our holiday. Mumma and Mum only used the stove for boiling water, so we lived on roast chicken with fresh bread and butter, chocolate milk shakes, and wafers with vanilla ice cream. It was bliss. Seven children and two scatty ladies all piled into a tiny four-person caravan, a car, and a station wagon. We even went opal mining. The man who owned the caravan park had a forty-foot mine shaft and a keen eye for my grandmother.

"I'll let you go mining," he told her with a wink, and, thinking it would be great sport for the boys, she agreed. We all trooped out to the opal fields, oohing and aahing at the never-ending holes, being careful not to fall into an uncovered shaft. The caravan-park man lowered a torch into the mine by a rope, and it fell to the bottom with a thud.

"It's like a well," I thought as he lowered us one by one into the shaft in an old tin garbage bin.

"Your turn," he said to me, after everyone else had been lowered below.

"No!" I answered. The fear deep in the pit of my stomach forced the words to spurt out from my mouth.

"Don't be scared; you can't fall."

Somehow I wasn't convinced. The man cajoled and reasoned, but I wouldn't get in the bin.

"Look," he said, nearly ready to give up, "I'll tie this rope around your waist, and then you'll be double safe." After a moment's thought, I agreed.

"Tighter," I said as he tied the rope around my waist. Then he picked me up and plunked me in the corroded bin.

Down I went, with a bump, a thump, and then a loud crack. The rusted garbage bin gave way, and I fell straight through its bottom, screaming and crashing against the mine shaft's walls until the rope around my waist jerked tight.

"You OK?" the man called.

I was bruised and scratched from head to toe.

"Yes," I feebly replied. He lowered me to the bottom, and we heard him laughing.

"I'll have to get meself a new bin. I'll be back in four hours to pick you up."

Shaken and feeling sorry for myself, I began to dig in the first tunnel with Mumma, Mum, and Tara. Much to our surprise, Tara found an opal big enough to make a small pendant. The boys went into the next cavern with a lantern and began to fossick for hidden treasures. The sound of dirt being chipped away mingled with hollow laughter, creating an eerie underground experience.

Mum didn't see the pickaxe until it landed an inch away from her nose. Benjamin had dug through the wall. Fearing the mine would collapse, Mum told us to stop digging. We spent the rest of the time scraping around in the dirt looking for potch and bits of petrified wood. It was an unusual holiday. It was a week away in no-man's-land, where sweaty heat and dust-ridden trails pushed aside all thoughts of returning home.

I often played dress-up in my mother's clothes.

"I have to go shopping now," Mum said. "I'm really in a hurry because I have to get back before your father gets home."

"Can I wear this?" I asked.

Mum laughed. "Of course you can, but don't twist your ankles in my shoes."

I hobbled down the hall in the high heels, singing to myself. I was dressed in my mother's green kilt and an old shirt pulled together with safety pins. I carried an oversized handbag and had a straw hat perched on top of my head. My mother watched me hobble outside and giggled because I looked like a miniature Second Hand Rose.

After she called the boys, we all piled into the Hillman and drove into Hornsby. Everyone was excited because the shopping center had recently been remodeled, and it now had a new doughnut-and-biscuit shop. When we arrived, a large crowd was gathered at the center court stage.

"It must be a show," my mother said.

"Can we watch?" we all cried at once.

"I suppose so. As long as you all promise not to move from here. Michael, look after your brothers and sister while I get the shopping. I won't be long." Mum made us sit down and then quickly went off in the direction of the supermarket. On the stage, children were getting up to sing. A funny little man in a brown suit and hat was talking to parents and writing things down on a clipboard. I wandered over to the stage so I could get a better view of what was happening.

"It's your turn now." A strange woman was standing in front of me. I stared at her because I didn't know what she was talking about.

"It's your turn to sing," she added.

I was confused. "Sing what?" I asked, and the woman clicked her teeth together impatiently.

"It's your turn now to sing, dear. You're in your costume; now hurry up, or I'll get someone else to have a go."

I looked at Michael for permission, and he shrugged his shoulders.

"I s'pose it's OK, 'cause I can see you from here," he said, and I took the lady's hand. She led me onto the stage, and I racked my brains for something to sing. I didn't know many songs, so in the end I chose one I had sung at school.

"Where's your music, dear?" the man at the piano asked me.

"I'm sorry; I don't have any."

The man in the brown suit looked at me and began to laugh. "Don't worry, sweetie; you look great, so just sing without the music."

I started the song. It was a cute piece about shopping, and I guess my age made it comical. Soon everyone was laughing at my rendition, as I impersonated a tired housewife, a bit like my mum going shopping. When I finished I received a huge applause from the giggling crowd, and then I headed back toward my brothers. By this time my mother was back from the supermarket, and we all turned to leave.

"Hey! Wait a minute!" the little fat man in the brown suit cried out. "She didn't sign the contract."

"What contract?" asked my stunned mother.

"The contract for the show…"

"What show?" Mum was totally confused.

"The show she just auditioned for." The man pushed the clipboard into Mum's hands, and she began to read.

"You've just auditioned for a kids' show, and they want you to sing on TV." My mum raised her eyebrows. "Do you want to do this?"

"Yes, please, Mummy," I quickly replied.

My mother wasn't sure. "You know it will be hard work. You'll have to practice…"

"I will; I promise," came my definite reply. My mother signed the contract and handed it back to the man in the brown suit.

"I'll be in touch," he yelled as he walked back to the stage. "Next!"

"When do I go?" I asked excitedly. "Is it soon?"

"In the holidays," Mum answered, preoccupied with her own thoughts.

"Shannon," she added, "don't mention this to your father."

The plate hit the wall above the stove with a crash. Sausages bounced off the linoleum. The gravy and mashed potatoes ran down the wall, leaving a sickly white-and-yellow trail. Peas dropped onto the floor one by one.

"You call that dinner, woman?" he shouted.

I looked at the food my mother had set out for dinner. It looked the same as every other night. His eyes became wilder, and he hit another plate. It fell, splattering more food over the floor.

"It's not fit for a bloody dog. It's shit."

As he walked out of the room, he turned and yelled, "I'll eat at the club."

Mum didn't answer. Every time she went to confession and asked the priest for advice, he informed her she was married for better or for worse. No one believed my father behaved differently at home.

"He's so charming," people would say when they met him, and we felt powerless to state otherwise. My mother sighed and looked at the food on the floor.

"Don't worry about it," she told us as she prepared to pick up the mess. "Daddy's just having another bad day."

But I was sick and tired of "Daddy having bad days," and to top it off, I was becoming aware that my family was different. Most children loved being at home, while the mere thought terrified me. At dinnertime the next day, when I walked past the steaming sausage mince, my eyes gravitated toward the open can of dog food on the kitchen bench. My mother's eyes followed mine, and she seemed to suppress a nervous giggle. I suddenly felt very angry and courageous.

"I'll do it," I volunteered, and I tossed the can's contents into the stew.

That night when my father returned home from work, we watched with mixed anticipation.

"You asked for a casserole," Mum said as she served out my father's dinner. Dad ran his fork over the plate's contents. He stopped momentarily. With his fork poised, he stared at a stray carrot and stabbed it. Mum stiffened, and her face went white.

"Better," he growled. "Much better."

Behind his back, my mother raised her finger to her lips and shook her head. The fork swooped down on the casserole as he shoveled it into his mouth. My jaw dropped open, and my eyes wandered over to where the carrots sat on the kitchen bench. The gravy packet was near the stove, next to the empty can of dog food.

"Food fit for a king," my father said, and I agreed.

It was the morning of my performance on *New Faces*.[li]

"TV studios are strange," I thought. "So big and cold."

For my costume, I wore one of Mum's dresses held in at the waist by an apron. I also had on Mum's high heels. The seven string bags I carried looked cumbersome, but they were filled with empty cardboard food containers. I had rehearsed with the piano, and the man had shouted at me. He said he didn't like my music. Then the producer got angry at him, and they ended up having an argument. I felt better when this happened, because I realized they were angry with each other, not with me.

"Just look at the camera with the light on and sing," the director said, pushing me onto the set, as it was time for me to sing my song.

"Shopping here, shopping there, things to eat and things to wear..." I warbled.

People were laughing. Mum had explained that I would be performing as a comedy act, so I was relieved the audience thought I was funny. Afterward, I was congratulated on my performance and asked to come back and perform in a different show. *The Super Flying Fun Show*[lii] was designed specifically for kids, whereas *New Faces* had adult performers in it. I didn't really understand the talent-quest concept, but I was more than interested in the fourteen dollars they offered me as payment. To me, fourteen dollars seemed like a fortune.

The bonfire crackled loudly, sending shivers down my spine.

Pop! went a piece of dry grass, making me jump.

His silver cross waved in the air. The Devil's voice droned on and on.

"What have we here?" he asked as he burned one of my mother's dresses. "So pretty...What a shame!"

He casually threw things into the fire. Receipts, photos, and old account books—assorted documents that belonged to my mother. I knew she'd be upset when she found the things missing. I tried to block out the thought of my mother crying, and my mind began to wander. Lately, I had spent a lot of time in the doctor's waiting room while Mum received treatment. For the past year, her body had been inundated with black bruises, my father's drunken rages targeting her body for his animalistic pleasure in pain. People were starting to ask her questions. Only the day before, Mrs. Peters had noticed the long gash on her arm.

"How did you do that?" she had asked, looking at the wound when she brought over some fresh tomatoes.

"I got caught on the fence," my mother replied.

Mrs. Peters didn't believe her. "That looks too straight to be a rip from a fence, Emma. It looks more like a knife wound to me."

The doctor also examined me. Afterward, Mum told me he had prescribed some small blue pills[liii] to make me relax. I took one that night, and it made me feel groggy. I began to panic.

"This is like the handkerchief," I thought as tiredness overcame my body. "How will I run away?"

Next morning, Mum said I had to take another pill, and I refused. She told me that the doctor said I needed the pills to calm me down. I told her that

I was calm and that I didn't need the pills. My mother, not wanting a struggle of wills, shrugged and gave in, suggesting I only take them at night. She put the pills on the kitchen windowsill, and when her back was turned, I grabbed them. That day at school, I watched the pills as they floated in the toilet. I quickly flushed them away, relieved to see them disappearing.

"You're the last thing I need," I thought. "If I take you, I can't think, and when I can't think, my nightmares become real…"

My thoughts came crashing back to the bonfire in front of me. The Devil was shouting at me.

"Listen!" he yelled. "Wake up!" I must have dozed off. I opened my eyes, trying to push away the rush of exhaustion consuming my body. He was hard at work. The fire crackled and fizzed when he threw things in it, sending flaming tendrils up into the air. The Devil dropped the makeshift cross on the ground and began to sing, dancing around the fire in savage abandon.

"Build a bonfire; build a bonfire. Put your mother on the top. I will blow her fucking head off, then burn the bloody lot."

He suddenly stopped and grabbed something out of his bag.

"Now what do I have here?"

"More photos and cards?" My reply was whispered. On the fire, family images were crinkling with the heat.

"Wrong!" his voice gonged like an admonition as his hand drew my doll out of the bag.

"No!" I shrieked, but it was too late.

The straw from Maudie's cracked face formed a golden ball, melting her plastic blue eyes and turning her black.

"You'd better be careful, little girl," he sneered, "or you'll end up dead like your dolly."

The silver cross waved inches away from my nose, and the chirruping notes of the madman boomed in my ear.

"Mummy's going to heaven soon, darling daughter, and you're going to hell."

Many hours later when it was night, his snores filtered through my thin bedroom walls as I wept into my pillow.

"There's no way out," I thought. "He's going to kill us all."

The bush exploded that night. The newspaper reported that a firebug had wreaked havoc upon the land.[liv] Five hundred volunteers were called in to battle the burning bush, and my father happily joined them. We didn't see him for two days. Instead, we played the waiting game with Mother Nature.

My mother hoped the wind would change and drag the fire off in a different direction, but the smoke from the blackened bush kept spiraling uncontrollably, corkscrewing ominously across the sky.

After the fire had been burning for two days, flames started to gallop toward the goat and chicken sheds at a dangerous pace. My mother moved all the animals up to the house and hoped the weather forecast for rain was right.

"They said on the radio there would be a storm," she said, looking up at the sky, "but it's hard to tell what is smoke and what is rain cloud."

The air was brutally hot when the thunder finally clapped. This tremendous noise was followed by a lightning shaft. It cut through the smoke and lit up the sky. A few large pellets of water fell on our heads, and we all screamed with relief.

"Let's do a rain dance," yelled Liam, and we all joined in. As the rain kissed our upturned faces, we jumped and hollered with glee. The downpour extinguished the inferno in our backyard and saved our house.

My mother told us to "say a prayer of thanks to the Infant de Prague," and in relief she muttered, "Someone's watching over us."

"That's funny," I thought. "The parish priest said the same thing." I had visited him recently to ask for his help, and he had shown me a statue of the Infant de Prague.

"When you need help, pray to him," he had said. "He'll watch over you."

When I got home after school that day, I picked up my mother's statue to pray to it, and its head fell off.

"Oh no," I thought. "The Infant de Prague has been in an accident."

I looked at the statue in my hand. His clay head had been sliced cleanly off and taped back on again with sticky tape.

CHAPTER 9

1969

I didn't like the Valdermeres' place. The weatherboard house originally had three rooms, but now it was just a shell, a shack rotting in the bush. The only things left in the house were stacks of old newspapers and pornographic magazines. In the kitchen area, rows and rows of chemical bottles[lv] filled makeshift shelves made of bits of plank held up by rows of bricks. These shelves of chemicals took up a whole wall.

"Don't touch them," Michael warned. "Some are dangerous poisons, and others will burn you. I know because we use some of them at school in science." Michael told me, "Mr. Valdermere must have been a mad scientist who was hiding from secret agents," and I believed him.

The Valdermeres' land had been vacant for about six months, and the Devil had moved in. When my father wasn't around, we would play by the Valdermeres' rusty old tank and bravely venture into the abandoned shack to play Hogan's Heroes.[lvi] Michael would put the cardboard Nazi symbols on my brothers' arms and march us around the bush shouting, "Heil Hitler!" and "Herr Commandant!" The Valdermeres' old shack was like a haunted ruin, a wreckage of asbestos-ridden fibro and tin. It was a forbidden zone, but we were much too curious to leave it alone. All this changed when a stranger came to stay.

It was Easter. Every year, my mother entered the goats in the livestock competitions at the Royal Easter Show in Sydney. When she won prizes, her sales of goat's milk would increase, and people would want to buy the kids for breeding. My brothers and I knew the showground like the backs of our hands. We all thought Good Friday was the best day at the show because it was closed to the general public, and we could roam the showground without getting lost in the tremendous crowds. Sometimes Liam would deliberately get lost so he could go to the lost children's tent and eat free ice cream. After a while, the police got to know him and just gave him the ice cream and told him to go back to the goat pavilion.

Marge Banning lived at the Royal Easter Show while it was on. She took on my mother's sister Tara as her new protégé. Marge had a small room at the end of the shed, while Tara slept in a sleeping bag up in the goat shed's rafters. Each day we'd drive to the showground to check on the animals and to bring the goats their feed. On one occasion Tara had an unusual experience with the police.

"What's going on?" Mum asked Marge Banning in alarm.

"It was a misunderstanding by the police," Marge replied, and then she went on to explain. "Apparently a girl about Tara's age went missing yesterday, and she was seen with a man leaving the grounds."

Marge went on to explain that the missing girl was blond like Tara, and an eyewitness had said it was her. They had both been called to the showground police station[lvii] to explain that Tara wasn't the same girl and that the man had been my father.

"Are you all right?" Mum asked her excited sister, and Tara nodded. "You'd better stay around here and not wander off," she added. "The last thing we need at the moment is for you to go missing."

The Easter show had not been as pleasant as in years gone by. The Devil had slipped my favorite goat, Sally, a musk stick lolly coated with poison, and she had died in agony. He finally put her out of her misery by filling her writhing frame with bullets. I lay on the bed sobbing, with my fingers in my ears trying to block out her prolonged bleating and screams. It was all too reminiscent of Binki, the goat he had destroyed when I was three.

My mother and I were still reeling from the shock of Sally's death when Mum's sister Jessica came to stay with us. She had a part-time holiday job at a petrol station down the road, and she traveled to work each day on the bus.

Jessica said she had seen a girl get off the bus and walk down the Valdermeres' track. She was carrying a suitcase, and she looked a bit like Tara. She was an extremely pretty girl, and although no one was sure of her age, we all thought she was about fifteen or sixteen. Anyone over thirteen years old looked like an adult to me, so I just accepted that she was the shack's new owner. The girl was very thin and had pale-blond hair that fell straight to midwaist. Her fair skin was clear except for a few freckles across the bridge of her nose, and her eyes were blue. She wore a shift dress and seemed lonely. Michael and I saw her when we were playing by the Valdermeres' shack. We noticed a movement by the window.

"There's someone in there," Michael whispered. "I'll take a look." He quickly sprinted behind the old tank to get a better view in the window. Seeming dissatisfied with what he saw, he headed back toward me.

"It's just a stupid girl!" he said in disgust. As if to prove just how uninterested he was in the female species, the nine-year-old boy began to walk home.

"Who is she?" I hissed after him, but he ignored me. My inquisitive nature soon got the better of me, and I crept toward the tank and peered in the window.

Inside the living area, a camp bed had been set up, and on it lay two gray army blankets. The mattress didn't have any sheets on it, and coils and bits of straw were coming out of it. On the floor, I saw some paper bags that could have contained food and two chipped blue cups with the handles missing. Lying in a pile of dirt, there was also a bent, tarnished silver fork. The girl was sitting on the camp bed reading, and she didn't see me at the window. I carefully made my way around to the other side of the house. The back room had once been a bedroom, and light was spilling onto the floor through a hole where the tin roof had been blown off in a storm. There was no real back entrance, as the walls had fallen down and pieces of smashed fibro lay on the ground. From where I stood, I could walk straight through the walls onto the bits of corrugated iron that lay scattered on the floor. I didn't venture inside, however; something warned me not to. Instead, I turned quickly and ran back home through the bush.

The girl stayed for approximately two weeks. Occasionally we would wander through the bush and see her. One day, Jessica, Benjamin, Michael, and I saw her sitting on a rock, staring out into the bush as if she were the most troubled soul on earth. She was crying silent tears, and we decided to approach her. The girl didn't run away. She smiled and asked us our names. The strange girl said her name was Tina. She didn't talk very much, and she obviously didn't want anyone to know very much about her. Jessica tried to make teenage conversation, and I listened. Then everyone said good-bye, and we headed back home through the bush.

The strange girl didn't enter my thoughts again until a few days later, when my father took me back to the Valdermeres' property. It was strange; we could have walked there, but instead we drove in his truck. He told me to wait near the burned-out gum tree near the fence. He went inside the shack, and I became sick of waiting. Bored and filled with curiosity, I made my way quietly to the windowsill. Tina was with my father. They were sitting on the camp bed, deep in conversation. Suddenly, Dad looked up and saw me. He walked menacingly toward the window, and I ducked down and lay on the ground outside, holding on to the childish belief that if I couldn't see him, he couldn't see me. I waited for what seemed an eternity, amusing myself by drawing in the dirt with sticks. Finally, my father came outside and told me to leave. I was relieved, and although I didn't fancy the walk home in the bush, I was glad to get away from him. I hurried back home by myself.

The next day I saw Tina for the last time. My father had been on edge all morning. He shouted at us for making random noises, and my mother jumped each time he yelled. He stormed outside and told me to get in the truck. I obeyed him immediately. He drove to the end of the dirt road, intent on visiting a man who had moved in recently. The man had built a house opposite the old deserted swaggie sheds just before the electricity poles. He said he was a lapidarist, and when I didn't understand, he explained it meant that he polished stones. He was foreign and spoke with a thick accent. A great stone wheel stood in his yard, and he told me he used it for polishing and grinding rocks into pretty shapes for necklaces and rings. His work was beautiful, and I watched in awe as he turned a shapeless rock into a shiny pink stone.

"How do you get the colors?" I asked him.

The man laughed and replied, "They are in the rocks. Look here!" He picked up a rock and doused it with water. "Can you see the color?"

Sure enough, the wet stone had tinges of blue beneath the surface.

"I'll polish it up, and it will make a lovely necklace."

He rummaged in his leather apron and brought out a rock. "Look, this is wood!"

I looked at the orange-and-brown rock swinging from the chain and felt it. I was confused. "It doesn't look like wood."

"It's petrified wood. It's been under the ground for years and years, and now it's as hard as rock." The man pushed the necklace into my hand. "I'd like you to have this. It's a little present."

"Thank you!" I cried excitedly, and I struggled to put the chain around my neck. The man helped me put the necklace on and said, "Beautiful."

The giant polishing wheel also served as a grinder, and I waited while my father had his axe sharpened. Soon the axe sparkled in the sunshine.

"There..." he said, handing Dad the axe. "It looks as good as new."

Dad handed him two dollars and then picked up an amber-and-pink bracelet.

"I'll take this!" he said, and then, with an afterthought, he added a blue stone that dangled from a chain. He paid the man and got into the truck.

"Come on; we'll be late," he yelled as he started the engine.

I clambered onto the back of the truck and waved to the man. As we reversed out of the drive and headed down the bumpy road, I felt elated. The wind caught in my hair as I stroked my precious new possession. I was unaccustomed to presents, and this one was so beautiful. To my surprise, the truck turned in to the Valdermeres' driveway instead of continuing down the road. I had assumed we were heading home, and I felt sick.

The truck pulled up, and Dad said, "Wait there." He pointed to a burned-out gum tree.

I jumped out of the truck and did what I was told. Disappointment set in when I realized I would be left waiting again. I sat down on the ground and began to draw in the dirt with a stick. He always took such a long time.

Finally, my father stormed out of the Valdermeres' shack. He looked furious, and Tina followed him, pulling on his sleeve so he would stop and listen to her.

"What am I going to do?" the girl asked.

He turned to look at her and said, "I don't really care."

The girl became more upset. "But you have to care…you love me…"

He didn't answer her. Instead, he turned his back.

The girl stared at the ground and softly said, "I could be pregnant."

As quick as lightning, my father turned and punched her under her jaw. On impact her neck gave a sickening crack, and she fell, crumpling onto the ground like a discarded rag doll. Tina didn't move. Her pale-gold hair fanned over her face, her neck sticking out from her body at a peculiar angle. Without looking at me, my father picked up the girl and carried her to his truck. He opened the passenger door and pushed her inside, making sure she was sitting upright as he did so.

"Shannon," he ordered, "get in the truck."

I slowly did as I was told and went to climb on the back of the truck, but he stopped me.

"Not there," he said. "Inside."

I walked around to the driver's door and climbed in. Dad got in behind me.

Tina looked sick. She was totally still, and her eyes looked strange. Her head was to one side, and her jaw fell slackly open, and I could see her tongue. I tried not to look at her. Dad started the truck and headed out onto the road. Up past acres of rugged bushland and scattered, desolate dwellings. Past the lapidary man's house, until we reached the top of the hill. The huge, triangular steel electricity post was on the opposite side of the road. It was linked to other posts by electrical wires, slung over the gorges, across the national park. I thought we were heading down the gorge toward the river, but when we reached the Steinmans' house, Dad turned left down an old fire track and sped down into the gully. As we turned, Tina slumped on top of me. I tried to push her upright, but she was very heavy. When the truck hit a rock on the road, she bounced forward, hitting the dashboard with a thump, and then flopped lifelessly into her own lap. Dad swore. Swerving dangerously all over the track, he leaned over in front of me and tried to reposition the girl. He pulled on the back of her dress, and she shot upright as he slammed on his brakes. He turned off the track and parked in a clearing near a second high-transmission power line. Tina fell forward again, and I began to cry.

"Quit bellowing," he hissed as he stopped.

Dad got out of the truck and went around to the passenger door. Meanwhile, I resorted to the only form of protection I knew. I began to pray. I knew something was terribly wrong. Tina was all floppy and limp, and she wouldn't stop leaning on me. The nuns at school told us that "Jesus saves little children," so I rattled off the Hail Mary in my head. The prayer always got mixed up with the Lord's Prayer whenever I became scared, and I panicked because I was getting it all wrong. Confused, I started the prayer again.

As the truck door opened, Tina fell out on the ground. Dad stepped over her and pulled me out of the truck in such a way that I seemed to fly over her body. I didn't fall. I just glided down to the ground, his hand firmly encircling my upper arm.

"Stand over there near that tree," he ordered. My father pointed to a very tall ghost gum on the opposite side of a flat sandstone rock. I walked over and faced the tree, staring at the trunk in the same way a disobedient child faces the corner. I waited for something to happen, not knowing what to expect, not daring to move, and fearing the worst.

Two rough hands grabbed me and twisted me around, forcing my back against the tree. My father had changed into a black raincoat, and he had a rope between his teeth. He crossed my ankles over each other and pulled my arms out to the sides, fastening me to the tree. I closed my eyes to block out his face, and then he walked away. I let out my breath and opened my eyes. My father had dragged Tina's crumpled form over to the sandstone rock, and he was staring at the sky.

"Get up and run, Tina," I thought. "This is your chance." But Tina didn't move.

As if he could hear my heartfelt pleas, my father walked over and grabbed Tina by the leg. He pulled her around and arranged her spread-eagled on the rock. Then he calmly walked to his truck and rummaged in the back.

"What is he getting? Is it a gun…a knife?" The questions raced through my mind as I struggled against the rope.

Clink. Clink. I heard the sounds of metal as he threw things from the truck. Dad walked toward Tina's inert body, carrying something by his side.

What was it? It was hard for me to see.

He whispered something in the girl's ear and then began to cry.

With uncontrollable desperation, he crouched, sobbing over the body. A black, hysterical frame, shoulders heaving, with tears streaming from his eyes. The blubbering mass wailed like a toddler, his massive fists pounding the ground. I struggled against the rope, wanting to block out all sound, but his cries did not stop. They fell on Tina's dead ears, her body becoming part of his shadow as he cradled it in his arms and rocked back and forth.

"Misereatur tui omnipotens Deus, et dimissis peccatis tuis, perducat te ad vitam aeternam…"[lviii] he roared to the heavens.

I saw it flashing in the air. Slick and sharp and landing with a madman's force, it entered her body all silver and shiny. Then it exited, red and repulsive. I gulped back my tears and tried to block out the hideous scene. The sharpened axe came down again and again. Tina's face was no longer distinguishable. Then I knew he had forgotten me, lost in his own world. I thought I heard him scream. My mouth was open, but the voice coming from within me seemed totally foreign. It mewed like a strangled cat, high pitched and hysterical. These sounds mixed with my breath, and my tearless gulps became so ferocious they seemed to claw at my throat. I prayed for it to end. I prayed for everything to dissipate into blackness.

That night I took off the orange-and-brown stone necklace and wrapped it in a tissue. For some reason, it had lost its attraction. I wanted to throw it in the bin, but I pushed it deep beneath my mattress.

"It will help me remember," I thought, hating the feeling in the pit of my stomach. I still have the necklace today. The blue stone necklace given to my mother and the dark brown stone that I feel was meant for Tina lie in the bottom of my jewelry box as reminders of the thin, pretty girl with the pale-blond hair. From that day onward, whenever my father gave me a present, I would give it away. I felt as though all his gifts were cursed and stamped with the memory of the girl's sad stare.

I reached my hands out and touched her enormous head. I could feel the blood pulsing through the paper-thin skin, beneath my fingertips.

"This is your brain, Rosalie," I whispered. "You won't die...not while the blood is pumping through your head."

Forced into accepting the fragility of life, I looked on Rosalie's frailty as a blessing. Her eyes rolled upward, and she laughed. Her trusting blue eyes were very close to mine, and saliva was dripping from the corner of her mouth.

"The Devil won't touch you, you know. He says you're a deformed beast."

Tears stung my cheeks. I had accepted that my father contained different people, but lately he had been switching characters as if they were hats. Whatever control he had was being challenged, and the Devil was becoming more pronounced. Rosalie looked at me and gurgled.

"But you're lucky," I whispered. "You'll always be safe here with your mother. She loves you, and so do I." As if on cue, Mrs. Peters came into the room and demanded to know what I was doing.

"I was patting her."

Martha Peters gave a rollicking laugh. Layers of fat rolled up and down until she composed herself and looked at the time.

"It's getting late, dear. Kiss Rosalie good-bye, and we'll see you tomorrow." Then she shooed me out of the way.

The Peterses' house seemed so safe, and whatever I told Rosalie went no further than her room.

"She's so good at keeping secrets," I told Mum later. "I don't notice she smells after I've been there awhile, and she never complains about anything." Rosalie had taught me one of life's most valuable lessons.

"No matter how big your problem, there is always someone less fortunate than you."

Michael had been out walking, and he was confused. Near Conrad's Caves, he had made a grisly discovery: dried dark stains that looked like buckets of blood. Bits of gore were rotting, filled with ants and maggots. Next to the scene, he found lots of magazines. There were scattered piles of embarrassing magazines—magazines with pictures of naked ladies in them.

When he arrived home, the house was in an uproar. Conrad had found a huge bone. The Labrador was covered with dirt, wagging his tail and dragging the bone along the ground.

"Wow!" shouted Michael. "This is fabulous. Mum! Quick! Come and see. Conrad's found a dinosaur bone." My younger brothers were whooping and hooraying when Mum came outside to check.

"Here, boy," she whistled, and the black Labrador bounded toward her with the bone.

"It's very old," said Michael in awe. "It must be a dinosaur."

My mother looked worried. "It only looks old because it's covered with dirt. We don't know how old this bone is because it's been buried."

Mum turned to Conrad and asked him, "Where did you find this, boy?" The dog wagged his tail for an answer.

"Will I be famous, Mum?" asked Michael excitedly. "Is it a dinosaur?"

"I'm sorry, Michael," my mother replied. "I don't know where it came from, but this bone looks human. It's a tibia."

My mother left the bone on the table until my father came home. He didn't look very concerned.

"It's just an old sheep's bone," he kept saying.

"I'm not stupid," Mum answered. "I know what a sheep's leg looks like. I'm taking it to the police station tomorrow. They'll know what it is."

Michael was filled with happiness. It wasn't a dinosaur bone, but a visit to the police station would be very exciting. We woke up the next morning and looked for the bone.

"It's gone!" we cried when we couldn't find it, and my mother panicked.

"It can't have just disappeared!"

My father, who was reading in the corner, looked up from his newspaper and said, "The bloody dog got it again. I chased him down the bush, but I couldn't get it back. He'll have buried it by now."

And so the bone was gone and, in a short time, forgotten.

It was an easy task to get rid of evidence. Pieces of hewn flesh could be eaten by wild animals or minced up and poured into sewerage tanks. Bones could be ground up and crushed with hammers, then buried in lime. If I walked in a straight line down past the goat shed and into the bush, I ended up on Picnic Rock. If you imagine Picnic Rock as the central point of a compass, you could walk into the gorge for about eight acres to the north, west, and east and find the same thing. In the bush there were pieces of wrought iron assembled to make a lean-to shelter. Also, behind the house to the south, a large meat mincer was set up on a makeshift table. The mincer at the north end of the gorge was different because it stood next to a big stone sharpening wheel. It was very heavy, and none of us could move it. We rarely went near the mincers, but when we did, the boys sharpened bits of wood on the wheel to make spears, and Jamie filled the mincers up with rocks and ground them down to sand.

In the past many of our pets had gone missing in the bush. In the beginning it had been an average of one every six months, but now the killing had escalated. Beloved pets like Sheba, Timothy, and Goldie had all met death, and now our golden retriever, Sharie, was nowhere to be found. My mother searched for Sharie for a week and then gave up hope of finding her alive.

I knew the Devil had a bloodlust, and the killing of animals was part of it. The animals were executed, not as a ritualistic practice to appease the Devil, but as a way of educating me. Through the drill of carnage, he hoped to gain absolute control of me. He hoped to annihilate my spirit and replace it with total subservience to his self-absorbed majesty. The trusting retriever had been his last victim, shot twice to teach me the lesson of silence. Sharie's remains were in the same sandy clearing where he had butchered Tina. The terror I felt enslaved me to secrecy and protected the Devil from the law.

After a month, I took my mother to the place where Sharie had been shot. Remnants of fur still lay on the ground, although any skeletal remains had been removed.

My mother and I both screamed when a neighbor from another property walked quietly up behind us and said, "Are you ladies all right?"

Mr. Steinman wore an Akubra hat and carried a rifle. To me, he seemed like a giant.

"I've heard some shooting down here lately, and I thought I'd take a look around," he said. "Some mad bastard has been taking potshots at the fishermen down at Crosslands. One poor guy even got pellets in his neck. The trouble is that nobody seems to know which direction the gunshots are coming from because of the rifle range across the gully. It's hard to distinguish the sound when it's a windy day; the gunshots just echo through the gorges."

Mum told Mr. Steinman that we were looking for Sharie, and he examined the fur on the ground.

"That's dog fur, all right. That explains why she's missing. The lunatic taking potshots killed your dog."

Jessica, my mother's sister, was staying with us while she worked at the petrol station in town. She walked down to the goat shed, deep in conversation with my mother.

"We'll have to leave him," Mum told her.

Jessica's blue eyes widened with this juicy tidbit of information.

"You shouldn't have told her," I hissed, sensing betrayal on the horizon. "She'll tell him."

But Mum wasn't listening; she was too busy feeding the goats. Jessica glared at me and mouthed the words "Shut up" from behind my mother's back. After pulling a face at her, I resolved to keep away and hoped nothing would come of my mother's soul baring.

Later that afternoon, I went to find my brothers in the bush.

"Maybe they're at the Valdermeres' old house," I thought after searching around Caveman's Cave. I walked back to Picnic Rock and then through the bush, until I saw the shack in the distance. It looked deserted. Upon drawing closer, I went to the open doorway and looked in. A man was on top of a girl with blond hair. I recognized the singlet and the brown pants loosened at the waist. The pants were falling down, humping and grunting, exposing grayish-white underpants and pink-and-white flesh. I tried to see who the girl was.

"It's not Tina," I thought. "Tina is dead."

The girl sensed my presence and looked over my father's shoulder. Her deep-blue eyes widened in recognition, and I took an involuntary step backward. The girl was my mother's fifteen-year-old sister, Jessica. I didn't wait for explanations; instead, I ran as fast as I could through the bush and back to the house. That night I heard him shouting.

"You told your sister you were leaving me."

"No," cried my mother.

"Don't lie to me; Jessica told me what you said. She also said Shannon wants you to leave."

I froze, the mention of my name spelling trouble.

"I hate that little bitch. Shannon is a liar and a troublemaker."

I recoiled inside and tried to block out the venom in his voice. My mind was racing, so many questions left unanswered. Why had Jessica told my father what my mother had said? Surely she loved her sister more than my father! Was Jessica a traitor, or was she a butterfly seduced by his web? Was she going to end up like Tina? Answer upon answer eluded me.

The next day, my mother took me into town shopping. I stayed in the park, playing on the swings, while Mum went off with Jessica. When she came back, I didn't recognize her. I waved to Jessica and kept playing.

"Hey," called out Jessica, "it's your Mum."

I stared in disbelief. She looked years younger. "What have you done to your hair? Did you dye it?" I asked.

Mum laughed. "It's a wig."

I was surprised. My mother looked so different, so pretty and young, almost carefree in her appearance. She warned me not to tell my father about the hairpiece, but as soon as he arrived home, Liam spilled the beans.

"We've got someone new in the house," he giggled excitedly, dancing around my mother and pointing at her. My father immediately demanded to know what was going on. When Mum produced the wig, my father grabbed it and put it on. Michael immediately fled to his room, and something inside me snapped. I ran screaming and crying from the house, with Mum following me. I heard her calling me and telling me not to be silly, but I had disappeared.

Visions of Grandma O'Leary flew into my head as I cowered under the house. She was dead, but she still visited through my father. When I was little, she only appeared in her house in Pymble. She never came to my house on Somerville Road. Gray wig, brown wig, or blond wig. The color didn't matter; they all melted into one. My unsuspecting mother had transported Grandma O'Leary from her own house to ours, by the simple purchase of a wig. Now I would never be safe from her overzealous eyes. Ever-tidy, ever-perfect Grandma O'Leary, who scrubbed sinners clean and forced soap into your mouth if you were bad. Her outlandish dress code, the curtains and bed-sheets, the makeshift dresses cut with a cross in the middle and draped over one shoulder with "elegant refinement."

When I got home, there was more yelling.

"What a waste of bloody money!"

A hurried "I'm sorry" from my mother sent us all scurrying to our rooms. But no apology would take the blond wig away. It had met up with an old friend, the personality my father kept closest to his heart.

His mother!

Michael huddled in the corner. He looked a sorry sight with the old gray wig perched precariously on his head. Bright-pink lipstick smeared his face, and tears filled his eyes. He didn't seem to remember how long he'd been sitting there or why. I mentioned his funny hair, and he cautiously put his hand up and felt it.

The wig wobbled in his hand, and he muttered, "That's right; I was with Grandma O'Leary."

I wanted to know more, but something told me it wasn't the time for questions. My brother pulled the wig off and threw it down in disgust.

"How come she was here?" I asked.

"Who?" he replied as he frantically rubbed at the lipstick on his face. It mixed with his tears and made him look all pink and messy.

"Grandma O'Leary," I prompted.

But he didn't seem to hear me. Instead, his hands kept wiping his face, erasing his memory as they did so.

"I have to go to the corner shop," Mum said, and I beseeched her to take me with her.

"I can't; the boys are out in the bush, and they will worry if they come home and no one's here."

"But Dad's here," I pleaded.

"Just keep out of his way," Mum warned. "I'll only be ten minutes."

"Ten minutes is long enough," I thought as she drove away.

As he heard her drive off, the singsong voice began. "Sha-nn-on. Sha-nn-on."

Like a nervous colt, I bolted. Down the driveway, through the lucerne patch, over the rocks, and out onto the road. Around the corner, until I reached Rosalie's house. The door was open. I hurtled past Martha Peters's lumbering frame and squeezed behind her fridge.

"What in the world?" she exclaimed, but there was a knock on the door.

"I'm looking for my darling daughter," my father said. "She ran over here."

"I haven't seen her," Martha replied.

"You bloody liar, I saw her come over here. I'll get her myself."

Martha Peters's giant frame blocked the door.

"She's not here." The big woman stood with her hands on her hips, a large pan poised dangerously in her hand. "I've already told you, Patrick O'Leary; your kid's not here. Get off my property and search your own backyard."

My father swore and turned to leave, hurling abuse as he retreated home.

Martha Peters came over to the fridge. "You can come out now, love," she said.

But I was afraid he'd come back.

"He's gone now," she added, "probably to get another drink."

Still no movement, and Mrs. Peters's patience was wearing thin. A strong, flabby arm reached behind the fridge and dragged me out.

"You'll get gassed, you silly beggar," she said. "He's gone now. Go play with Rosalie till your mum comes, or better still, do my washing up."

I laughed. I certainly felt I owed her something. As I started to wash the dishes, I heard my mother's voice at the door.

"I won't leave her with him again," she said in a troubled tone. "I don't understand it; he always says he hates her."

"For someone who hates her, he certainly chases her around a lot," Mrs. Peters snapped back. Later, Mrs. Peters gave me a brand-new twenty-cent coin.

"That's for all your hard work," she said, "and for being a brave little soul."

That night, he paid me a visit. It was to be expected, because whenever I managed to avoid him, he always sought me out. He was singing outside my window softly, almost in a whisper, the song "You'll Never Walk Alone."

It was the right tune, with the wrong words. "You'll never be alone…"

The tractor boots paced up and down, crunching on twigs and squashing the grass. Back and forth, outside my window. Scratching sounds, like fingernails on glass. Ever so quiet, but deafening to my ears. It had become a weekly ritual. He would say he was going to the club and drive off in his truck. Then, after a night of drinking, he would head home again. However, instead of turning in to the driveway, he would stop up the road and cut through the bush. He'd end up outside my bedroom window scratching softly on the glass. The strange predator was never seen. He crept silently, never suspected in the black, powerless night. He traveled alone, his pocket full of Mars bars and his breath stinking of alcohol. Sometimes he'd force chocolate into my mouth, chanting "Good girl" into my ear. I don't know what I hated more—the window, which didn't have a lock, or the bittersweet aftertaste of regurgitated chocolate mixed with semen. In these incidents I did not throw up because of the oral sex. I'd choke on the chocolate, and he'd come in my face. Afterward, when I finally fell asleep, I'd have more nightmares.

One time the dream was different from the rest. A long line of people were standing in single file near Caveman's Cave, down in the bottom of the gully. They were waiting for my father to speak. There were about twelve females, all with different faces, some familiar and others very alike in their features.

I was at the head of the line, and my father was brandishing his rifle as he shouted, "Which one will I kill first?"

"Kill me!" I pleaded, but he laughed, his face sneering into a smile.

"No, my *darling* daughter," he said in an apologetic tone, "you will be last. You have to watch."

As the nightmare progressed, he shot the people one by one. The strangers were first, followed by a group of blond, blue-eyed girls, like Jessica and Tina. He then shot my brothers and Sister Luke. Not a word was spoken as he pulled the trigger. It was like a domino effect. A silent line of people fell down dead as the rifle exploded into their chests. He laughed as he shot my mother, and then he turned to me. The eyes projected cold, calculated hatred as he pulled the trigger. In my sleep, I felt the bullet rip through my chest with undeniable clarity, its force rocketing me bolt upright in bed. Awake and bathed in sweat, I shook uncontrollably. My mouth was dry, and my hands were clammy. Heart pounding, I fell back down on the bed, wide awake and unable to resume my fitful slumber.

The doctor sent my mother to marriage-counseling sessions at Lifeline.[lix] On a Thursday night, a lady gave us a lift into Hornsby. Meetings took place in a big, old mansion in the middle of the park. My brothers and I would wait in a room upstairs while the adults talked downstairs. We'd take our pillows and blankets and try to stay up as late as possible, playing practical jokes, eating biscuits, and watching *Marcus Welby, M.D.* on TV. Unbeknownst to us, on our fourth visit, my father turned up to the session. Up in our TV room, the night seemed to drag on forever. After asking Michael the time, I crept downstairs to see what was happening.

"It must be nearly the end," I thought. "It's after nine thirty." I peeked through the glass door.

"Dad's here," I thought, my heart leaping into my mouth. I felt sick. The room held a circle of people, some of whom looked very nervous while my father talked to them. My eyes traveled around the circle and came to rest on my mother. She was sitting opposite him, frozen, like an alabaster statue. Dad's arms waved, and I noticed something on his lap. It was his gun. He rose to leave and spotted me behind the door. He dragged me inside immediately, but I broke his hold and ran behind the largest potted plant I could find.

He screamed, "You're coming home with me."

"No!" I yelled in defiance, dodging his clasping hands and breaking leaves off the plant as I did so.

He stormed out of the room with his gun in hand, yelling wildly, "I'll take the boys then."

Everything was in turmoil. All the adults scattered, grabbing their belongings, eager to leave the room. The boys had come downstairs, and my father ordered them outside. During this time my mother was begging my father not to take them home.

"They're my kids, and I'll do what I like," he screamed. "Go and get in the truck."

My frightened brothers scampered over the backboard, and Dad drove off, leaving Mum and me to get home with our lift. The lady was very frightened, and she didn't want to take us all the way home. She dropped us off at the top of the street, and we started to run.

Our feet pounded on the road like a heartbeat in time. I had a stitch in my side, so I tried to concentrate on the sky filled with stars and a big, full moon.

"I have to keep running," I thought, willing myself to push onward.

Mum was staring straight ahead, praying out loud while she ran. "Please don't kill them. Please don't kill them," she said over and over again.

I decided to pray too. "Don't let them be dead, God, but if they are, please let him kill me first. I don't want to watch my mother die," I prayed in silence.

Finally we could see our house in the distance.

"Stay here," my mother said, and I collapsed on a rock. "If I don't come out in ten minutes, run to Mrs. Peters and get the police."

I sat panting on the rock and tried to calm down. I didn't own a watch, so I tried to count ten minutes in my head. All was silent. There was no shouting, just a dark house in an eerily quiet night. Black ink spots danced in front of my exhausted eyes, and I tried to focus on the moon and stars in an effort to stay awake.

A hand! It touched my shoulder, and I jumped out of my skin.

"It's OK," whispered Mum. "The boys are asleep."

"What about Dad?"

"He's asleep too. He's so drunk, he'll sleep until morning."

We walked toward the house, hand in hand. Both of us were diminished in energy and age. Like three-years-olds we crept into my room. I got into bed while Mum took an old blanket and slept on the floor.

The next day, Mum got the camp bed out and began sleeping in my room. The night was filled with whimpering noises. They were desolate and frightening.

"No, no," my mother cried, tossing and turning in her sleep. The camp bed squeaked under her weight, and I tried to see her in the dark. The room was too black.

"Is she being attacked?" I thought.

I heard more strange sounds—muffled moaning and crying. I slid off the bed and crawled across the room on my stomach, hoping to drag her out of the room. Finally I reached the bed.

"No!" Mum screamed and sat bolt upright in bed.

My arms waved over the top of her, trying to feel whether he was there, but I found nothing. Instead, Mum's hand connected with my jaw, knocking me flying.

"Ow!" I yelped.

She whispered, "Shannon?"

"Yes," I whispered back. "Be quiet. It's only me. You're having a nightmare."

"Go back to bed," Mum whispered.

"I thought you were being attacked," I whispered.

"I'm all right. Did I hurt you?"

"I'm fine."

As I crawled back into bed, I felt strangely relieved by the fact that my mother had nightmares too.

"Everyone must have them," I decided, taking comfort in this newfound normality.

After that, sitting with my father on the concrete steps of the patio became a daily ritual. Each session lasted for about half an hour. His arm would grip like a vice around my shoulders, tightening with each repetition.

"Why don't you love me?"

"I do love you," I'd have to answer.

His singsong voice chanted on and on. "Why are you afraid of me?"

"I am not afraid of you."

His fingers dug into me, and my shoulder ached. "Why don't you love me?"

The same questions, over and over again.

"I do love you."

"Why are you afraid of me?"

"I'm not afraid of you."

My neck would hurt from my attempts to keep my body away from him. The pressure of his fingers on my shoulder would increase until it forced my rigid body back toward him.

"Why don't you love me?"

I tried to focus on resistance while my mouth answered, "I do love you." I'd repeat my answers, my facial muscles unmoving and my eyes fixed to the ground.

Over and over…

Again and again.

The questions and answers never changed, the repetition stifling and hypnotic. I would lose all contact with time as the recurrent theme of a demoniac played havoc with my psyche. My hysterical heart screamed fear and repulsion. It was always the same, an endless, disenchanted déjà vu.

That night I heard the bedroom cupboard door in my parents' room slide open. It was a sound I was familiar with, the ominous noise of my father reaching for his rifle.

I reached under my pillow for the five-cent piece.

"If he kills me," Mum had told me, "you must run to the phone box and dial zero zero zero for the police."

The five cents had been under my pillow for months. There was also one under the Sunshine milk can in the laundry, but I wasn't sure when I should run to the telephone box. I could hear Dad through the wall, hitting and kicking, thumping the walls and my mother. I waited, and when I didn't hear Mum speak, I crawled toward her bedroom door. My father pulled my mother from the bed and threw her on the floor. He knelt on her shoulders and punched and slapped her in the face. The pounding and her screams woke Michael, and he came to see what the matter was.

"Get the hell out of here," my father shouted as he held my mother up with one hand. I ducked behind the door, and Michael ran for cover while my mother was thrown back on the bed.

Sobbing hysterically, she pleaded, "Don't!" I couldn't watch anymore, so I crawled back to my room and sat in my cupboard with my fingers in my ears, waiting for the noise to stop.

The next morning my mother needed medical treatment.

"My head is spinning," her strained voice said from behind black sunglasses. "I need to see the doctor." Her hand was holding up her jaw, and a great black bruise covered the left side of her face.

Her face was black and blue, and her cheek was broken. The doctor told her to report the injury to the police, and she went to Hornsby Police Station and filled out a report.

"We can't really help you, madam," the constable said. "We're not allowed to interfere with domestic violence cases."

Mum was crying. "But what if he kills me?"

"Then we can interfere," the officer replied.

When we returned home, Michael looked at Mum's bruised and battered face. "Did Dad do that to you?" he asked, as if the memory of the previous night had vanished.

"Yes," she croaked.

"Then we should leave."

Relief! Mum had left me in the park to play on the swing. Relief! She had taken Dad's two rifles to the police station, and they had said they would keep them. Relief! I looked at a fluffy white cloud and thanked Grandfather for protecting me!

When we arrived home, we found pandemonium. The sounds of metal pipes clanking and smashing against one another filled the house. Things were lying around broken, and ripped photos and papers were scattered on the floor. The phone was lying in a splintered heap, and bits of plaster lay on the floor where the electrical cord had been ripped out. Suddenly, the banging stopped. My father came into the room, sat down, and stared at the wall. He hadn't changed for days.

"He smells," Jamie had whispered the night before, and we had quickly shut him up. Dressed in a filthy singlet and underpants, Dad sat, caressing a new gun. His boots were filthy, but he wouldn't take them off.

"These boots were made for walking," he sang. "That's what I intend to do. One of these days these boots are gonna walk all over you."

He had just finished disconnecting the water.

"I can shower at the club," he shouted. "You can rot, you stupid cow."

My mother watched him in silence. Around him, we tried to continue on as if nothing unusual was going on. I stayed close to my mother, helping her with the chores. We got some water from the tank and brought it into the kitchen. Then Mum poured it into the sink and began to wash up. Her hands shook as she stacked the plates up on the sink.

At these times, his alcoholism usually saved us. We'd wait for him to be overcome with the need for a drink and leave to go to the club.

Suddenly, Dad jumped up out of his chair and screamed, "No one will leave here! I'll kill you all."

The gun pointed in all directions, like a commando poised for combat. My mother and I froze against the wall.

"Where are the boys?"

"They're out playing," Mum answered without expression.

It was always best to speak in monotone because it wouldn't provoke a reaction. Lately when they weren't at school, my brothers seemed to appear only for meals and then run off into the bush. At night, Michael stayed in the bedroom reading encyclopedias. They were the only books in his room other than his well-worn copy of *No, No, Nannette*, a story about a girl and her goat.

Having his family under siege gave my father a strange feeling of contentment. Secure in the knowledge he controlled us, he sat down on the chair and watched us. We continued washing up in silence.

"I'm going out." Dad said. He suddenly lurched forward, grabbing the gun and pointing it at Mum's head. Mum froze.

"Don't you dare leave this house, woman, or I'll blow your fucking head off." He marched into the bedroom to change. Soon after, he left to go to the club.

My mother immediately ran outside to the Hillman. The car wouldn't start, and she opened the bonnet to see what was wrong. Part of the engine was missing. He had made sure we couldn't leave the house. We were trapped, waiting for the hunter to pounce.

June 7, 1969

I woke up feeling nervous and sick. The day had come when we were going to leave. I was strangely relieved, excited, and terrified all at once. We had no money, but we were going to escape. For the past few weeks, it had been my job to arrange the kitchen cupboards so they looked full. I'd pack all the food tins and containers in a line at the front and hope Dad wouldn't notice the empty spaces behind them and become suspicious. It was Saturday, and my father was going to play golf. After he left, we all piled into the car with the dogs and cats and rode to a strange house. The lady who owned the house was a member of Lifeline, and she had offered her services as a babysitter so Mum could move out of the house. I felt safe with her because my father had never met her.

In the past, my mother had been to the local police station several times to ask for help and she had been told they were powerless to help her. On this occasion however, her pleading finally convinced them to send two policemen to help us move out of the house. They impounded two more rifles and remained stationed in their car outside while she got her belongings. She didn't have much to take—only a few household items, our beds, a few toys, and clothing. The hardest part of the move was taking the animals. The goats were taken to Auntie Marge's house, and Mum gave the chickens to some people who lived down the road. We would get them back when we had somewhere permanent to stay.

I still recall this as being one of the longest days in my life. I sat for hours rocking and trying to will time to go faster. To break the waiting cycle, I'd go out to the back of the house and pat our dogs, which were chained to the clothesline and waiting good-naturedly. Then I would go back to rocking again. My heart was filled with the nagging fear that something terrible would happen to my mother. I relived scenarios from the past, replacing dead people with images of my mother. The long day was a horrific exercise in strength and patience, one that I never wish to experience again.

CHAPTER 10

RELOCATING

For the next six weeks, we stayed in a cramped weatherboard house with Ella, a single parent who had also survived a traumatic marriage. She moved her two-year-old daughter into her bedroom, and my mother slept in the little girl's bedroom. My brothers slept on the veranda, and I slept on a dusty, old lounge.

We were all sworn to secrecy.

"Don't tell anyone where we are living," Mum pleaded. "It will take him longer to find us." But our escape from my father was short lived. We had only moved one suburb away, and we still attended the same school. Within a couple of days, my father knew where we were living. He'd watched us board the school bus and followed it to Ella's house. He'd park outside, smiling and waving, laughing as we raced hysterically from the bus stop to the front door. During the first week of our stay, I went for a bushwalk with a girl from down the road. We didn't get very far because three children came tearing out of the bush screaming.

"Don't go down there," they shouted. "There's a loony man running around starkers."

"What does he look like?" I asked.

"He's naked," they cried.

"No, what does his face look like?"

"He's got fair hair and is speaking some weird language. He's got a cross as well."

The Devil had returned. Our cat went missing, and we found her about half a mile away, near the railway, poisoned. This new incident created a snowball effect. Spiraling fears and paranoia gripped me, and my nightmares returned. We all realized our bid for safety would be short lived.

One night, I woke to the chill of a violent electrical storm. Water pelted down on the metal roof, and thunder blasts filled the lounge room where I slept. The noise from the storm was deafening. The argumentative sky burst forth bullet rain. Lightning flashed and cast eerie silhouettes on the yellowed fibro walls.

One lightning strike revealed a macabre black figure sitting on the end of my bed. I felt its weight with my toe and quickly drew my knees up toward my body. I pulled the blankets up over my head and waited for a hand to grab me, but nothing happened. After a few more blasts of thunder, I peeped over the covers. The room remained dark until lightning lit it up again. The figure had disappeared, retreating as silently as it had appeared. I could hear Conrad barking. It was a disturbed, wild kind of barking, and I thought he was scared of the storm. The dog yelped, becoming more distressed, and I could hear him pulling on his chain as he tried to break free from the water tank. His howling frenzy sent shudders down my spine, and I pulled my blankets up around my ears. The barking kept on and on, and I crept out to see what was wrong.

The black figure was standing near the dog trying to grab the chain, but Conrad snapped and snarled. Then the man raised his hand to strike, but the dog was too fast. The black Labrador leaped into the air and bit the arm hard. The figure began to swear, and there was a flash of silver. Growling and yelping. Savage teeth gnashed flesh once more, and then the chain was broken. Our protective canine fled into the night. He was mortally wounded, felled by the knife-wielding vision in black.

My mother got a job as a bookkeeper at the local bakery. This provided us with the steady income of thirty-nine dollars and eighty cents a week. Coupled with the four dollars Mum made as a market researcher, it meant she could get a loan from her solicitor to buy a house. There was a tiny two-bedroom house in town that had a backyard big enough for a small chicken coop and goat shed. My mother got a mortgage, and the house became ours. She converted the dining room into a lounge room and used the lounge room for the boys' bedroom. She partitioned this room with a wardrobe so that Michael thought he had his own bedroom. Mum slept in the front bedroom, which looked out onto the street. She acted like a quiet sentinel, watching through the window, in case my father decided to call.

The most prized possession in the house was the bright-pink flushing toilet. Gone were the maggots of the old bush dunny and open, smelling drains. At our old property, my father had built strange "no-go" areas. He'd set up about five large clay pipes around the house and topped them off with square-meter slabs of cement or pieces of wood. These pipes didn't connect to anything. Instead, they led nowhere and provided random, unfastened cement wobble boards, which my brothers sometimes balanced on. In summer, these pipe structures emitted a vile, unforgiving stench. Gut-wrenching, they reeked of rotting blood and gore. In winter, this alien putrefaction became immersed in the damp smell of the land.

Of course my father found our new home in no time. We didn't move far because of my mother's work and my brothers' and my schooling. He monitored our movements from his parked truck. He turned up at school, at bus stops, and along our way home. We'd get strange menacing calls from his personalities, so we stopped answering the phone. Often, he'd drive his truck slowly beside us, stalking us and letting us know he was a presence to be reckoned with. He'd even come to school and take me out of class for imaginary doctor's appointments.

In the new house, I had a small room at the back. When the door was closed, the room was very dark. When possible, I avoided looking out the window, especially at night. I kept the curtains drawn at all times, and if I heard scratching on the window, I refused to open it. We ate in the kitchen at a small secondhand card table that wobbled whenever we put weight on it. I remember Liam and Jamie playing Three Stooges[ix] and pushing pies in each other's faces.

"They'll never do that again," said Mum after watching them.

Sure enough, she was right. We had no money for food, and my brothers had to scrape the pie shells off their faces and eat them or go hungry.

It was meant to be a secret, all hushed and spoken about in soft voices. Leah was pregnant.

"I'm going to have a baby," she told Mumma proudly, "and you can't stop me."

My mother and grandmother shared hushed, desperate conversations and looks of disbelief.

"Who is the father?" everyone probed. But there were no answers.

"I can't tell," she kept saying. "It's a secret."

Mumma was distraught. "She never goes anywhere by herself. Who could the father be?"

My mother wondered the same thing. Leah never went out without a chaperone because she wasn't capable of looking after herself.

My grandmother arranged for a forum of psychiatrists to decide whether Leah was physically and emotionally capable of looking after a baby.

Leah didn't pass the evaluation; the doctors allowed her pregnancy to be terminated and her tubes to be tied. This didn't put my grandmother at ease, however. The experience left her feeling totally inadequate as a caregiver.

"I can't look after her anymore," she said. "This pregnancy proves I will have to find a shelter where she will be more cloistered."

Mumma decided to send Leah to a church facility in the country.[lxi] There, the church cared for girls with varying physical and mental challenges and taught them life skills.

One Saturday we were told we had to visit my father.

"It is my right to see them," he had shouted at my mother. "They belong to me."

The old house still looked the same, but Dad had been working on the bathroom in order to reconnect the water. In the lounge room, he had taped a large color photograph of my brothers and me to the wall. It had been taken a few years earlier, and a huge butcher's knife held it up. This knife was positioned so it stabbed me through the head.

My father saw me staring at it and laughed. "Got a headache?" he inquired.

He was an expert when it came to sarcasm. His words could cut you off at the knees, crippling all conversation and leaving you stricken in silence. I sat in the corner and hoped time would pass quickly. I felt no motivation for play, just gave the pretense that I was enjoying the visit. The boys watched wrestling on TV until my father demanded we play a game with him.

"I have a new toy," he told us.

He had a cassette player plugged into the wall. The Games Man quizzed us, pretending he was a TV host and we were the contestants. We all failed to answer his questions correctly, and he quickly became bored with the game. He then said he wanted to "play something" to me.

The tape recording was muffled, and it was very difficult to hear what my mother was saying on the tape. It had been recorded through the wall or the floor.

"You shouldn't have said that," he warned and pointed to my photo on the wall. "One more false move, and you're dead."

Our conversation was cut short when Liam gave an excited shout. "Shannon's on television." I turned to see my brothers cramming around the TV to watch me singing.

"Not for long," said my father as he pulled out the TV's plug. "I bet I'm not the only television viewer doing this."

Suddenly his voice became higher as his personality switched. He clasped his hands in front of his chest and pursed his lips, bending toward me until he was close to my face.

"You think you are so good," he carped, waving his hands in the air, "but you're just an ugly girl with no brains. You can't sing. You can't act. You have no talent at all. You are a big, fat nothing, and you'd be better off dead."

Confusion left me barren of anger, and while part of me wanted to watch my performance, the rest of me was glad the image was gone. Embarrassed by the heckling and reprimands of false vanity, I longed for a big, black hole to crawl into. "The actress," as he called me, was left in a corner feeling incredibly ugly and foolish. I didn't feel hurt or angry. Instead I felt numb.

"Yes, I would be better off dead," I thought.

"Please don't let him have it," I pleaded with Sister Luke. "He'll only kill it." I hugged the tiny black kitten to my chest, and it mewed in protest. It was a stray, born to the cat that took shelter under the school, and I had picked it up on the road.

"It can't stay here," the nun tried to explain. "It needs a home."

"We can't take it," my mother added. "I can't afford another cat." I looked at the kitten and started to cry. The hand came down and grabbed it from me.

"Stop being stupid; you can visit it. It can live with me." My father threw the kitten in the truck, jumped in, and started the engine. His parting words resounding in my ears as he drove off: "You can come and visit."

We went on Saturday, and, to my relief, the kitten was playing on the porch.

"We call him Blackie," a little girl with blond hair told me.

Dad said she was his new housekeeper's daughter. The housekeeper said her name was Marie, and she had just come to stay. She had three children, two little boys about two and three years of age and a little girl, Amy, who was older, probably about four or five. The house smelled like wet nappies and was in a terrible mess.

My father kept calling Amy my name.

"Shannon," he'd call. "Shannon." The sound of his words made me feel sick.

"Her name is Amy," I told him, but he didn't seem to hear me.

Later that week, my father came to my school. When I saw him walking across the playground, I ran into the staff room and hid under a table.

"Don't let him take me," I sobbed, gripping the table leg tightly. "Please. I don't want to go."

The head nun looked perplexed, while other teachers stopped and stared.

"Get up off the floor and stop being silly," she reprimanded. "You are being very disobedient. Get off the floor and go outside immediately, young lady." I felt a hand on my shoulders, and I was pulled to my feet. "You're not allowed in the staff room. Now stop being silly, and go with your father."

I refused to move, and the nun's voice became louder as she dragged me toward the door.

"Do as you're told at once!"

The figure waiting for me took my arm and led me to the truck.

Later we were headed down the road into the bush. I looked down and noticed I no longer had my school uniform on. I was only wearing my singlet and pants. My head felt fuzzy, and I was having trouble keeping my eyes open. We drove past my father's house and on toward the bushland clearing where Tina had been butchered.

Someone was lying in the clearing, her outstretched arms attached to tent pegs driven into the sandy earth. The woman had a large wound to her left temple, leaving the side of her face distended and blue-black. Her matted brown hair was caked with blood, and her feet were tied together, like a human crucifix. Clothes lay in a discarded heap beside her, and she wore only a bra and pants. My father pushed me up against a tree and tied me up while she lay on the rock, unmoving, for what seemed an eternity. I stood staring at her in a state of shocked paralysis, uncertain whether she was still alive.

My father changed into his black raincoat and went toward the woman, carrying a pair of pliers. He kicked her, but she didn't respond. Then the vulture swooped down onto his prey, forcing her mouth apart by pulling down on her lower jaw. Bending down over her, the pliers still in hand, he attached them to her tongue and pulled hard. The woman's body jerked up and then fell down again on the rock, so he changed his position, placing his feet beside her head. A crunching sound ensued, assaulting my ears as he stood on the woman's shoulders and forced the pliers down her throat. He pulled again with great difficulty, grunting like a wild pig and panting with exertion.

I'm not sure if the gurgling sound was ripping flesh, but the tongue didn't come out properly. It came out a bit and then stopped. Dissatisfied, the Devil reached into his pocket and pulled out a white bone-handled knife and hacked at the tongue. Finally, it came free.

He left the dead housekeeper and walked toward the truck. I couldn't see him, but I knew he was searching for something. I tried to turn around, but the rope was too tight. Soon afterward he walked past me, his axe in hand. I closed my eyes so I wouldn't see it come smashing down. As the axe came down, the sound of crunching assaulted my ears and then stopped. I suddenly felt myself being shaken roughly. He untied my hands and feet and dragged me over to the dead woman's side. I didn't want to look at her, but my eyes wouldn't look away.

There was blood everywhere.

Blood covered his hands and his raincoat. There was blood on the ground and blood splattered on my singlet and pants. Repulsed, I wanted to be sick. The Devil's eyes fixated on mine as he raised his hands and deliberately licked each finger. Then his hands attacked her body and pulled out a lumpy bit of flesh. He was chanting gibberish and smearing the bloody mass around his mouth when he unexpectedly turned and hurled it away into the bush. Whistling and awash with blood, he wiped his bloody hands on the raincoat and walked back toward the truck.

I heard him laughing at me as I tried to run in the opposite direction, down the track. I also heard the truck starting, so I stopped and lay flat on the ground, hoping he would drive past me. He did, and I started to run again.

I ran and ran. Then suddenly he was in front of me, dragging me back to where he had parked the truck farther down the road. After throwing me inside, he drove me back to his ritual rock again. During this time he was speaking, but his words were alien to me. Maybe he was speaking in Latin, maybe in gibberish, but whatever the words were, they seemed to make sense to him.

The body was still there, isolated in the bush where no one knew of its existence. He instructed me to kneel beside him and watch as he pulled whatever he could out of the body. Everything was red and bluish purple, and drying blood carpeted the ground. My father got a baking tray and a torn white sheet out of the truck. He ripped the sheet into bandages and twisted them into coils. Then he stuffed them into the body, mumbling incoherently as he did so. The bandages soaked up any moisture that was left in the woman.

The Devil motioned for me to do the same, but I couldn't touch her. Instead, I just coiled the strips and threw them randomly in her direction. Overcome with nausea, I felt myself gagging on my own bile. As I turned to run again, the hanky overpowered me. My brain numbed, and my body collapsed at the knees. I hurtled into a timeless void where pain and reason could not reach me and where everything went a merciful black.

It was dark in the corner of my room.

"Our Father, who art in heaven."

I felt the sticky, red blood on my hands.

"Hallowed be thy name…"

I smelled the blood while seeing the life force extinguished in front of me.

"Thy kingdom come, thy will be done…"

I heard the grunting, uncomfortable sounds and watched, knowing I was powerless to help. I couldn't remember the next line.

"As it is on earth…" The prayer eluded me. "Forever and ever, amen."

I was filled with memories of the gurgling and the choking sounds, consumed by the Devil's hostility and my alienation. I desperately wanted the woman to know how sorry I felt.

"Guilty!"

I rubbed my hands together. Red blood flaked off into my palms. It was all over my hands, and I had no water to wash it off. It was so hot, the heat of the air mingling with flesh and sweat. My head was damp, and my hair was filled with dirt. That stupid prayer kept preying on my mind.

"Our Father, who art in heaven…hallowed be thy name…"

I had recited this prayer on a daily basis for years, and whenever I really needed it, I couldn't remember it. I was guilty. He kept saying so.

"Shut him out," my brain shouted while my head revisited the broken prayers. I could not help her in her hour of need. My broken sentences couldn't bring the dead back to life, but Jesus could. He brought people back to life and forgave everyone. Jesus said, "Suffer the little children," and I was suffering. I wondered whether Jesus would meet me if I were dead and whether the lady had gone to Jesus. I remembered her. She didn't look at peace. She didn't look happy. She was a mutilated mass of blood and gore, and I wondered if I would go to hell with my father.

The housekeeper was gone, and so were her children.

"Here one minute; gone the next," he said to everyone with a snap of his fingers. "They've done a moonlight flit."

I heard my brothers ask, "Why did they leave all their stuff here?" but my father didn't answer. The next time we visited him, the housekeeper's and her children's clothes were gone, and the house was an empty shell again. There were no traces, just nightmarish pictures in my head and countless unanswered questions. I thought I saw a baby hanging but didn't know if it was real or a dream. It was tied to a gum tree, unmoving and naked except for shoes.

This apparition followed me into adulthood and forced me to relive past monstrosities. Stuck in my mind, it was imprinted with an overpowering force. It can bring my adult senses to their knees and whirl me back into childhood, forcing me to recollect the past. The vision of the child in the tree denies me compassion, the mercy to know the difference between reality and phantoms. At these times my heart churns and my body freezes in denial. I lie in catatonic fear, seeing and feeling nothing while I relive my human reactions to an inhuman action. At these times I cannot analyze. I don't want to feel, so I breathe in shallow, short breaths and just lie still. Eyes shut tight, curled up in a ball.

A few days after the housekeeper's death, I was taken from school once more. Gulping for air, I was chased down the road again. Intent on escape, I ran over the grass mounds and down into the bush. I looked for an old hiding place, but when I crawled into the tank, the stench was overpowering. The predator's approach, however, drove me inside, and I hid in the darkness. I listened to his footsteps, cowering like a baited animal, as he stamped around in circles outside.

I hated the rusty, old tank, but my need for a hiding place far outweighed my fear of snakes and spiders. As I huddled in the shadows, I tried to avoid the beam of light that shone in from the circular hole at the top. The footsteps became slower, and I heard the dragging and kicking of tin. He always knew where to find me, as my childish brain was no match for his.

I heard his fingers tapping along the outside of the tank and stepped backward. I had expected to feel cold tin against my back, but instead, I came into contact with cloth. A small group of creatures started to crawl on my hand, and I panicked. I tried to flick the creatures off, accidentally hitting the material with my hands. The material was attached to a solid base, and my movement caused it to lurch forward on top of me. I could feel even more creatures crawling on my skin and hair. Hysterically, I jumped away, but the weighty object followed me. It flopped like a beanbag into the shaft of light, where I could see its face.

There, writhing on a lump of decomposing flesh, was a nest of maggots.

I screamed! The woman's face was eyeless, her matted hair a battered reminder of the housekeeper I had seen on the rock. Her face was a muddy, mutilated piece of pulp, encrusted with dirt and debris. I pushed the body away from me and heard a laugh. The Games Man was laughing at me from the top of the tank. I heard the scraping sound as he lifted the sheet of corrugated iron from the ground. The tank thundered out in protest as the iron fell with a clatter over the entrance, blocking out the light and sheathing the faceless woman in black.

Our golden retriever barked and scraped at the floor with her paws.

Mum and I stifled a giggle, and we went to get some pots and pans. With a clatter and a bang, we let them drop, banging them together as loudly as we could in the process. The metal pots hit the floor and bounced onto one another.

Bing! Bang! Thump! Cling! Clang! Over the part of the floor where the dog had told us my father was hiding.

"That will make a good tape," I whispered to Mum, and she smiled, picking up the saucepan and letting it go with a clatter.

It had become an everyday occurrence. Sometimes my father would hide under the floorboards, while at other times he'd break in and squeeze himself into the manhole in the roof. He'd tape record our conversations and use them as evidence against us. We spoke in whispers when our faithful dog pointed at the roof or barked at the floor, informing us of the intruder's arrival.

Once at about two o'clock in the morning, I heard screaming and hollering outside.

"Let me in. See what you've made me do. Let me in, or I'll do it again."

My mother looked out the window. My father was in frenzy, banging on the door, threatening to wake up all the neighbors.

"Go home," she told him through the locked door. "Go home before someone calls the police."

"I've already been home," he sobbed, the baby in him coming to the fore. "Let me in, or I'll do something drastic."

My mother opened the door, and his foot came in with a thud. Wild-eyed and smelling of alcohol, he raved as he pushed her aside. Around his neck he had tied a thick lump of rope in a hangman's noose.

"I tried to hang myself," he cried, displaying the rope burns around his neck. "And if you don't come home, I'll kill myself."

This episode and the constant break-ins made my mother even more worried about our safety. Looking over our shoulder had become a daily ritual. He was everywhere, watching and waiting. Sometimes he stared with silently pleading baby eyes, while at other times with cruel fanatical menace. My mother was afraid he would kidnap us, the problem of our being latchkey children until she came home from work an ever-present threat to our safety.[lxii]

"You are not to go home after school anymore," she said. "There will be no more walking home by yourselves. Instead, you must catch the bus into town and go to the library. You'll be safe there, and I can collect you after work."

Mrs. Jack, the librarian, was very proud of her library. She was forever telling people to "Shush!" as she stamped borrowing cards. If books were overdue, she would demand a fine, and customers would place the money on the palm of a tin African American boy who greedily gobbled up the coins.

This money box was a fascination for many children. Some deliberately kept their borrowed books so they could be fined. When I borrowed books, I'd read them overnight, consuming them like chocolates. I had read all the books in the children's section and started reading the reference books. As I was there every day after school, Mrs. Jack made it her business to teach me to catalogue and file. I'd ride around on the library trolley as if it were a scooter, returning the books to the shelves.

The library provided drama and art classes after school. The teacher, Oliver, had a large garage area set up as a studio, and for twenty cents you could paint, draw, make wax or clay sculptures, or study other simple craft techniques. Oliver sported an Afro hairstyle and wore a beaded shirt. He told me he lived in a flat under the Sydney Harbour Bridge and kept a tarantula for a pet. Oliver worked as an artist making TV stills for cartoons. He often brought in the unused slides so we could copy them during class. On Wednesdays, after the library had shut, Oliver also taught drama. He had a passion for history, so most of the plays we'd create revolved around ancient themes. These classes became my passion. I vented my emotions with such force that often the other children would stop to listen to my solo performances.

Michael also enjoyed the lessons. He had a flair for accents, and everyone would roll around in stitches, laughing at his impersonations. Drama classes became the highlight of our week and our major source of therapy. They allowed us to become someone or something different, transporting us away from our traumatic lives.

On special occasions, we'd visit Leah in the Southern Highlands. She had settled into her new lifestyle at the church home, and she worked sealing envelopes at the mailing center. Every year, the home held a fete to raise money, and we would go. Leah would make scones and craft items, and we would have a picnic in the home's beautiful European garden.

At the fete in 1969, Leah let it slip that my father had kept in contact with her by mail and that on several occasions he had visited her.

About a week later, my father said he had "started working at the Mercy Convent" across the road.[lxiii] This meant he could sneak down the church alley and into the school playground for a surprise visit. At lunch one day, Dad grabbed my arm and told me I had to go with him down the church lane. He half dragged me out onto the road and then down toward the convent where he had parked his truck.

"Get in" was all he said.

He started up the truck, and we headed up the road toward the golf club.

We passed the club, and my father turned the truck left, over the railway line. He sped up the highway and stopped outside a house within walking distance to the railway station.

My father got out of the truck, walked around the back, and rummaged among his tools. He then came back and threw me a paper bag.

"Put them on," he ordered.

In the bag I found some clothes. I picked up the pink woolen cardigan and an orange-and-pink striped dress. After I had finished changing, Dad walked me to the Mount Kuring-Gai railway station, and we caught the train back to Asquith.

Waiting for us on the platform was a girl of about sixteen years of age. She wore a green school uniform and had protruding front teeth, and her hair fell to her shoulders in thick red waves. I thought I had seen the girl before. This might have been at Leah's home during the fete, but I wasn't sure. The girl knew my father, and they started to talk. I wasn't introduced, and I watched them both like a silent spectator.

I remember looking up and seeing some children from my school walking over the railway overpass. My father's eyes followed my gaze, and he quickly told the girl to wait where she was and to look after me.

"I have to go," he said. "I'll be back in a minute." He pointed to me. "Whatever you do, don't let her get on a train."

The girl watched his retreating figure and said nothing in reply. We didn't speak as children from different schools filtered onto the station. I then realized that school was over and everyone was waiting for a ride home. A train pulled in to the station, and I saw some children from my primary school getting onboard. One girl from my class was watching me as the train pulled out of the station. She waved at me, but I pretended not to notice. I stared at the ground, feeling nervous and self-conscious, wishing I could go home. It seemed as if we were waiting for an eternity, so I began to hum to pass the time. The red-haired girl still remained silent.

The station was practically empty when my father returned carrying two milk shakes. He handed the girl the chocolate one and kept the strawberry one for himself. They chatted happily, and I noticed they weren't really interested in their shakes. I was hungry and wished I had one too.

We boarded the next train to Mount Kuring-Gai, and I wondered if the girl lived there. It must have been after four o'clock, and the train was practically empty. We got off at the station and waited until two other passengers left the platform. My father went over to the ticket office and looked around.

The station was empty.

Dad walked toward the end of the platform, but instead of leaving, he walked down a dirt ramp to the railway line. The girl and I hesitated before following, but he called to us sharply, "Hurry up! I've work to do."

We both slowly walked down the ramp.

My father grabbed the girl's milk shake container and pushed it toward me. "Wait here," he instructed, and he gave me his milk shake as well.

I sat down and placed the milk shakes on the ground. The girl's container was empty, while my father's was still half full. I picked up a stick and started to draw on the ground, and as I did this, my foot knocked over the strawberry milk shake. I tried to pick it up, but it was too late; the container was empty.

The girl and my father had disappeared into a tiny railway shed, and they were taking a very long time. If only they would hurry up.

Finally they emerged.

The girl had changed her clothes, and Dad was carrying a small rail spike. He told us to walk up the railway line. The girl walked first, I was in the middle, and my father was at the rear. From out of the corner of my eye, I saw my father pick up a large rock and throw it at the girl. The rock hit her in the back, and she tripped.

"My leg, my leg," she yowled like an animal. "You've broken my leg."

It dawned on me that the girl could have been mentally handicapped, as she seemed slow, like Leah.

My father walked up to where the girl was lying on the ground and rolled her blue trousers up to the knee. He examined her leg and drew a line above her knee with his blue pen.

"Maybe I'll have to cut your leg off." He laughed, and my blood went cold.

The girl was frightened. "No, please don't cut it off."

My father pulled the girl to her feet. "Get up! I told you I'm in a hurry." He walked off down a bush track to the right. We followed him until we came to a small clearing. In this area there were two large pipes that resembled septic tanks and two rusty orange road graders. They had been left there in preparation for the construction of the new expressway to Gosford. The area was deserted, and the equipment would be needed when the roadwork commenced. The girl sat down on a rock and began to take her sock and shoe off. While she did this, my father walked up behind her and pulled something out of his pocket. It was a guitar string.

The girl's hands flew toward her neck as he strangled her. They flayed around in the air as she choked and grunted her last living sounds. The girl fell forward into her own lap, and the wire dangled loosely from my father's hand. It had blood on it. Dad stared at the girl as if he didn't know what to do with her; then he put the wire across her forehead and pulled her backward. She flopped back on the ground, and I noticed a thin bloody line across her forehead where the wire had cut her.

My eyes locked with my father's as he picked me up and carried me to the concrete pipe. Without speaking, he dropped me inside the pipe. I put my hands up, held onto its concrete rim, and tried to lift myself up, grazing my knees as I did so.

I could see my father as he pushed the railway spike into the girl's mouth. I heard a crunching sound, and the spike seemed to go through her head.

Blood seeped out onto the sand, and I felt nauseated. Once again I was forgotten as he became lost in his own world of different personalities.

The spike was his weapon, and he used it mercilessly on his victim.

As he proceeded to rape the dead girl with the spike, I couldn't watch anymore. I slid down the sides of the pipe to the earth below and hugged my knees into a fetal position. I rocked and prayed. Prayed and rocked. I don't even remember how I got home again or any of the events that followed. I could have spent half an hour in that pipe or even three hours. On this occasion, time and hysteria melded everything together, liquefying my memory and leaving it void.

Every Sunday evening we went to church. Michael liked church and nagged my mother if she suggested we give it a pass. We even started going to church on Wednesdays to pray the Novena. Mum thought these rosary sessions might help us enlist God's help, but they seemed excruciatingly long and made my knees ache. It didn't matter what church we went to; Dad always showed up. His stalking always paid dividends, and we just accepted he was following us. Dad demanded I pray for his marriage. He said that Mum wanted to give the marriage another try and that we would move to Rockhampton to start a new life. I prayed this wasn't true.

Mum said going to church was good for our stability.

"You have to have faith in something," she said.

I asked her what she believed in, and she told me, "Hell is here on earth."

I asked about penance and martyrs.

"It's courageous to die for a belief, but it's hard to tell if it's just an easier way out of living," she answered.

I asked her why she didn't take Communion anymore.

"In the eyes of the church, I'm a sinner, and I'm not supposed to have Communion," she said. "I want a divorce, and the pope says it's a mortal sin."

With this revelation I decided to give up Communion too, deciding that I was a sinner as well because I also wanted my parents to get a divorce.

The Baby was back again, making me wince with embarrassment. He was down on his knees outside the front door, begging us not to leave him.

"Get up, Patrick," Mum said quietly. "The children don't want to see you this way."

He blubbered and spluttered, wailing loudly so the neighbors could hear. "You're so cruel. You've hurt me deeply. Don't you know I love you and can't live without you?" The crying continued. Mum walked away, searching for the front-door key in her bag.

"Are they crocodile tears?" Jamie whispered. "Or are they real?"

"A bit of both," Mum whispered, but I disagreed.

"He doesn't love us. He thinks he owns us," I hissed back.

"Yes," whispered Mum as she opened the front door. "I think you're right."

We walked past him in single file, trying not to look at him. He grabbed my hand and forced me to stand in front of him. I dreaded these scenes. The manipulative baby always tried to get his own way.

"Why are you all so nasty to me? I can't stand it anymore. I'm going to kill myself." The Baby said he had a gun and was going to use it. "I'll shoot myself, and you'll be sorry."

These words always worked, alarming my mother and terrifying my brothers. As soon as he saw he had won, the Baby disappeared, and my father took his place. Bad-tempered and aggressive, he'd push his way indoors and begin to interrogate and subjugate my mother.

We had spent the day at Mr. Brecht's house. My mother had offered to sew some curtains for him if he would fix our car. Mr. Brecht had three sons, twins who were seven years old and a boy who was eleven. He was Dutch and was waiting for his bride to arrive in Australia from the Philippines. He had decided that his house was too masculine and that my mother could help him by adding "the female touch" to welcome his new bride.

Mr. Brecht was a kind man who had taken my brothers and me out with his children to the Museum of Applied Arts and Sciences.[lxiv] Michael and I had been amazed because it was the first time the plastic lady with all the light-up organs had been on display in Australia. Afterward, when we walked to the car, it began to rain. We all got soaked, but we didn't mind, as our heads were filled with science exhibits and inventions. Mr. Brecht took us to a café, bought us hot chips, and delighted us with our very first hot chocolate. We had great times playing at Mr. Brecht's house. He was an excellent woodworker who had made an enormous cubbyhouse for his children in his backyard. His boys owned two albino pet rats, which were tame enough to run up our arms and sit on our shoulders. I thought the Brecht children had a perfect life and hoped some of this would rub off on me.

Mr. Brecht cut me a piece of wood and gave me some of his tools so I could chisel a woodwork picture. It kept me busy for a whole day. My mother sewed while I chiseled. At five o'clock it was time for us to leave, and we went outside to get into the car. We were met by my father, who was walking up the road with a machete in one hand and a lump of rope in the other. His shouts called out to the neighbors in the street, and they came out to watch the scene that was unfolding.

"I'll kill him," he shouted to Mum. Then as he walked toward Mr. Brecht, he added, "I'll kill you, you fucking bastard."

My mother screamed at us to get in the car, and the neighbors watched silently. Mr. Brecht was a tiny man, no bigger than five feet tall, and my father seemed to tower above him.

"I'll chop you up into little pieces," the madman bellowed. My father swung the machete high above his head and began to hurl more abuse at the confused Dutchman.

"Put it away, Patrick," Mr. Brecht tried to reason. "I don't want to hurt you."

With those words my father began to laugh hysterically. "*You* hurt *me*? Give it a rest! I'll break your bloody neck…I'll hang you from that tree."

Mr. Brecht turned to my mother and said in his thick Dutch accent, "Get in the car, Emma. I'll deal with this lunatic."

My mother got into the car. She was deathly white and shaking all over.

"Is he going to kill Mr. Brecht?" I asked between sobs.

"I doubt it," my mother answered. "Mr. Brecht has a black belt in karate. If anyone gets hurt in this fight, it's more likely to be your father."

I watched silently as my father advanced toward the Dutchman, and the two men started to speak. I don't know what Mr. Brecht said, but he certainly changed my father's mind about fighting. As quickly as he had advanced, my father retreated. As he was leaving, he brandished the machete at the five of us in the car.

"I've changed my mind," he screamed. "I won't kill him; I'll kill you instead!"

I heard my mother's indrawn breath as she quickly started the car.

"He means it!" she cried as she slammed her foot down on the accelerator. My father ran toward his truck, hurling abuse as we sped past him. My mother drove as fast as she could, all the while thinking of somewhere we could hide.

"Can't we go home?" my little brothers cried.

My mother didn't answer them. I crawled onto the floor in the front of the car and began to rock.

"Shannon's hysterical again," said Michael mockingly. "She is so stupid!"

Something snapped inside me, and we began to fight. It was as if my mother couldn't hear us. She was so absorbed in her own fear she needed all her self-control to drive. We just kept on driving round and round until it was night. Finally the car made an enormous swerve into a car park and stopped.

"We'll be safe here!" she said, and no one spoke.

Four frightened faces glared at her in the dark, and she breathed a defeated sigh.

"Who wants a doughnut?"

Liam and Jamie immediately came to life.

"Doughnut? In the middle of the night?"

The boys were hungry, and I was sick from crying. I got up off the floor and looked around. We were in Hornsby Hospital's car park.

"He'll never look for us here," my mother assured me. "He'll look for us at home or at Lifeline."

As we made our jumpers into pillows so we could settle down for the night, I hoped she was right. Mum went to the hospital canteen and bought us some hot doughnuts and lemonade to chase the cold away. After eating, my brothers drifted off to sleep. I heard Mum getting out of the car, and I sat up.

"I need to make a phone call," she explained.

Mum rang a man, and he came to the car park to help. They sat and talked for ages. At around three o'clock in the morning, the man escorted our car back to our house. Dad was waiting for us, but when he saw the man, he decided to leave.

"You're all dead!" he hollered as he sped off in his truck.

A few days after the incident with Mr. Brecht, Liam dropped a bombshell.

"I want to go and live with Dad."

We all stared at him in shocked silence. We knew he was afraid of my father and couldn't understand his decision.

"He said I can have steak every night and a room to myself."

My heart sank. I knew all too well what would happen. Liam would become his new playmate, endangered and tormented by the Games Man. My father had been slowly killing the pets we had brought to the new house. I was his macabre living token, unwillingly dragged by his side to be his silent witness. My presence provoked his maniacal memories and gave his savagery impetus. One afternoon he held my finger and forced it down the throat of my beloved guinea pig so he choked to death. On another occasion, I was home sick from school, and he broke into the house. I woke up to find him offering me a chicken sandwich for lunch. Inside the two slices of bread was the head of my favorite chicken, Gertie. Her body was discarded in the yard and her death blamed on savage dogs. I felt Liam would be next.

My mother tried to reason with him, but he had the resolution of a stubborn child.

"I want to live with Dad."

That night we all watched as Liam's bed was lifted onto Dad's truck.

When Mum hugged him good-bye, she was a gray-white color. It was as though all the blood had drained from her face.

"How can he do this?" I asked.

"It's his decision," she answered as the truck sped off. Then she turned and went to her room. Michael and Jamie went for a walk, and except for Mum's sobbing, the house was silent. I peeked into her room, and she was lying prostrate on the bed, her face in the pillow, crying.

I went to a friend's house.

"Please, Mrs. Hall," I asked her mother, "can Brittany help me clean the house? Liam's gone to live with Dad, and it's broken my mother's heart." Mrs. Hall gave me a strange look and nodded her head.

"You can go for half an hour," she told Brittany, seeing we were on an errand of mercy. "After that I need you at home."

Brittany and I had become friends when we moved. She thought I was a bit odd, but we both had the same interest in performing. She could play the piano, and I could sing. Michael went to school with her older brother, and we had met by default on the bus. She was a year older than me and was the epitome of a good daughter. She was going to be a nun when she grew up, and she tolerated me as long as I stayed at arm's distance. We both went back to my house and did the washing up. We swept the floor and cleared the table. We cleaned everything we could think of until it was time for her to leave.

Then I had nothing to do except wait. I sat in my room and wondered if Liam was eating steak. I was so afraid for him. Why did he put himself in danger? I asked my mother why she had let Liam go.

"He would have gone whether I liked it or not," she said. "If I had stopped him, your father would have persuaded him to run away. I know where he is, and eventually he'll come home."

"If he's not killed first," I said, and my mother didn't answer.

Liam stayed with my father for only two weeks. He came home with us because it was Christmas Day. Jamie was ecstatic that his brother had returned for a day of play. Santa had left us a large Christmas hamper full of presents and food. It was all packed neatly into a washing basket on our doorstep. With tears in her eyes, Mum brought it inside and placed it under the Christmas tree. I silently read the attached card.

"With love from the Salvation Army."

We had a field day! Our main diet was mince on toast. We didn't have any Christmas food, and Mum had no money for presents. The basket of food was heaven sent. Christmas crackers, lollies, pudding, tinned ham, tinned vegetables, and custard. There were also chocolate-covered nuts and sultanas[lxv] and a variety of toys. Mum made us all promise to give the Salvation Army a donation every year at Christmas so we could one day repay their generosity. Then it was off to see Mumma to wish her Merry Christmas. Little did we realize that after this visit it would be over a year before we saw our beloved grandmother again.

CHAPTER 11

1970—Boxing Day

I woke up to find my mother packing my brothers' clothes into an old cardboard box.

"We're going on a holiday to Rockhampton," Mum said to my excited brothers. "You can choose two toys to take with you."

Previously, my mother had warned me we were moving, and I had given any toys I had to St. Vincent de Patrick because they wouldn't fit in the car. My brothers each grabbed a toy from the hamper. Jamie packed his train set away in his bottom drawer because it was far too precious to take on a holiday. I didn't have a special Christmas present I wanted to take with me. I had been given a beach bag (a tradition that would continue for the next four years) and notepaper. All I really wanted for Christmas was to run away.

I was surprised to find that a man was coming with us. His name was Bill and he had served in the British Navy. A bomb blast during the war had left him stone deaf and he had taught himself to lip read. Bill was a tall man with an excellent physique, and I noted that he was twice the size of my father. This observation filled me with childish hopes of protection and reassurance.

The journey away from Sydney was fraught with problems. Liam, Jamie, and I were riding in Bill's station wagon, while Mum and Michael followed us up the Oxley Highway. They stopped constantly. My mother was terribly ill and couldn't stop vomiting. She looked like an anorexic spider. Her skin was gray, and her eyes were like large saucers in her face, red rimmed and luminous. You only had to look at my mother's face to feel her despair. Hearts are wretched things when hurt beyond repair.

It took us two days to get halfway up the North Coast. Conditions were cramped. We were squeezed in among mattresses and cardboard boxes—three cats, two guinea pigs, one dog, and four children. We spent the first night sleeping under the stars on the side of the Pacific Highway on the Bulahdelah Pass. Bill told my brothers to behave like men, but we were all scared of the dark. We talked and giggled nervously, not noticing the lumpy ground until exhaustion waved its magic wand and we fell asleep.

The next morning we stopped at a telephone box, and Mum fervently went through its pages. The telephone book contained thousands of names. Smith, Harris, and Muldoon were the most popular, so Mum decided on Smith. I hated the name from the beginning, but she was sure it would bring us anonymity. For the next five years of my life, I was called Shannon Smith. No one questioned the name or asked for my documents of identification when we enrolled at our new school. The change was as easy as sliding into a new dress. However, I hated this "dress," and I knew I couldn't change out of it.

The country town where we stopped had about fifteen hundred residents. Reliant on the tourist industry, the townsfolk suffered the holidaymakers and rejoiced when they were gone. They didn't trust city folk, and newcomers had to prove themselves to the locals. We found a local caravan park that was very cheap and allowed pets. I made up a bed on the table, and the boys slept in the car with the cats. There was a tiny gas cooker, a fridge, some small benches, and a double bed. The cupboard space was limited, but as we had no possessions, that didn't bother us.

My mother considered the water suspect, so she was forever boiling it. It was just like being on holiday. We lived on cornflakes, toast, and hot chips and spent our free time exploring. None of us were good swimmers, so although the beach was a novelty, we weren't driven to spend all our waking hours in the sand. The pool seemed safer, and Mum let us swim for hours while she went in search of a job.

Bill was a habitual creature. He was Scottish, strict, and excessively critical but totally in love with my mother. We were told to call him Mr. Bill and to be patient with him because his naval experience had rendered him deaf and emotionally scarred. Bill had tanned biceps and triceps acquired from years of swimming. He reminded me of Tarzan in the movies. The Scot in him drank and smoked to excess. He'd go on the plonk[lxvi] and then lecture anyone who'd listen about humanity's downhill slide into chaos. He said he was an atheist.

"God is for fools and idiots," he'd expound, hitting the table, and then he'd expostulate in Gaelic.

He had a gentle and protective side, which he displayed to my mother. In the early days of their relationship, he'd give her Robbie Burns recitations and moral support. She honestly believed he had saved us from hell, and I followed suit. Bill hated weakness of any kind and considered his deafness a curse—a curse thrust upon him by the "bloody Japs and rotten slanty-eyed bastards." He hated "fairy boys, Nancy boys, faggots, and lezzos." Later, I found out his homophobic attitudes stemmed from the fact that his only son was gay.

When we left Sydney, my mother and Bill called us all together and told us that Dad was going to kill us.

"What's new?" I thought.

We were told that none of us were to communicate with him in case he found out where we were hiding.

"No communication!"

My response was euphoric.

The first night we ventured out of the caravan park, the town was celebrating New Year's Eve with its annual talent quest. It was my tenth birthday. We happened upon the free show in the park by accident and sat down to watch. A few older locals, ranging from guitarists to hopeful rock 'n' rollers, made up the show. There were no children in the show, but the man kept asking for new entrants, as they didn't have the contestant numbers to stretch the show until midnight. Mum kept encouraging me to have a go.

"You could win this," she kept saying, and, looking at the acts, I believed her. After performing "The Hippopotamus Song," I eventually tied for first place with a male guitarist. It was a windfall: fifty dollars. We hurriedly put aside the shared prize money for school fees and shoes.

We lived in the caravan for six weeks until my mother got a job in the local fish shop. Bill also got work bricklaying. We then rented a two-bedroom house on Church Street. My brothers slept on the enclosed veranda, and I had my own room. It was far better than what we had been used to in the past. My mother enrolled us at the local Catholic school. The classes at St. Joseph's were tiny, with one class for every grade. There were twenty children in sixth class, and only six of them were girls. On the first day, I made a stupid mistake.

The most popular girl in the class asked me, "What does your father do for a living?"

I answered without thinking. "Don't talk about him. He kills people."

The reaction was immediate.

"Liar, liar," the girls chanted, and I wished I were invisible.

"I was only joking." My feeble reply was as tortured as their unrelenting taunts, and I came to the realization that making new friends was not going to be easy.

The principal, Sister Geneva, was my teacher, and she wore a modern habit. History interested me, and, to my delight, we studied convicts and their settlement in the local area. English, however, was another story. For the third year in a row, I was given the SRA Reading Syllabus.[lxvii]

"I've already finished this," I told Sister Geneva. "Twice."

"Impossible," she replied tersely. So I resignedly settled down to a year of scholastic boredom.

We had been in the area for about six weeks, and we were coming home from school when we saw my mother running toward us.

Panic-stricken and red from exertion, she yelled at us hysterically, "Go back to school! He's found us." I felt my stomach drop into my shoes at once. My mother was shaking and frantically yelling at us, "We have to go back to the school, or he will see us."

Logic prevailed when I said, "He was parked outside our house. He already knows we live there."

"But he didn't try to come inside," said Mum.

"That's because he's playing with you."

My mother shut up and stared at me with a confused expression on her face.

"Why don't we go home by another road, and if he's still there, we can call the police?"

Mum calmed down and decided to take my approach. We turned around and started to walk home by another road, praying he would be gone. Questions rocketed through my mind.

"How did he find us? Is he going to kill us, or is he stalking us until he decides what punishment he'll inflict upon us?"

These questions remained unanswered because my father was gone when we arrived back home. My mother decided that his parking near our house must have been a coincidence and life continued on. We realized he knew where we were, but thankfully the distance from his home to where we were staying, the close proximity of neighbors, and Scottish Bill's presence in the house made it harder for him to terrorize us.

CHAPTER 12

1971—THE SHOP

My mother got a loan of $16,000 from the bank. We bought the shop and boatshed, as the two went hand in hand. Andy Gilmore owned the boatshed, and his sister owned the shop. Andy was an alcoholic who was raising two children, a girl called Polly and a son who was his namesake. He and his children lived about two miles away in a broken-down shack. His children were always sick with the flu and covered with impetigo. They both had vomiting attacks and occasionally had hepatitis. Whenever I saw these children, I stopped feeling sorry for myself. My brothers and I were healthy, and my mother always made sure we were clean.

The shop soon became our new home. It seemed to give us a feeling of purpose, a sense of hope for the future. It didn't matter that it was made of rotting weatherboards and fibro. It made no difference to us that holes dotted the roof and that only a thin partition separated the shop from the enclosed veranda that would become our living quarters. There were no bedrooms. My mother partitioned a small corner of the veranda by placing a wardrobe across it. This became her bedroom. I slept in the area that remained. My bed was a board precariously balanced between two chairs. I spent the night slipping off it and onto the floor, as I was a very restless sleeper. In the end, I gave up trying to balance and slept on the floor.

My brothers all slept in an old train carriage. Smelling of rising damp and mildew, it was a cockroach-infested tin shell without wheels. The carriage was suspended on small brick foundations that wobbled every time someone jumped. If a strong wind blew up, everyone worried the carriage would turn over. When it rained, everything got wet, and my brothers kept tins and saucepans handy to keep the excess water in check.

Outside, we had a rickety bush toilet filled with green swamp frogs and spiders. The council cleared the refuse every week. Occasionally, swamp rats lurked in this part of the yard, and the cats would devour them. They ate mice, cockroaches, rats, and fish, as all were in abundance.

The yard also contained a large wooden shelter that had no walls, just a roof and a raised platform area where all kinds of wood were stored. There were bits of metal, old pieces of refrigerators, wooden signs, and boards. The platform was so high we needed a ladder to climb up onto it. There wasn't a bathroom, so Mum hooked a hose over one of the shelter's beams and made an outside shower. In winter the water was freezing, so everyone jumped in and out, screaming with cold. Then Mum found an old disused copper cauldron. She'd fill it up with water and light a fire underneath it. When the water was steaming, we'd fill up an orange plastic garbage bin and pretend it was a bath. I would squat down, being careful not to move because the bin would topple over. It was a warm alternative, much better than the shower or a cold dunk in the river.

Millie Ann McDonald waddled into the shop. Stringy hair and gray-green teeth were set amid freckles and a protruding forehead, her distorted body heaving with the effort of walking. Millie didn't see me reading behind the counter; she only saw my mother stacking shelves.

"I'll have some of them lollies," she said, pointing a chubby finger at the caramel buds on the shelf.

"Please," added my mother without thinking.

"Please." Millie Ann raised her eyes to the ceiling. "Five cents' worth!"

The dwarf waited until my mother's back was turned and then proceeded to stuff lollies into her pockets from off the counter. Mum turned and gave her the caramels.

"That will be five cents, please."

"What about the rest?" I spoke but didn't take my eyes off the book in my lap. "She's got at least twenty cents worth in her pockets."

Millie Ann swore and unzipped her school uniform pockets. Lollies fell out onto the floor as she jingled her change around, searching for twenty cents. She slammed the money up onto the counter and bent down to pick up what she had dropped.

"Shitheads," she muttered under her breath. "I never stole nothing!" While stuffing lollies into her mouth, Millie Ann trundled toward the shop door.

Growling, she turned to me and said, "I hate you, Smith."

Traveling to school became a problem after the incident with Millie Ann. She had unlimited support and protection from the children who lived on the Point. Most were her cousins, and they were all used to getting away with thieving. The only way to get to school was on a double-decker bus. The bus left at eight in the morning and arrived home at four o'clock. As it was the only transport to town besides private car, often adults would hitch a ride. I was lucky because the bus conductor and I got on very well, and I was allowed to stand up in the back of the bus and chat for most of the journey. My brothers sat upstairs, sometimes enjoying the experience and sometimes becoming the subjects of cruel bullying.

If it was too windy, the bus would be canceled, and we would have to walk to school. Most kids on the Point took the day off and went swimming, but not us. We were the goody-goodies. The people who lived on the Point were a mixed breed. I honestly do not know how my mother coped, as she had very little in the way of literate conversation. Instead, she had character after character coming into the shop to chat. Most times, they wouldn't buy anything; they'd just gossip and ask what was in the newspapers. Most couldn't read, and my mother would show them the pictures and explain what was going on in the world.

Sunday was our only day of trade. If the weather was fine, we would sell bait and tackle to tourists wanting to fish in the river. We sold hamburgers, Chiko rolls, and pints of milk with a scoop of chocolate flavoring to doped-out surfers who drove beat-up sin bins. Bronzed and bleached, they'd pound on our door at five o'clock in the morning, demanding petrol and cigarette papers.

Around three o'clock in the afternoon, we'd usually hear shouting near the ferry stop. We never worried about the noise because it was only Jim the Scotsman. Jim lived by himself next to the ferry stop on the other side of the river. During the week he'd drive the ferry, and on Sundays he'd go to town. Dressed in his kilt, with his bagpipes in hand, he'd march up the Point Road toward Port Macquarie. Sometimes people who knew him would give him a lift, but often he'd make the trip by foot.

Between three and five o'clock in the afternoon, he'd religiously return home from the pub, drunk as a skunk and shouting in Gaelic. No one ever knew what he was shouting about, but he obviously felt it was important. Sometimes Jim would start a scuffle with people waiting for the ferry, and this would usually result in his ending up face down in the dirt.

"I've been hit," he'd shout. "Call the bloody coppers!" But no one ever took any notice of him; after all, he had provoked the tussle. When he was in a melancholy mood, he'd sing and play his bagpipes near the cars waiting for the ferry. When people asked him to stop, he wouldn't take any notice; he'd just continue bellowing and playing. Finally the ferry would arrive, and Jim would go home, swearing and shouting, seeking solace in his bagpipes. If the wind was right, we could hear him playing from across the river. It was an eerie sound, all reedy and swept up in the river's natural sounds.

It was a Sunday occurrence, funny in all its pathos. Jim's bagpipes broke the cone of silence that sheltered us from the outside world. The melodies would bounce across the River Hastings and drown swiftly, softly consumed by the salty night air.

We soon discovered that most of the people on the Point had skeletons and secrets that they didn't want to share with those who lived in town. The setting was idyllic, but the few people who lived there were misfits. Some were hiding from the law, while others were eaten up by drugs and alcohol abuse. Most were dirt poor, and the Point provided a boundary that housed them in a kind of anonymity. This allowed each and every one to create his or her own peculiar recipe for survival.

The savvy apricot cat never strayed, but he was missing.

"Maybe the wild cat got him," everyone said when we mentioned Samuel's disappearance. All the fishermen and children on the Point believed in the "wild cat." Rumor had it that the feral cat was four feet long with long, pointed teeth and glass-edged claws. It could kill a cat or small dog with one swipe of its paw.

Samuel had been missing for a week when Jamie found him. Up in the rafters, Samuel was in a deadly sleep, his throat slashed from ear to ear, his bloated feline remains filled with gas and maggots.

We also owned the boatshed by the ferry stop. It was a shed with a wharf that flooded during king tides. We sold bait and petrol from the boatshed and hired out tinnies.[lxviii] The boatshed was built directly over the river. The sound of the water made me feel tranquil and safe. The place was most beautiful at sunset when red, gold, and magenta rippled through the skies and down onto the water. I could stare at the river and sky for hours, as it had breath of its own. Its chameleon moods would stretch my imagination and inspire me to write. Song after song, poems, and prose poured from my heart, purging the past.

The ferry chugged across the river at different intervals, conveying cars and people to the other side. Our boatshed was the last petrol stop for miles, and it only made money during the summer holidays. Through the front entrance of the boatshed was an antiquated olive-green fridge. It stretched across in front of the visitors, chopping the room into halves. The fridge threatened to blow up at any tick of the clock, and it doubled as a service counter and bait storage. We sold lots of fishhooks and sinkers, and these were in assorted boxes next to dusty cards hanging from nails on the walls.

A thin partition cut off the rest of the shed, and a rotting laminated table-top was nailed to the back wall because there were small holes in the wall.

The boatshed was dingy and dirty. The walls concealed dead cockroaches and kerosene, and methylated-spirit smells permeated the walls. Large kero drums and two large gas cylinders stood in the far corner, while rowlocks, oars, and fishing tackle decorated the walls. All these hung on makeshift hangers that threatened to collapse within an eye blink. At first we owned three boats, two twelve-footers and one fourteen. We stored these, accompanied by their motors, near double garage-like doors that opened out onto a boat ramp.

In order to keep the boatshed running, we had to catch and buy bait. Our two main sources of bait were two local characters called Ariel Smythe and Eddie Badrock. Ariel Smythe was a nomad, living on the beach in summer and camping with the fishermen in the cooler months. Sometimes I'd see Ariel on the side of the river with her fishing mates. She was always the only woman. Ariel and the fishermen would yell and laugh at one another, drinking metho and whisky for days at a time. These escapades would often end in fistfights, with Ariel giving as good as she got.

One day she came screaming into the shop with blood gushing out of her mouth.

"He's knocked me bloody tooth out!" she yelled like a true fishwife. "I'll kill the bastard." We never found out who the culprit was, and in all my eleven years of wisdom, I couldn't see what the problem was. After all, Ariel had only three teeth to start with.

Ariel Smythe owned a rusted motor scooter that traveled about ten miles an hour, and she often went around town selling bait to boatsheds and fish shops. Ariel looked about seventy years old, but she really wasn't more than forty. Her face was leathered from years out on the beach, lined and tanned, with large freckles interlocking like birthmarks. She had dyed her hair bright orange and set it in baby-doll curls that fell down past her shoulders. She had bright-blue eyes, and she carried a whisky flask in her belt. Ariel's wardrobe was always the same. In winter, she'd wear a Driza-Bone coat[lxix] with a worn Akubra hat spiked with fishing hooks. In the summer, she'd wear a filthy purple-and-yellow ribbed top with a short black woolen miniskirt. She stuffed her spindly legs into dirty white bobby socks in sandshoes. When I saw Ariel from the back, I could swear she was a badly dressed teenager, but from the front, she looked like Bette Davis in *Whatever Happened to Baby Jane?*[lxx]

Ariel would come to our boatshed twice a week to buy petrol and sell us worms. We could see her traveling down the road from a distance, her baby-doll curls flapping in the wind, her neck draped with giant beach worms.[lxxi] She would zoom toward our petrol bowser,[lxxii] avoiding a collision by inches by slamming on her brake. She swore like a trooper and knew the tides like the back of her hand. Ariel would boast she was the best worm catcher on the North Coast, and I believed her. Whether it rained or hailed, Ariel would always know where to catch her bait. Once, I asked her how she knew where the worms were hiding, but she refused to tell me.

"If you come to the beach and see me one day, I'll show you," she promised, "but I won't tell you nothing."

Now it just happened that one day we were at Point Plummer, and I saw her down on the beach. She beckoned to me to come over to her and watch her catch the bait. Ariel was holding on to a thick lump of rope that was tied to something in the water.

"It should be ready now; they've had half an hour."

She heaved and puffed as she pulled the rope up the beach, and I watched in fascination. A hideous vision was revealed. The rope was fastened to a decomposing horse's head. It was covered with crabs and infested with worms. They crawled inside the horse's eye sockets and ears. Overpowered by the smell of salt and decomposing flesh, I wanted to throw up. Ariel saw my look of horror and laughed.

"The stinkier the burley,[lxxiii] the better!" she cackled, her hands diving into the horse's skull to catch the beach worms. They writhed slowly as they were exposed the hot sun, which depleted them of moisture. As Ariel gathered them up, she strung them around the back of her neck and let them fall toward her chest. She wore the worms like broken medals, half-dead trophies exhumed from salt water and rotting horse flesh. I ran away, but the worm catcher didn't notice; she was cackling like a chook, too absorbed in what she was doing.

Eddie Badrock, on the other hand, was a totally different kettle of fish. Over six feet tall, he'd lope along in his old navy overalls, picking things off the ground and then discarding them again if he didn't find them interesting. He was a seventy-year-old bowerbird taking commands from his eight-year-old mind.

"I'm not stupid," I would often hear him say. "I was just standing behind the door when God gave out me brains." Eddie loved my mother and called her "Mum."

"You don't think I'm stupid, do you, Mum?" he'd ask day after day.

My mum would always give him the same reply: "Of course not; you're the best pipi catcher I know." Eddie would collect us pipis (small shellfish-like mussels) in a bucket from the beach to sell for bait. He'd get up at first light and spend the day looking for pipis, clawing the beach with his feet and hands in the cold, salty surf. Later, he'd walk into the shop and pour the buckets out onto the counter.

"There's at least one hundred pipis there," he'd always say as Mum handed him some money. Eddie couldn't count, so in some buckets there would be dozens of pipis and in others there would be none.

Next to wandering on the beaches, Eddie's greatest love was collecting rubbish. He loved anything that glittered in the sun. He'd bring me delicate shells to make necklaces, and he knew where to find the most exquisite wildflowers.

"I've brought you some flowers, Mum," he'd sheepishly say as he hid the flowers behind his back. "They're your favorite, aren't they?"

My mother assured him that she treasured whatever he gave her, and that was probably why he loved her. She made him feel he was appreciated and that he was doing something worthwhile. She always told us to be polite to Eddie and listen to him when he spoke.

"Even though he is like a child, you should treat him with the respect you would give to any old person," she'd say. My mother was convinced it would help him become more confident.

"I'm going fishing today," he'd shout to her from the ferry. "I'll bring you back a whopper!" With this statement, he'd indicate with his gnarled, old hands the size of the fish he was going to catch. It was always enormous!

Mr. and Mrs. Blackspool lived down the road in a tiny fibro house surrounded by vegetable gardens. Mrs. Blackspool had three daughters, Amy, Daphne, and Jasmine. Daphne, who had been born with Down syndrome, was married to a man she called Alfie Baby. They lived in a beat-up caravan next to the house. Alfie had thin, greasy hair, which he wore combed over his balding brown head. He wore tight tartan pants and a flannelette shirt with the sleeves rolled up. His clothes were caked with oil patches, dirt, and fertilizer. Alfie smelled like cow dung, and Daphne never bathed. Her peroxide hair stood up in tufts on her head, thick and chopped short by a blunt pair of scissors.

"Gentlemen prefer blondes," she'd tell us when she came to buy tobacco. We often saw Daphne sauntering down the Point Road. She looked like a large yellow omelet, all round and eggy. Yellow dress, yellow thongs, yellow teeth, and yellow hair.

Alfie was forever jumping in front of cars in order to keep his invalid pension. We'd often see him near the ferry stop, waiting to dive headfirst into the way of an unsuspecting motorist's vehicle. He'd sport his broken arm or leg around like a lottery win.

"Got myself a beauty." He'd grin, waving the plastered limb in the air. "Got a good six months out of this one."

Amy was thirty-six and had a daughter aged seven. The little girl never went to school; she just trailed behind her mother, pointing at things and screaming. Amy would tell us her child was "touched," pointing to her brain and drawing circles in the air.

"She thinks a crab's a lobster and a worm's a snake," she'd say, crying as if it were the end of the world. Amy and her daughter lived with her younger sister, Jasmine, in a one-bedroom shack. Jasmine never uttered a word, and she was thinner than Popeye's Olive Oyl.[lxxiv] She had a rancid mouth, which revealed decaying black tooth stumps when she smiled. Mum told us the Blackspools were a bit like the Beverly Hillbillies.[lxxv]

"They believe in the land and the gun," she said. "They've never been to school."

One day we heard an appalling noise outside the shop. It was Daphne.

"Dad's gone to the Lord," she screamed to Mum, "and now they want to dig him up." Poor Mr. Blackspool had died three days beforehand, and the family had buried him near the vegetable patch.

After the news spread, the police wanted to exhume the body and put it in the cemetery, but Mrs. Blackspool and her daughters stayed in the house, guns in hand, screaming, "You're not taking our dad. It was you who killed him. If he hadn't had that operation in the hospital, he would have been all right. You killed him with the water. You even gave him a bath."

A day later, it was discovered they had moved the body farther down into the swamp. With each rising tide, the body floated upward, but the Blackspools kept a vigilant guard. Not wanting to stir up a hornet's nest with the old lady and her mentally challenged daughters, the police kept watch on their house. They sat in their car and waited. I was glad because they bought hamburgers and coffee from the shop. Eventually their chance came, on pension day. After the pensioners and schoolchildren had piled onto the bus to go to town, the police dug up the old man and buried him in the local cemetery. They must have received permission from one of the family members to do so, but most seemed none the wiser.

In fact, a year after Mr. Blackspool's death, Mrs. Blackspool brought Mum some tomatoes.

"Lovely red ones, aren't they? I always knew the old man would make good fertilizer. Our vegetables have never been so good."

Nine months after we bought the old shop, the council gave us permission to build a new one. It was to be a double-faced shop, complete with a living area and two second-story flats. Bill said he'd complete the building by himself, and my mother went along with the idea. A giant lorry and crane winched the old shop up and moved it to the vacant lot next door. Bits of wood snapped off the floor and roof, but we didn't care. The wheels of progress had been put in motion, and we thought we were headed for better times.

We set three rough planks up as stairs so people could walk in and out of the building and we could continue trading.

"Bill will build the new shop," my mother informed us.

"And you'll dig the foundations," he told us.

Steel sheets were delivered and left out in the rain to rust. Bill didn't seem in much of a hurry to start building. Eventually he pegged string areas around the vacant block and told us to start digging—six-foot foundations dug by four children and their mother, pickaxes nearly connecting with our feet and heavy shovels grazing our shins.

The task was monumental. I liked to dig after rain because the ground was red clay. This meant it was concrete hard in hot weather and soft and gluggy in winter. One day, my mother gathered us all together and handed us rubber gloves and rolls of steel wool. Hours later, sunburned and exhausted, we were still scraping and scrubbing, the rusty steel smearing our faces and arms with red powder. It felt good when we placed the steel in the ground, our aching feet and hands no longer an issue. Bill filled the foundations with cement, and the area was ready for the concrete building slab.

However, there was a problem. We had run out of money! Our white elephant came to a standstill.

There were a few legitimate landowners on the other side of the river and farther up the Point Road toward Port Macquarie. There were also some farms and the caravan park farther down the road.

At the end where we lived, however, there were fishermen who lived in makeshift huts or shacks along the water's edge. They would disappear at the slightest whisper of police because many of them were squatting illegally in the mangrove swamp. I suppose they were a bit like the original swagmen, except these swaggies lived by the water in the swamp rather than in the bush. On pension day, they'd all come out to collect their checks and buy supplies, consisting mainly of petrol, metho, bread, and tobacco. They all seemed to be related in some way, and they all seemed to be old, their faces weathered and lined from sun and salt.

Windy was the jolliest fisherman, and I liked him a lot. He lived on Pelican Island in a hut he had built out of pieces of iron and driftwood. Windy was an enormously round and wobbly old man with twenty dogs. He had a balding head with long, gray tufts of hair that streamed out from behind his ears. This, combined with the fact that he had no teeth, made him resemble a crinkled-up Halloween pumpkin. You could spot his gummy smile from a distance, like a beacon, floating down the river on his boat.

He had built an amazing raft, which he and his dogs would ride on. On the raft he had built a strange captain's cabin, a bit like an outside toilet, and this perched precariously in the middle of the vessel. Windy paddled his raft up and down the river, catching fish and chortling as he threw them to his dogs. I'm sure he had collected every stray mongrel in the area. The mutts scampered around him in all shapes and sizes, fat and thin, wildly loyal to their renegade master.

Windy was a man obsessed by the sea.

He said he was a sea captain, but no one knew if it was true. To be on the safe side, we'd occasionally call him Captain to keep him happy. He was a hermit by nature, and except for his visits to our shop, he only ever spoke to the fishermen he met out on the river. Sometimes he'd disappear for weeks on end. We would just reconcile ourselves with the possibility of his death, and then he'd suddenly appear at our shop counter. Windy would demand his supply of Tally-Ho tobacco and matches and then launch into a seafarer's tale, his great belly wobbling with laughter and his story making no sense at all. My mother and I always had time for Windy. He was a true-blue Australian character. He stank of fish and rotting burley, but his kindness to his dogs reflected the man within.

Then there was Tom, Windy's cousin and Andy Gilmore's brother. Everyone in the area was related. Unlike Windy, however, Tom only had one dog. Bluey was a mangy cattle dog, and he followed the old man everywhere. Tom was also a fisherman, although I'm sure he drank more than he fished. He lived in a shack in the middle of the mangrove swamp.

I only ever visited him twice, once to deliver an important message and once by mistake, when I got lost in the swamp. Visiting him wasn't a very pleasant experience because both times I got covered in leeches. Tom shared his shack with a lot of feral cats. He always had tiny kittens and lots of old tins and metal plates lying around, filled with fish and cat food for them to eat. His cats never went hungry. In fact, they probably ate better than he did.

On my eleventh birthday, Tom gave me a kitten in an oversized cardboard box.

"It's a mangy cat," he told me, "a bit like you. He don't like anyone 'cause his father is a wildcat, and he won't get on with me other moggies."

Tom waited for my reaction. The old man rubbed his stubble with his chopped-off finger stub and continued, "If you don't take him, I'll have to drown him."

I must have looked upset. He hastily added, "Happy birthday!" and pushed the box toward me. I went to put my hand in, and the six-week-old fur ball hissed and tried to scratch me.

Tom was right! The orange-and-white kitten was the most antisocial feline I had ever met. Beautifully marked, he had a face straight out of *The Aristocats*.[lxxvi] As he was part Persian, he had a furry squirrel tail that was much too long for his tiny body. The cat managed to scratch and bite everyone in the family, although after realizing my mother was a hand that would feed him, he soon warmed to her. I called him Prince Julian of Prowsville, but everyone called him Doodles for short. After a lot of cajoling, he became my best friend. Doodles loved living in the boatshed. He must have thought he was a dog, because he followed our golden retrievers everywhere. When they'd go down to the river, he'd jump off the wharf with them and go for a swim. Rab, the male dog, would shepherd flathead fish up on the beach, and Doodles would be waiting. As soon as the fish were in shallow water, Doodles would dive in and catch his dinner. It was an amazing sight to watch. He was a totally independent soul. I once saw a fisherman standing on the side of the river reeling in an enormous bream. Doodles was watching from underneath the wharf. The fish was out of the water and halfway up to the rod when the cat made his move.

Up the beach he sped, straight toward the unsuspecting fisherman. Then, with a mighty leap, he jumped up and grabbed the fish. The fisherman let out a mighty roar as his rod flew out of his hand and unreeled while the cat raced down the sandbank. Doodles kept running until the line eventually broke.

Afterward, he came slinking back to the boatshed with the fish in his mouth, the fishing line tangled around his legs and his fur all matted.

We had to cut the fishing line off him, and upon close examination, we discovered that he had chewed the fish off the hook. His mouth was torn and bleeding because the fishhook had embedded itself in his jaw. My mother's dental skills immediately came into play, and she operated on the cat with a pair of pliers and scissors. Then, after sterilizing a needle over a flame, she put two stitches in his mouth with fishing line. The cat stayed still the entire time, trusting that we could help him. He was better in no time, his tough immune system fending off infection as he rapidly healed.

I found out that my father had made friends with a family who lived farther up the road. He had a new job as a carpet salesman, which allowed him to travel interstate. Whenever he was going up the coast, he would turn up unannounced, usually during school holidays or on a weekend when he knew we would all be home. He obviously planned his visits well, because every time he arrived, Bill was out or away somewhere.

He visited one night when it was very late. I was woken by the black plastic that was hanging over the broken window above my bed on the shop's side veranda. It flapped from side to side in the night breeze and caused shadows from the moonlight to dance across the walls. I inadvertently shuddered. How I hated shadows; they left too much fodder for my imagination to feed on. I thought I had heard a noise, a scraping noise, and I hoped it was just the wind.

"It's probably a cat," I said to comfort myself.

Suddenly, a flash of silver caught the moonlight and entered through the window. I lay completely frozen as the old-fashioned pistol waved above my head. It looked like a cowboy gun, the kind cowboys used in movies. The person had to be standing on something outside my window, and I was sure from the position that the person could not see me. I wanted to go to the toilet but knew the person would become aware of my presence if I moved. I pulled the blanket up over my head and closed my eyes tightly, trying valiantly to erase the picture of the gun that hovered above my head. I stayed under the blanket until slumber overpowered me.

When I woke up, it was dawn. Light was breaking outside, and I felt safer now that I could see the new day. I got up slowly and ventured outside to the toilet. I tentatively looked out the back door to make sure no one was around. Everyone was asleep. Only the dog was awake, and she padded softly beside me as I made my way to the old bush toilet. The door was closed. It hung on two warped hinges and required pressure to open it. I put my shoulder to it and pushed. The door moved, and I went inside.

The hand came out of nowhere and grabbed my arm while another clasped my mouth shut tight. I looked up at the figure hiding behind the door and saw his hideous smile. His teeth had started to rot, and the gap where his tooth was missing on the upper right side of his mouth had become more pronounced. A sick feeling from the pit of my stomach enveloped me. It couldn't be him, but it was. I pushed against him with all my might, and I heard a loud crash as he hit the wall. As he released his grip, I ran out of the toilet and alongside the fence. The long flannelette nightdress I was wearing hampered my escape. While I scrambled over the fence, something caught the back of it, and I fell to the other side.

Thump.

I hit the back of the fence and landed on the ground. On this side of the fence, there were overgrown paddocks and then the swamp beyond these. There was also an abandoned chicken coop. It had half fallen down, and overgrown bushes and weeds covered it. I was dragged into the coop as the hand covered my mouth in case I screamed.

But I didn't scream. I was terrified. I was a whimpering, pathetic creature who never fought back. My feet hurt, full of prickles, and my hands kept clawing at the air. My face hit the dirt as he pushed me to the ground, and when he sat on my back, I found it difficult to breathe. A searing pain ripped through my scalp as he pulled my hair, using it to pin my face to the ground. I felt something cool on the side of my face and realized it was the gun pointed at my head. I heard my own silent screams as he lifted my nightdress and his fingers invaded me. And then his weight shifted as he lay on top of me.

I felt pain with overwhelming fear and anger. I wanted to stab him as he was stabbing me. My fingers kept tearing at the dirt, and then, suddenly, he forced my face to his and kissed me. The alcoholic fumes overwhelmed me as they mingled with the scent of his unwashed body.

The rape was over. He had finished with me. I vowed it would never happen again. From that day on, whenever I saw him I would run away. I sought protection in other people, only seeing him face to face when there were others around me. I knew he would only reveal his secret personalities if we were alone. It was as though I suddenly discovered that I had legs and I could run away.

Polly Gilmore was an overweight girl with oily black hair and a ferret face. Her mother had died when she was three, and she was left to manage her meager household. This resulted in her wearing filthy clothes, as she had no washing facilities. Her brother, Andy, was the same. Children completely ostracized him, refusing to sit near him on the bus because he stank of urine. His nose was always running, and he never looked anyone in the eyes.

The area was filled with uneducated misfits who lived with bottles in their hands and sired dysfunctional children. Polly and her brother would roam around the Point looking for food, covered in bruises. Everyone knew their father beat Polly and Andy, but people turned a blind eye because many children were subject to their parents' violent outbursts.

When we first moved into the shop, Polly tried to befriend me. She was a slow-witted girl who told terrible lies, but I was lonely, and I felt sorry for her. Polly was nearly fourteen, and even though I knew she was poor, she always had an unlimited supply of money and lollies. Soon after our arrival at the Point, she told me she had to deliver a message to old Cockeyed Kettle. She invited me to go with her, and Mum agreed as long as I wasn't away for more than half an hour.

Cockeyed Kettle was a scrawny, stinking little man with bulbous blue eyes that were eternally bloodshot. He had long, spidery arms and was missing three fingers on his right hand. Rejected by society, he lived down the old bush track that led into the mangrove swamp. His caravan was a rotting, empty shell. It had broken windows and had been dumped in the swamp many years previously. Upon discovering it, Cockeyed Kettle had decided to set up camp in it.

Cockeye would stumble into our shop about once a week. Drunk and often incoherent, he would buy Drum tobacco and methylated spirits. When he went outside, he'd mix the metho with brown boot polish and drink it.

As Polly and I walked to Cockeyed's caravan, she told me she could make five dollars off Cockeye today, ten if she was lucky. Then she rambled on about sex, telling me to beware of the man's germs because they could make you pregnant. She told me if you got pregnant, you would have to go to the butcher's and get an abortion. Then, she said, you'd get sent to jail for being a slut. I took everything she said with a grain of salt, not knowing what to believe. After all, Polly was three years older than I was.

Cockeyed Kettle was waiting for us to arrive. He stood in the rusted doorway and then lurched toward me. I immediately took two steps backward because he emitted a putrid, pungent smell.

"Here!" he croaked. "Have some of this."

Cockeyed coughed and spat out yellow phlegm from the side of his mouth. Part of the spittle leaked down the side of his chin, making bile churn in my stomach at the sight.

"Have some," he said, offering me the contents of his hand. "It's good stuff."

There, on his nicotine-stained fingers, lay a rusty syringe. It was filled with heroin. The sight was enough to cause me to bolt. I called to Polly. She didn't answer, so I quickly ran all the way home. Polly didn't follow me; she stayed behind. Sometime later, she returned from Cockeyed's caravan with bleary eyes, proudly waving a ten-dollar note.

"This could have been yours," she said. "What's wrong with you? Are you chicken? It's easy; you don't feel nothing if you take the stuff."

Poor Polly; she was only fourteen and earmarked for a life of drug dependency and prostitution. I was glad I was terrified of needles. From then on I stayed away from her. Two years after this event, Polly moved to Sydney. We heard on the gossip vine that she had ended up in a remand center for soliciting. I felt torn, hoping somehow intervention would help her. But deep down I knew it was too late. She was a product of her environment who fought for survival in the only way she knew how.

When I began high school, I was the youngest by nearly two years. I spent my early mornings and late afternoons working in the shop. On the weekends I served the few-and-far-between customers with my head stuck in a book. I devoured Shakespeare, Dickens, and works by the Brontë sisters, living through their language and imagination. I didn't have the option of going out to play, so I immersed myself in theatrics, literature, and music. The library was my main port of call both at school and in town.

When the time came to demolish the old shop, Mum, Bill, and I had nowhere to sleep. So my mother bought an old school bus for ten dollars. Bill and Mum slept at the back behind a curtain, and I slept on a wooden plank bed attached to its side. The bed was too narrow and short, so I had to sleep in a fetal position on some old foam. Every time it rained, water poured through the sliding windows and soaked the bed. My brothers continued sleeping in the cockroach-infested train carriage, and Bill built a tin shed for Mum to cook in.

The corrugated iron shed had a hole for a window and a red dirt floor, which often turned to mud when it rained. Cooking was the least of our problems, as Mum could only afford mince or sausages. We'd catch fish from the river and eat the leftover bread from the shop. Mum scorched all these "delectables" in her trusty frying pan over an old gas stove.

Bill also built a makeshift bathroom in the boatshed. He placed an old bath behind bits of Masonite next to a bench. He didn't plumb it into anything; the water flowed straight into the river through a hole in the floor. He did not nail the Masonite walls around it to anything either. They balanced precariously around the tub to simulate privacy, but there was a big hole in the wood, so anyone could look through. I learned to have my baths in five seconds. I had no time to relax. It was like a military exercise, as I had to jump in and out before the walls fell down on top of me.

The farthest corner of the boatshed smelled of urine because Bill refused to go outside to the toilet. Instead he would urinate over a hole in the floorboards into the river beneath them. He was often drunk, and then he missed the hole completely. I dreaded having to pull the boats out of the shed and down the slip because it meant I had to work near the stench of stale booze and urine.

I had lots of problems at school. I found it hard to communicate with others, and I rocked continually when anxious.

"I hate...I hate...I hate."

I'd write the words over and over again.

It was a mindless exercise, and I didn't realize the strength of what I was writing. It was automatic. The writing flowed through my fingertips, drawn in circles and artistic doodles on the page. It was as though an alien force were guiding me. Then suddenly I'd realize what I was writing, and I'd stop.

"I hate...I hate...I hate what?"

I'd crumple the paper in my hand, distressed and embarrassed.

"I shouldn't write those things," I'd reproach myself, realizing I hadn't been aware of what I was doing.

Old Sam grew the nicest strawberries around. He and his wife lived in a little weatherboard house about half a mile from the boatshed, and they rarely left their house. I happened upon this couple purely by accident. I had missed the school bus, and as my home was six miles away, I started the journey by foot. It was a hot day, and I was very tired. I tried to work out a shortcut home and decided to cut across the Petchells' farm and then across the mangrove swamp. This, if my calculations proved correct, would make my journey shorter and bring me home to Settlement Point Road, about a mile away from home.

I managed to cut across the farmland easily, and except for a confrontation with a few angry cows, nothing happened. When I came to the swamp, however, it was a different story. High tide was coming in, and when I put my foot down on the mud flat, my foot sank with a sickening squelch into the ground. The swamp was like a vacuum cleaner. It sucked my foot down until my whole leg was submerged up to the knee. I screamed and pulled my foot out, losing a shoe as I did so. Gingerly, I put my hands into the slimy hole where my foot had been and groped around for my shoe, praying in earnest that the yabbies[lxxvii] wouldn't nip my fingers as I did so.

At last I found it! Relieved, I decided that the swamp at this time would be too dangerous, and I set out walking toward the property in the distance. This property belonged to old Sam and his wife, Bonnie. I had never met them before, but I knew they were related to the Blackspool family.

I hiked up to their dilapidated back fence. It was overgrown with choko vines and honeysuckle, and it had huge holes in it where the palings had fallen off. I squeezed through a hole and tripped over the vine, falling headfirst into a vegetable garden.

If there was a vegetable heaven, this garden resembled it! Huge, leafy cabbages and lettuces were everywhere, and spinach grew in a thick miniature forest. I felt as if I had just stepped into Peter Rabbit's forbidden garden.[lxxviii] The out-of-control tomato vines grew in a cobweb fashion, all over the ground. Big, red tomatoes had fallen off the vines, and they lay soaking up the sun, while a few played host to fat, greedy worms. I picked myself up off the ground and tried to walk carefully through the patch. Then I saw them! They were the biggest strawberries I had ever seen. I picked the biggest one I could find and prepared to eat it.

"You'll pay for that strawberry!" The voice nearly frightened me out of my wits. I turned and saw a tall, skinny man who looked at least 104 years old. "You'll pay for that strawberry, or you won't be leaving my property."

Old Sam pointed his rifle at me and waved it around. His overalls were stained and worn. I was too terror-stricken to answer him.

"What's wrong? Cat got yer tongue? They'd chop yer hand off in Arabia for what you done." I still couldn't answer him. "Yer a bloody thief," he continued.

Something inside me snapped, and my voice came out in a croak. "I'll pay for the strawberry, but I've got to go home and get some money first."

"How do I know you only ate one?" came his terse reply.

"I guess you'll have to trust me."

"Trust you! Yer a bloody thief!" The old man's look of disbelief made me uneasy.

Suddenly, I became aware of something squishy in my hand. It was the strawberry, still uneaten.

"Here," I said, pushing it toward him. "You can have your strawberry back."

Sam took the strawberry and examined it. He gave an exasperated sigh and threw it against the fence.

"All right, then," he muttered. "You can go."

I quickly said, "Thank you," and I tried to walk past him.

"Not so fast, girlie," he said, grabbing my arm. "Yer have to meet Janie first."

I looked into Sam's cool, blue eyes and wondered what was in store for me. Then he smiled. "Janie'll like you. She never sees no one no more." He pulled me toward the house. A small, plump lady stood at the back door, her hands on her hips and her feet tapping impatiently.

"Who's that?" She gestured to me as if I were an inanimate object.

"It's a girlie," he replied. "She's come to visit Janie."

"My name's Bonnie," she said as she extended her hand.

By this time I was quite confused. I had no idea who Janie was. As I walked inside their house, I heard a pitiful voice crying. The voice came from behind a closed door.

"Janie!" shouted Sam as he thumped on the door. "There's someone here to see you." He opened the door and pushed me inside.

The stench of urine was overpowering, and I took an involuntary step backward. It was too late, because Sam had come inside and closed the door. On the floor in front of me was a half-starved woman dressed in a soiled nightdress. She was groping wildly at the floor, searching for something.

"Where are you?" she shouted as she scratched the floor and cried. "Where are you hiding?" The old woman turned to us and held on to her head.

"I can't have visitors, Sam. I've not done me hair, and I've lost me teeth."

Sam pointed toward two yellow dentures on the bedside table. "There's yer teeth. The girlie can stay for ten minutes, and then she's got to be off home."

Sam shut the door behind him as he went out. I was so uneasy I felt like giggling hysterically. Ten minutes seemed a long time away. I looked at the bemused figure on the floor. Her long, thin, waist-length hair was matted together in knots around her shoulders.

"She looks like a witch," I thought.

"Get my teeth," she pleaded. "Please, girlie."

Janie's eyes were like big, sunken blue wells. Tears threatened to overflow at any moment, and I immediately felt sorry for her. I found a tissue in my pocket and picked her teeth up.

"That's better!" she said after she had snapped them into her mouth. "Now, can you put me back in the bed?"

I tried to help her, but she was all wet.

"I had an accident," she apologized. "The bed's all wet too."

I searched through her drawers until I found a nightie, and I went to find Bonnie to change the sheets. When all this was done, I helped Janie back into the bed. She hardly weighed anything, her thin, skeletal frame protruding sharply through her translucent, blue-veined skin.

"You can read to me." It was more of a command than an offer. I picked up the book she was pointing at and read its title.

"The Holy Bible."

I read to her for about five minutes while Janie sat listening with her eyes half-closed. Occasionally, she would drink foul-smelling cough mixture from an old bottle. When she liked what she was hearing, she would cackle, and when she disapproved, she'd grind her false teeth together, crunching madly, as if she were chewing nuts. Old Janie eventually fell asleep. I placed the book back on the bedside table and started to leave the room. Her eyes darted open immediately.

"You'll come back again? Please, girlie?"

I promised her I would. Maybe I felt sorry for her, or maybe she was just lucky that I had read *Pollyanna*.[lxxix] Whatever it was, a strange friendship was born.

After this episode, I spent many hours reading to Janie and picking her up off the floor. Sometimes I would hide her cough medicine, as I soon realized it was a mixture of cheap brandy and scotch. When I hid her precious bottle, Janie would spend her time hurling abuse at me. When this didn't work, she'd try other tactics, such as yowling, crying, or pleading.

"You'll go to hell, girlie!" she'd shout. "Without my medicine, I'll die."

But it wasn't the lack of medicine that caused Janie's death. Chronic alcoholism caused her to have violent physical attacks accompanied by severe bouts of depression. After two hospitalizations, Sam and Bonnie threw her out into the street, and she went to live in the two-room shack that belonged to the Gilmore family. There, the supply of alcohol and drugs was limitless.

One Saturday I was in the boatshed with my mother when we heard a terrible howling. Suddenly, Polly Gilmore burst into the shop, her face red with crying and her eyes darting hysterically. Poor Polly was covered in soot and ash.

"She's done it," screamed the girl. "Call the police quickly."

My mother settled Polly enough to find out what was going on. In half cries and sobs, Polly told us that Janie had burned their shack down. Janie didn't have enough money for whisky, so she had started drinking methylated spirits instead. This had caused her to hallucinate, and she had lit the fire to burn away her demons.

Like a fish gasping for air, Polly gulped. "Everything's gone, even me mum's picture."

I quickly put on my shoes and walked back with her to the smoldering shack. It was a pile of rubble and corrugated iron. Polly's tears fell freely as she tried to poke sticks at smoky piles of debris to see if she could salvage anything.

"Where's Janie?" I ventured.

"I hope the old bitch is dead," came her reply.

"Did she die in the fire?"

Polly laughed! "Not bloody likely. She ran off into the bush with her dress on fire." Polly imitated her. "'Help me! Help save me from them!' She's a bloody fruitcake."

"Was she badly hurt?" I ventured.

"No! Dad put her dress out…He punched her out and then wrapped her in a blanket. She was here when I left to get help, but she's gone now."

The police searched for Janie and eventually found her hiding in the swamp. They took her to the local hospital for treatment, and she lasted for about two weeks before she died in her sleep.

"Dad's here!" I said as soon as I woke up.

"Don't be silly," said Mum. "Anyway, how would you know?"

"I can feel he's here," I told her flatly.

I walked out of the bus and toward the end of the block. Sure enough, there he was, smiling the smile that made my blood run cold and waving his hand as if in slow motion. He had parked his car near the boatshed, and he had the side door open so it shielded his body. I could see he had gleaming white leather shoes on, and he was wearing a tight white jacket and pants. The look wasn't very flattering, although he certainly looked as if he had money.

At that moment Michael and Liam walked past me.

"Hello!" Dad called.

They stopped in their tracks and then called out, "Hi."

"I've bought you a Christmas present," he shouted. "Get your mother."

I felt sick. As we walked slowly toward him, Mum and I held hands like seven-year-olds. We were both shaking, yet we did as we were told. We walked as if we were hypnotized toward the man who was waving a silver butcher's knife and holding a giant leg of ham. In slow, deliberate strokes, my father cut off two bits of ham. He gave each of my brothers a piece and then gave my mother a fruitcake. Then he suddenly laughed, got in the car, and drove away, leaving us standing there like shocked fools. No one ate the ham, and I forced my mother to throw the cake into the bin. I was terrified the food was poisoned.

That night one of our cats died. She had been fed a mixture of meat and ground glass, suffering an agonizing and barbaric end.

For many months I had been teaching myself the piano on a tiny children's toy made of plastic. I had bought it from the charity shop, and it only had twelve notes. Armed with the toy and a book from the library, I'd sit up all night teaching myself the notes and trying to play tunes. My mother knew how desperate I was to play, so she begged Mumma to send me up her old piano for my thirteenth birthday. The baby Beale piano eventually arrived. I was ecstatic. It was scraped and battered, but it had retained its beautiful tone. The piano immediately became my soul mate, and people would hear me thumping away as the sounds got caught up in the river breeze. I spent hours writing music and songs, my poetry delivering me from the demons in my sleep.

During this time my mother endured a messy four-year divorce trial. The laws at this time were antiquated, and my father's never-ending accusations and false affidavits thwarted her reach for freedom. Her financial struggle was constant. We had no money and no customers. We lived on her meager wage as a dental assistant and made concoctions to eat out of carrots, chokos, and nasturtiums. One of the fishermen once gave us a marlin, and Mum mashed it up and mixed it with stale breadcrumbs. She then froze dozens of fish cakes in the old shop fridge. It seemed as if we ate marlin fish cakes every night for months.

On a couple of occasions, the rain started and didn't stop for days. This deluge caused the river to balloon, and it cut us off from town. No one could ever predict how high the floodwater would rise, and the boatshed would be caught between the bursting river and the backwash of the swamp. During one flood I stood on the boatshed's counter and refused to get off. Instead, I watched as terrified water rats and snakes swam past me, joining the mullet and flathead in the gushing torrents. When it flooded, water rushed all over the Point, and we were forced to ride out the storm.

As soon as we received a flood warning, Mum and I packed what little produce we had in the shop in boxes and put the boxes up into the rafters of the boatshed. My brothers would drag the boats into the boatshed and secure them so they couldn't float away. We'd also park the bus on the highest piece of ground, and with strong ropes, we'd winch my precious piano up in the air so it would also be safe from the rising water.

Upon our arrival in Port Macquarie, my mother, my brothers, and I had joined the Amateur Theatrical Society. Acting, like music, became an integral part of our lives. The local ballet teacher, Abby, befriended me, and she shared my enthusiasm for performance. We'd creatively brainstorm about stage shows, directing, and all things theatrical. Although she was twenty years older than I was, she became a great friend, role model, and mentor. I'd babysit her three children while she choreographed and rehearsed in local theatrical productions. By babysitting her children, I could escape my life in the boatshed and Bill's ever-increasing alcoholic episodes.

Abby encouraged me to perform in all the local productions and supported me tirelessly when I jabbered on about new ideas and had imaginative bursts of energy. Every year, I entered the Taree Eisteddfod[lxxx] and won prize money for singing, comedy, and drama. I also produced my own mini productions around the town, and people got used to reading my name in the local paper and hearing me on the radio. I wrote poem after poem, song after song, and musical after musical. I was an odd fish trying to heal myself by hiding behind a wall of piano notes and poetic verse.

On one disastrous day, Bill told me he had to see Mr. Montgomery, who owned the upmarket boatshed farther up the river. Bill had become very neurotic; his alcoholic binges fueled the paranoia he felt due to his deafness. Bill suspected nearly everyone of talking about him. He had stopped working, and my mother was supporting him, accelerating his low self-esteem.

Mr. Montgomery bought and sold speedboats, and Bill wanted to buy one. While he negotiated with his friend, I walked down to the water. After some time, Bill called me back because it was time to go. Back at the car, I said hello to Mr. Montgomery, and he smiled and asked me how school was. We joked and I laughed, and then we went home. After arriving home, I opened the shop, and Bill went off to drink at the RSL Club. It had become a nightly ritual. He'd drink and come home drunk. When he was in this state, he'd often speak Gaelic, and none of us could understand him. Our lack of response would then make him snap. He had once lost his temper with Liam and punched him in the face. Blood had gone everywhere, and Liam had had to deal with a broken nose.

That night, after going to the Montgomerys' boatshed, Bill came home in a very black mood. Everyone knew he was at boiling point, so we shut the boatshed and bolted the door in silence. The boys went off to their room for fear there would be an argument, and Mum and I cleaned up. By this time Bill was halfway through a cheap flagon of red wine.

Suddenly, Bill let out a wild yell and smashed his fist through the boatshed wall. My mother and I both stopped what we were doing and waited for the tirade to begin. We thought he'd start yelling and shouting, but that night something was different. Bill turned and started toward me. I saw him coming, but my feet wouldn't move. I just stood there while he screamed at me. Bill's hand came down with a crash, knocking me off balance as he hit me across the face. My mother tried to run to stop him, but he was twice her size. He pushed his great arm across her throat and held me with his free hand by the clothes around my neck. I felt myself being lifted into the air, and then I saw stars.

Bill head butted me in the face, like a soccer ball, and let me go. I fell to the ground and tried to crawl toward the boatshed door. Bill kept kicking and hitting me until I reached it, and then he turned toward my mother. I managed to lift up the bolt and open the door.

As I ran down the road, I heard my mother yelling, "Stop!"

I was a hysterical mess and I had no where to run and hide. I stopped and sat down on the side of the road, sobbing and swallowing tears until my mother caught up to me. She told me to calm down but I had already gone into shock. Shaking uncontrollably I rose to my feet and slowly started walking. Time dragged at my heels as if I was in slow motion and my vision was blurred with tears. They fell unabated as I had no power to suppress them. Later I managed to crawl into bed fully clothed. I pulled the blanket under my chin and curled up, rocking in a fetal position. I couldn't sleep so I stared at the door while I cried and gulped for air. I recall my mother coming back to see me for a few minutes later that evening. We didn't talk about what had happened; she just asked me if I was all right. At that point in time, I had no idea what she felt about my torment and I had no idea about hers. I knew she had tried to stop Bill from hurting me. As a result of this intervention, her neck and shoulder were bruised from where he had pushed her back against the wall when she tried to stop him from hitting me. My mother had also run after me when I had raced hysterically down the road. She had left Bill swearing and shouting insults at her from the boatshed door, choosing at that moment to follow me rather than to stay with him. The events of that night had taken its toll. We were both emotionally torn. Psychologically scarred and heart wrenchingly unable to communicate our feelings to each other. I couldn't reach her, and she couldn't reach me. We were both traumatized.

Something inside me snapped that night. Within my psyche, my self-enforced containment of memories dissipated. Feelings I had previously grappled with rushed to the surface, and hysteria flooded back. My mind filled with panic, terror, paranoia, and self-loathing. My blackest feelings pitted my positive will against itself and turned my soul into a chaotic chasm of despair. I didn't feel in control anymore, and I wanted out. I felt totally unloved and alone, but I didn't know how to change my situation. I felt powerless to do anything, and for once, I didn't even have the strength to write my feelings down.

After Bill hit me, I had a constant ringing in my right ear. It lasted for about three months and then became intermittent. The worst part about the attack was that it seemed to have shattered the wall I had built up in my early childhood years. Without warning, I would begin to shake and shudder for no apparent reason, and this really frightened me.

My first shaking episode happened the day after I had been hit. I was walking around the school playground when I suddenly felt very cold. I started to shiver. No matter how I tried, I couldn't stop shaking. I became frightened and decided to tell a teacher. The nun told me to stop it, and I told her I couldn't. My body had gone into remote control and wouldn't listen to what I was saying.

I certainly acted strangely. Shaking, rocking, locked in thought. My paranoia about my own self-worth intensified, and I constantly felt embarrassed and nervous. I would write abstractedly in class, often not realizing I was doing so until I saw what I had written before me. I didn't understand why, but my pen seemed to have a mind of its own.

There, on the page before me, would be written the words, "I hate..." or even, "I hate me..."

Embarrassed, I'd quickly scribble the words out and draw something nice, like a flower, but the words screamed to be let out, and I continued to write them when I wasn't concentrating. Sometimes, when I was immersed in thought, teachers would ask me questions and feel that I was ignoring them by not answering. This made them very angry, and it would result in my being punished. I became an expert at taping five Biros together to write the copious numbers of lines that the teachers dished out to me each day.

When they asked me what I had been thinking, I'd reply, "I don't know." This wasn't a lie, as I sometimes couldn't remember what I was reliving in my head. I was drifting in and out of shock, always remembering and forgetting the past.

I became filled with doubts and questions about the whole theory of Catholicism. Previously I had tried to become very religious and better myself through prayer and the Mass. However, I had become more analytical in my teenage years. I would sit listening to the priest, the bloodshed of the Old and New Testament evoking past shadows and migraines. I came to the conclusion that church was not for me. I stopped going to confession. I stopped going to Communion. Symbolism or not, I hated the thought of eating someone's body and blood. Jesus had died and had walked willingly to his death. This was suicide, so had God sinned too? Religion was all too confusing and too much like a scenario in a play. There were miracles for the masses in the subtext, a bloody crucifixion as the finale, and a resurrection as an encore. I doubted all this was for the sake of poor sinners like me. In the end I decided I was an atheist or an evolutionist—anything but Catholic.

My reoccurring dreams continued. Nightmare after nightmare repeated themselves and surrounded me in blood. School became a jumble of teachers and headaches. Lack of sleep prevented me from concentrating, and I often felt myself falling in and out of a doze. I tried desperately to remain calm in a school, where our family had become the misfits. We were the charity kids to be laughed at and picked on. My brothers and I heard the taunts. So did the teachers.

"Peasants…Fat, ugly pig…Midget…Goody-goody."

We heard their shouts on a daily basis, and they increased in volume when others joined in. I soon lost all respect for the system, in which they preached kindness but allowed such savagery to desiccate children's hearts.

A nun who had taught me at St. Joseph's later told me that our family had been placed in the "too hard" basket.

"You were so pathetically poor," she said.

CHAPTER 13

A New Life

I sang everywhere and spent hours at the piano. It was my solace, my soul.

Everyone on the Point became used to the constant flow of music. I loved to read Shakespeare and Shaw; I'd recite my verses and dramatic excerpts when no one was around. My world filled with make-believe characters, and the writers' textured language energized me.

One day a tall, thin man of about thirty came into the boatshed carrying an armful of heavy books.

"These are for your daughter," he said with a refined tone. "I've been listening to her practice each evening from the water's edge, and I feel that she will love these books as much as I do."

"Thank you very much," my mother replied, "but I'm sorry. I can't accept such an expensive gift."

The man pushed the books into her hands.

"Of course you can. I am not a well man, and I would love her to have them." He looked at me directly, and I felt embarrassed. I knew my Shakespeare wasn't brilliant and thought it odd that anyone would offer me anything for nothing.

"You'd like the books, wouldn't you?"

I nodded.

The man gave a flowery wave of his hand and said, "Then you shall have them!"

My mother went to speak, and he quickly intervened. "I ask for nothing in return, except that she read them and look after them as I did."

My mother took the books, and I thanked him. We watched his retreating back, and she cried out, "I hope you get better soon."

"There's little hope of that," he shouted back. "I've only got six months to live."

We never saw the man again, but I still have his books. It was the beginning of a series of many good turns. People who had noticed I could perform offered to give me free singing lessons, dance and drama lessons, and even piano lessons. My mother could never have afforded to give me these opportunities, and I am forever grateful to the people who gave their time and imparted their knowledge so generously. These people unwittingly saved my sanity and, through their kindness, helped me to realize life is not all about anger and violence. Bill left us and got a job building a motel in Taree. Mum was relieved. She tried to live day to day without the stress of arguments and financial worry; however, I knew she still didn't feel safe. Unbeknownst to her, I knew she slept with a tomahawk under her pillow, and I slept with a hammer.

One night my father tried to break into the bus. I heard the window sliding open and saw his hand reach for the lock. I got the hammer from under my pillow and hit him on the hand. He let out a yell and woke the dogs. They came running across the yard, and one bit his arm as he ran off into the darkness. Mum and I stayed up all night, the bus rocking uncontrollably as we shivered in fear. The next day my mother bought a rifle. She kept it by her bed and grabbed it whenever she heard a noise outside at night.

We needed money desperately, so my brothers and I got jobs after school. I had one at the local coffee shop on the weekends and one at Woolies on Thursday nights, and I also ran a small drama-and-singing class after school on Fridays. Michael packed shelves at another store and spent all his spare time studying and playing his guitar. He hoped to escape to university the following year. My school life had become a blur. Constantly tired from lack of sleep, I drifted in and out of daydreams, headaches, and fits of worrying. I would sometimes sit as if in a trance thinking and then snap out of it feeling nervous and unsettled. Without my mother's permission, the nuns sent me to see a counselor for a psychological assessment because I had such odd behavior and often rocked. A nun took me from school in the middle of the day and drove me all the way to Taree. She took me there without my mother's knowledge, and I didn't know where we were going until we reached our destination. I read the sign on the door and realized that I was going for some sort of test.

When we got there, no one suspected I was a trauma survivor. I still had a fake surname, and no one knew my real history. The counselor gave me the usual IQ test and questions and said, "Your results are excellent. You passed with flying colors; in fact, you got top marks."

"You sound surprised." I smiled. It all seemed so surreal. I was laughing off my situation to put him off the scent. I knew I was different. I knew I didn't fit in, and I was always looking over my shoulder, waiting for the stalker to strike. Over the years I had built up hundreds of what-if scenarios, escape plans to help me avoid danger. I also lived in fear of being taken into care by child welfare and being separated from my mother.

The psychologist's secretary rang Mum and told her where I was so she wouldn't worry, and we set off back home. On the way back to Port, our journey was delayed because a truck and some horses had collided in a horrific accident. It was a somber ending to a terrible day. The nun who was driving me was very angry with me and wanted to know why I hadn't been more demonstrative and had shown the weird behaviors I exhibited at school. She felt I had wasted her time, gave me a lecture, and then refused to talk to me for the rest of the journey. This gave me time to think. Depression fell in waves around me, and I gulped back tears. The silence in the car and the austerity of the nun driving hammered against my heart. I knew then I had to leave my surroundings or suffocate in my unhappiness.

I started to formulate a plan to move back to Sydney.

I waited for six months and then rang my mother while she was at work. I told her I was going to Sydney to look for work. She knew I was unhappy and agreed upon the condition that I live with her sister. Mum promised she'd move down after me, a promise she held true to three months later. I immediately changed my name back to the original one. I reclaimed myself, dragging myself out of anonymity and vowing never to change my name again.

Within the first months of moving to Sydney, I put on a show with local primary school students. This show secured me a trial position at a private boys' college as a drama and music teacher. The Christian brothers would mentor me and facilitate my doing a bridging course so I could teach for them. At the time, I was the youngest teacher in NSW. I was fifteen. My role was to teach and to write and direct musical performances for the school. I also taught art and singing, and I was lent out to other schools to help with their productions.

The brothers were very kind to me, and they made allowances for my own pursuits as an actress. They allowed me to audition for shows, and eventually I was offered the job as a presenter on a children's television show. I worked on national TV for five years and then moved onto the stage. I formed my own production company, married, and worked extensively in cabaret and children's entertainment. Throughout this time, I had five beautiful children, and I continued my studies, collecting eight degrees.

My mother and I are still best friends. She has been my confidante, my lifeline, and my true and trusted friend. We share a bond that will never be broken. For years we lived in silence, never sharing our torment. As a teenager, I listened to my brothers screaming in their sleep and knew that they, too, relived the horror of the past. It was not until thirty years later that we realized we all shared the same nightmares. It was only then we discovered the reality of our trauma, and the pieces of the jigsaw began to fit. My mother had lived many years as a broken, tormented woman, often too weak to stand, but she eventually broke free from the violent repression. All the females in our family remained silent about their abuse, my mother's little sisters included. Years later, we all accept the truth and know that our personal agony was the whole family's tragedy.

The police had been told. They had been given guns several times during our time with my father, and my mother had pleaded to them for intervention. They were retold the story again thirty years later. But without physical evidence, they could do nothing. Our accusations became hollow echoes from the past.

I will never know if my father collected personal trophies from his victims. After all, he had me—a living, silent, walking reminder of what went on. When I was in my twenties, he would follow me or park across the road from where I worked. He'd sit for hours watching me, quietly stalking me and keeping my feelings of terror alive. My mother and I got used to the anonymous or aggressive phone calls, and we learned to leave the receiver off the hook when we got calls in which music played endlessly. We'd get warning notes from him, and sometimes he'd send us odd bits of jewelry, which I threw in the bin. He also occasionally sent us plastic bags of butchered animals, which were left on the doorstep for us to find. After I had my children, I'd get messages from him asking if they were "safe."

A killer walked among us. He was not consumed by his conscience. He was protected by his personalities, his manifestations of himself. Was he the perfect criminal? Did his personalities ever meet or cross over, showing him what he was doing? With each premeditated murder, the Devil sang sweetly of his success, but when he disappeared, another personality took his place, his actions vanquished into the dungeons of his mind. Maybe he walked from one mind's room to another, closing the door and memories as he went.

As a child I looked at him and, because of my bloodline, had to call him father. But now I ask, "How red is my blood? The blood on my hands?"

I do not love him. I refused to see him anymore. I do not hate him. Terror surpassed hate long ago. The moment his personalities were introduced to me, I was enshrouded in fear—fears that lived long into adulthood and refused to go away. I lie in bed nearly forty years later and wonder when the night terrors will stop. I have woken up every night of my life at midnight, then at three in the morning, and then at six. The pattern rarely varies. It has been this way for years. A nocturnal clock ticks, ever fearful, in my heart, and I watch the shadows. My nightmares still continue, but one day I am determined to sleep unafraid. Eventually I will be rid of the bolts on the doors and the bars on the windows, and I will live without fear in my heart.

As a child I wanted to fly.

To spread my wings and transcend the black spots.

To capture my mother and brothers and take them with me.

To feel freedom.

Away from lying, angry eyes.

Eyes that filtered change as though it were water.

Forcing change and demanding I take note of it.

There were games. Games children play. Games that become bizarre replicas of our parents' actions and abreactions. Childlike games played without vision, unhampered by the future. There were games we played that must have affected other children. Doctors and nurses, mother and child. Fathers turning into devils and naked reenactments of strange rituals. We played our games in childish good faith, but they were twisted with adult intrusion. Adulthood's knife cut away our innocence and left us floundering. We were seen as the odd children with unusual behavior. Other children thought us strange, but we were secure in our abnormality, thinking every family was the same, not realizing things were different until we were older.

As a child I needed to live without terror. I needed more moments of peace.

I didn't need the adrenaline hit or the rapid-fire decision making that dictated whether I lived or died.

I needed sleep.

Deep, restful sleep.

Without the black spots.

Without the chloroform.

Without the ether.

Without living a madman's nightmare.

Epilogue

THE PHONE CALL CAME.

He died May 16, 2009.

It was as if the bell jar shattered and the clawing, scrambling mouse was free.

The devil had died, and necromancy was impossible.

All contact was severed, and immediately my nocturnal time clock ground to a halt. I no longer woke at midnight and then again at three in the morning. The sequential wakening and wandering that had followed and spurred me into sleepless action night after night were gone.

My sleep patterns changed.

My nightmares lessened.

It was as though someone had magically turned off a switch, and the allurement of sleep took on its natural course.

Forty-nine years of repression and terror that had been carved deeply into my subconscious dissipated. The madman's habituation had become imperceptible to others and sometimes even to me. His stamp in my formative years was intrinsic and hidden beneath layers of conditioning and self-resolve.

But on May 16, 2009, past cycles were broken.

With his passing, shock, coldness, and an inevitable hollowness enveloped me. My years of pushing against the wind suddenly stopped because the cyclone of time had been vanquished. I had to steady myself for fear I would fall over. No more looking over my shoulder; no more paranoia or fear. I will never be able to explain the depth and breadth of the psychological hold he had over me, the ever-present, deep-rooted terror in my psyche that held me back for all those years.

With his death I also felt an overwhelming sadness because I grappled with the knowledge that his victims' identities would never be discovered. In essence, I grieved for them and for the tragic knowledge that they disappeared undiscovered and that their passing remains unresolved.

Notes

MANY YEARS LATER:

In 2007, on a sunny Father's Day, the author took me and her three youngest children to Hornsby to show me the places she has described in her book. At the site where she believes Tina was murdered, I felt compelled to examine the immediate area to try to gain an insight into what might have become of the victim. If her father did not remove the body in a vehicle, the alternative would be to hide it in the vicinity—dumped either in a shallow grave or where no one was likely to find it.

To hide it, the easiest method would be to drag it down the gully. A couple of hundred meters would certainly be far enough in that difficult terrain. In the Australian bush, many people fear what may lurk under rocks and in dense undergrowth, and as such, most people will stick strictly to the tracks. Therefore, a body can lie for years undetected just meters away from where bushwalkers may wander.

With this in mind, the author's youngest son and I climbed down into the gully below and found a small cave. When we explored the cave, we discovered an old car seat, which someone had attempted to bury under piles of rocks. We also found two knives along with other odd items in a small plastic bag. Could this have been her father's secret bush den?

A few days later, the author and I revisited the cave to explore it more carefully. I spent an hour removing rocks to get the car seat out, and the author explored all the crevices around the cave, where she found another knife, so badly corroded that it blended in with the surrounding rock. It took me nearly a minute to work out what it was.

We removed the knives carefully, using rubber surgical gloves, and took them home. I made the decision that night to inform the police, and the author agreed. To their credit, the Hornsby police detectives took the matter seriously, and they called us both in for interviews and asked us to show them the site where we had found the knives. They interviewed the author's mother some days later and began an investigation.

I decided to help by going through old newspaper records to try to find evidence of missing people or any other clues that might be of help. A number of facts came to light almost immediately. Police records have all been updated, and many were incomplete or destroyed before the introduction of computers. Therefore, there were no surviving records of guns being handed in, of police intervention from the 1960s, or of the earlier interviews conducted by the police in the 1970s. Missing-persons records have only eight missing persons registered for the 1960s, yet a page-one headline in the *Sun* in November 1974 quotes a report to State Parliament that said that between 1968 and 1972, 299 girls under the age of sixteen went missing and were never found. The report was tabled in Parliament by Mr. C. Mallam, Labor member for Campbelltown.

What became of those girls is worrying. Certainly some of the girls must have covered their tracks carefully so that they would not be found, but a large number must have come to serious harm. People cannot just disappear forever and live a new life without some clue turning up at some point in the future. These people do not appear to have applied for birth certificate copies, applied for driver's licenses, applied for passports, opened bank accounts, or done any of the other formal administrative tasks that everyone else must perform at some point in life.

So where are these girls? We know that there are serial murderers out there because we read about their awful crimes after the bodies are discovered or when the criminal is caught. But how many Patrick O'Learys are out there, serial killers who are clever and lucky?

Remember, the public becomes aware that terrible crimes have been committed only when some evidence of this comes to light. Patrick O'Leary died

May 16, 2009, a free man because, to date, no remains have been found, and the victims the author and her mother saw are unknown. All my efforts to identify possible victims to support the author's story have so far been fruitless.

Australia has made significant changes to the child protection laws since the 1960s and 70s. There has also been a focus by government and advocacy groups condemning domestic violence. Media and educational campaigns have been implemented encouraging the public and victims to report incidents to authorities.

Special activist fundraisers—such as White Ribbon Day[lxxxi] for domestic violence and Bravehearts[lxxxii] for child sexual assault—have increased public awareness and are developing a community mentality of moral responsibility to protect one another.

Mandatory reporting of child abuse and neglect has become the moral responsibility of welfare and community groups, and this enables the early detection of cases that otherwise may not come to the attention of helping agencies. There also has been a focus on professional training to develop an awareness of cases of child abuse and police screening for those who work with children. Mandated regulations have also been put in place to protect those who report suspected child abuse. It is the aim of these Australian laws to encourage a culture which is more child centered in order to protect vulnerable children at risk of abuse and neglect.[lxxxiii]

In 2015, Rosemary Anne "Rosie" Batty, the Australian domestic violence campaigner, was made the Australian of the Year.[lxxxiv] Despite these developments, a NSW Bureau of Crime Statistics and Research study analysed all 169 homicides in NSW between 2005 and 2014 and found two-thirds of domestic violence victims did not contact law authorities about their violent partner. People who suffer this kind of abuse are still disinclined to seek help.[lxxxv]

C. MacKenzie

ENDNOTES

i. The first Commonwealth Census was in 1911, and censuses were subsequently conducted in 1933, 1947, 1954, and every five years from 1961 onward.

ii. The *Land* was a newspaper publication established by the rural lobbyist Jack Irving Campbell (1861–1942) in 1911.

iii. Nellie Melba (1861–1931) was Australia's first internationally recognized star. The opera star toured the world and received fame worldwide for her beautiful soprano voice.

iv. James Cassius Williamson (1845–1913) founded the Williamson Opera. He was an American actor who later created Australia's foremost theatrical management company, J. C. Williamson Ltd.

v. Raymond Longford directed the film *Sweet Nell of Old Drury*. Based on the play by Paul Kester, the film premiered at the Sydney Lyceum on December 2, 1911, and was screened for approximately six years.

vi. *The Fatal Wedding* (1911) also opened at the Lyceum cinema in Sydney. It was the first film directed by Raymond Longford (born John Walter Longford in 1878), who was Australia's most prolific director of the silent era.

vii. Brookvale Park was transformed into a showground in 1921. The Warringah Agricultural, Horticultural, Amateur Sports and Athletic Association established it. In the 1970s, after approximately fifty annual shows, the Brookvale Show moved to St. Ives Showground.

viii. The Marist Brothers founded Marist College North Shore in 1888. The Catholic school had a strong academic foundation and followed the Christian ethos *"Virtus ubique vincit,"* or "Courage conquers all."

ix. The Marquess of Queensberry rules provide a code of accepted sporting rules for competitive boxing. They were named so because the ninth Marquess of Queensberry publicly endorsed the accepted rules for boxing in 1867. This code of conduct was developed to protect competitors in professional and amateur boxing matches from serious harm.

x. The family kept Patrick's nervous breakdown secret until after he married. They felt too ashamed to acknowledge he needed help. When the expulsion occurred, only Patrick's older brother and his wife were privy to the situation, as they lived with the family at the time. Patrick O'Leary's mother took him to a farm in Narrabri. Ethel had a good friend who worked as a housekeeper on the property, and she arranged for Ethel to get work as a cleaner while Patrick recovered.

xi. In the Second World War (1939–1945), almost a million Australian men and women served their country. Over thirty thousand Australian servicemen were taken prisoner, and approximately thirty-nine thousand gave their lives.

xii. The Syrian Campaign (June 7 through July 11, 1941) was fought between Allied forces in Syria and Lebanon against the Vichy French, as a pro-German administration had assumed control of the area following the fall of France in June 1940.

xiii. The New Guinea Campaign started when Japanese forces occupied Rabaul and the northern New Guinea coast in early March 1942. Australian soldiers fought the Japanese in the Coral Sea and established a base at Milne Bay, preventing a seaborne attack against Port Moresby.

xiv.   Georgette Heyer (1902–1974) wrote approximately fifty-one novels. She pioneered the Regency England genre of romantic fiction.

xv.   Liam was admitted to Hornsby Hospital in December 1963 with phosphorous poisoning caused by exposure to a pet shampoo that had been released as a veterinary wash in 1961. Doctors could not ascertain how the child was poisoned, as he had not ingested or been seen to have any immediate contact with the pet shampoo.

xvi.   In Australia, "poker machines" or "pokies" are officially termed "gaming machines." To "play the pokies" means to gamble on slot machines.

xvii.   Tupperware began its Australian operation in 1961. It originally involved independent salespeople selling kitchenware and Tupperware products in a party-plan style.

xviii.   The Saanen dairy goat originated in the Saane Valley in Switzerland. The breed was brought to Australia in 1913 by the New South Wales Department of Agriculture.

xix.   Johanna Spyri (1827–1901) wrote the book *Heidi* as a juvenile fiction story. Set in the Swiss Alps, it tells the tale of orphaned Heidi, her grandfather, her friends Peter and Clara, and their goat herd.

xx.   When buck kids were born in the Tresco stud, some were donated to Taronga Zoo to be used as fresh meat for the animals, but Rissole was used in a breeding program at the zoo.

xxi.   "Hansel and Gretel" is a fairy tale of Germanic origin written by the Brothers Grimm in 1812.

xxii.   On February 15, 1964, a three-mile fire front swept through the Hornsby Valley and burned out three square miles of bushland.

xxiii. Oral history from locals at the time told of a tramp's body being discovered in a cave after the fire.

xxiv. *Ranunculus repens* are creeping buttercups. They are native to Europe, Asia, and northwest Africa, and they are classified as a perennial weed in the Hornsby Shire.

xxv. The Dick and Jane reading series started in the 1930s and was revamped in 1965. By that time, new characters such as Sally, Stanley, and Spot the Dog were included in the primers. Helen M. Robinson, Marion Monroe, and A. Sterl Artley wrote the series, and Bob Childress illustrated it.

xxvi. *The Goose Girl* was a small print of the painting by Stanley Royle, RCA, RBA, ARWA, the British landscape artist (1888–1961). The original, painted in 1922, is in the National Gallery of Ireland.

xxvii. The British cream shorthair is a comparatively rare shorthair breed. The cat's coat is a pale, pinkish cream. Occasionally they appear in tortoiseshell litters, but they can be bred successfully from pink and gray-blue sires.

xxviii. Latin for the beginning of the Lord's Prayer: *"Pater noster, qui es in caelis, sanctificetur nomen tuum."*

"Our father, who art in heaven, hallowed be thy name."

xxix. It was not uncommon for parents to leave children at home by themselves for short periods of time, although no one talked about it or advertised it to others. In 1968 nearly one million children under fourteen years of age were left alone to look after themselves while their mothers worked. This figure had doubled by 1978, with nineteen thousand to thirty-seven thousand of these children being preschoolers (Soman

2003). These figures were predominantly due to inadequate daycare and after-school services; however, a woman in a volatile domestic situation had a moral obligation toward male self-fulfillment, as men's desires came first in the 1960s (Barton and Douglas 1995).

xxx. A popular barbiturate made by Abbot Laboratories, Nembutal (pentobarbital sodium) came in a fifty-milligram white tablet dosage in the 1960s. It was a nonselective nervous system depressant used primarily as a sedative-hypnotic. The family had supplies of the drug for veterinarian purposes associated with goat breeding.

xxxi. In posttraumatic stress syndrome, child witnesses to violence demonstrate four types of symptomology:

1. Children describe the event as so traumatic they will never forget it.

2. They reexperience the event through traumatic play or dreams.

3. They exhibit mute/subdued behavior or adopt a third-person/journalistic attitude (psychic numbing).

4. They exhibit avoidant behavior of trauma-specific reminders or sleep disorders. (Frederick 1983)

xxxii. Oral history from Marge Banning collected before her death.

xxxiii. Opium poppies were grown in Australia on a limited scale during World War II. Cultivation ceased after the war, but during 1960 and 1961, trials were undertaken in New South Wales, Western Australia, South Australia, and Tasmania to see if poppies could be sustainable crops for medical research. People could also grow opium plants from untreated overseas seeds, as only poppy seeds grown in

Australia were treated so they could not produce opiates. These seeds were sometimes available from gardening shops.

xxxiv. Despite new regulation constraints for the pharmaceutical sector during the 1950s and 60s, many drugs could still be obtained over the counter. At this time, policy makers and the industry felt the laws imposed constraints on business, and unless products were proven unsafe, consumers could still buy them.

xxxv. Selective mutism, elective mutism, and traumatic mutism are symptoms of specific anxiety disorders. These include social phobia, separation anxiety, and posttraumatic stress disorder (Black and Uhde 1995; Anstendig 1999).

xxxvi. If women contract German measles, known as rubella, during pregnancy, it can cause miscarriages, infant deaths, mental retardation, and serious birth defects in the newborn. Vaccination for rubella has been available in Australia since 1970, and mass vaccination of schoolgirls began in Australia in 1971.

xxxvii. During the 1950s there was a rise in violent crime. The domestic violence movement had slowed, as the country had just experienced two world wars and the Depression. The 1950s prompted a reevaluation of family violence, which was also facilitated by the feminist movement of the 1960s. However, prior to the 1970s, there was little or no state or federal funding for domestic violence shelters or help for abused women and families (Gelles 1999).

xxxviii. In the 1960s family violence was considered rare, because the abusers and abused kept it secret. Government agencies did not require health professionals to report child abuse or domestic violence cases. Before 1970, hospitals failed to categorize patients upon admission as abused or nonabused cases. Police did keep brief records of domestic violence or disturbance calls, but these records often included only the name and address of the complainant. They also were often incomplete or inaccurate. A case of wife beating was often recorded as a disturbance rather than an abuse or violence case. This is because the streets were deemed more of a danger for women and children, as the home was meant to be a safe haven (Gelles 1999).

xxxix. "Hydrocephalus" comes from the Greek words "hydro," meaning "water," and "cephalus," meaning "head." This condition is often called "water on the brain." Despite the first shunt being implanted in the brain in 1949, hydrocephalus was virtually inoperable because of high postoperative mortality rates. In 1960, the combined invention of artificial valves and silicone led to a worldwide therapeutic break-through in the treatment for hydrocephalus, but by then Rosalie was too old and too severely brain damaged to undergo surgery.

xl. The book read was *The Land and Wildlife of Australasia*, part of the Life Nature Library series. This edition was written by David Bergamini and the editors of *Life* and published in 1965 by Holland Time-Life International.

xli. Arterial thrombosis is the presence of a thrombus in an artery, and arteriosclerosis refers to the group of chronic diseases in which thickening, hardening, and loss of elasticity of the arterial walls results in impaired blood circulation.

xlii. Professor Julius Sumner Miller was on the groundbreaking science TV series *Why Is It So?* on ABC TV from 1963 to 1986.

xliii. *It's Academic* was a children's quiz show originally aired on the Seven Network from 1968 to 1978.

xliv. The black and tricolor ants of the subfamily Myrmeciinae are the common bull ants found in the Hornsby Shire.

xlv. In 1965 Vatican II was introduced, and it was no longer mandatory to recite the liturgy and the Mass in Latin. These rites could now be proclaimed in English so everyone could understand what the priest was saying.

xlvi. "Misereatur tui omnipotens Deus, et dimissis peccatis tuis [May Almighty God have mercy on you and forgive you your sins]." This quotation is taken from the Absolution, in which the penitent makes a sacramental confession of all mortal sins to a priest and prays an act of contrition. The Absolution is an integral part of the sacrament of penance and reconciliation in the Catholic religion.

xlvii. In 1898 the Dog Act and the Goat Act were consolidated into a single Dog and Goat Act. This statute regulated the control of dogs and goats in the state of NSW. The Dog Act was revised in 1966, but the part of the act pertaining to goats was never revised, leaving its application to domestic goats in alignment with the 1898 law.

xlviii. A goanna is any of several Australian monitor lizards of the genus *Varanus*.

xlix. Under the dynamic leadership of Rev. Alan Walker (now Rev. Dr. Sir Alan Walker), in 1966, a unique "church in a theater" called the Wesley Centre opened in Sydney. The church also had a fellowship that helped runaways and troubled youth.

l. The heart is surrounded by three major coronary arteries. If a blood clot develops in one of these arteries, the blood supply to that area of the heart muscle will stop, and the person will suffer a heart attack (or, in medical terms, a coronary thrombosis or myocardial infarction). Arteriosclerosis is the presence of a thrombus in a hardened or thickened artery.

li. *New Faces* was an Australian talent show that preceded the British show of the same name, produced at GTV-9 Melbourne.

lii. The *Super Flying Fun Show* was a live weekday morning television program aimed at children. It was made at TCN 9 in Sydney, Australia.

liii. The small blue pills were Diazepam; these pills were prescribed in 1960s for anxiety and light sedation.

liv. There are many articles in the *Hornsby Advocate* (1962–1968) stating that a firebug was loose in the local area. It also has articles about random sniper attacks and animal cruelty and poisonings in the area. The perpetrator of these crimes was not caught.

lv. From the 1930s through the 1970s, chemicals were readily available to the general public. Chemistry kits were all the rage, and the chemicals, which would be banned today, were easy to come by. Small businesses supplied them directly to home chemists and chemistry hobbyists. These chemicals were sold as individual sales items. Today the law prohibits individual chemical sales.

lvi. *Hogan's Heroes* is an American television sitcom set in a German prisoner-of-war (POW) camp during World War II. It ran for 168 episodes, from September 17, 1965, to April 4, 1971, on the CBS network.

lvii. Oral history from Tara, who was interviewed by the police with Marge Banning in regard to a missing girl at the Royal Easter Show.

lviii. Latin for the Confiteor: "May Almighty God have mercy on you, forgive you your sins, and bring you to life everlasting."

lix.   Lifeline is an organization that provides free counseling and crisis support.

lx.   The Three Stooges were an American vaudeville and comedy act of the mid–twentieth century, best known for their numerous Columbia short-subject films that are still syndicated on television.

lxi.   Westwood, at Bowral, was a residential education center for girls over sixteen years old with mild intellectual disabilities that opened in 1965. It was run by the Methodist Department of Christian Citizenship. It was transferred to the Uniting Church in 1977 and closed down in 1979.

lxii.   During the war years in Sydney, Australia, a survey of thirty-eight schools proved that over three thousand children went home to empty houses or roamed the streets until their mothers came home from work. In other cases children younger than six were left alone in locked houses during the day. This trend progressed in the 1960s, when single parents, stepfamilies, and low-income parents had to work in order to support their families. This shift was a significant social reflection of the times, and the introduction of television into mainstream homes served as a babysitter when there were no childcare resources available for minors.

lxiii.   A Mercy Convent interview indicated he never worked there but had been seen there while nuns were at vespers in the church across the road. My father was seen staring out of the window in Sister Luke's bedroom by another nun, and Sister Luke had reported an intruder.

lxiv.   The Museum of Applied Arts and Sciences is now Powerhouse Museum in Ultimo, Sydney.

lxv. The term "sultana" refers to golden-colored dried grapes, which are also sometimes called "golden raisins."

lxvi. "Plonk" is a nonspecific term for wine used primarily in Britain and Australia.

lxvii. SRA Reading Scheme consisted of large boxes filled with color-coded cardboard sheets. Each sheet included a reading exercise, each of which was designed to teach independent reading and comprehension. SRA stands for the Chicago-based publisher of educational materials Science Research Associates Inc.

lxviii. A small tin boat usually eight to ten feet long.

lxix. E. Le Roy and his good friend Jack Pearson created the Driza-Bone coat more than one hundred years ago, in 1898. It was originally made from old ship sails treated with oil. This made the coat waterproof and kept the Australian sailors "as dry as a bone." Hence the coat became known as a "Driza-Bone."

lxx. The film *Whatever Happened to Baby Jane?*, directed by Robert Aldrich, was released in 1962. It tells the story of two sisters, Jane Hudson, a former child star, and Blanche, who is a crippled movie star. Baby Jane still wears doll-like makeup and curls her hair in ringlets in the same way as when she was a child star. The sisters live in their decaying Hollywood mansion and torment each other until the movie's horrifying conclusion.

lxxi. Australian beach worms can be a red to greenish color on the head with a white body. These worms can be found in sandy areas throughout the southeastern Australian coast at the low water mark and can exceed 2.5 meters in length.

lxxii.   A petrol bowser is the machine at a filling station that is used to pump liquid fuel into vehicles.

lxxiii.   Burleying is similar to the American practice of chumming, where animals are lured by throwing bait into the water. In order to catch beach worms, meat was used to lure the worms to the surface.

lxxiv.   Olive Oyl is a cartoon character created by E. C. Segar in 1919 for his comic strip Thimble Theatre. The strip was renamed Popeye in 1929 after the sailor character became a member of the cast.

lxxv.   *The Beverly Hillbillies* is an American sitcom originally broadcast on CBS for nine seasons, from September 26, 1962 to March 23, 1971.

lxxvi.   *The Aristocats* is an animated film produced by Walt Disney Productions and released on December 11, 1970.

lxxvii.   The common yabby (*Cherax destructor*) is an Australian freshwater crustacean in the *Parastacidae* family.

lxxviii. "Mr. McGregor's Garden" is in *The Tale of Peter Rabbit*, written and illustrated by Beatrix Potter. It is a British children's book that was printed independently by Potter in 1901.

lxxix.   *Pollyanna* is a best-selling 1913 novel by Eleanor H. Porter that is now considered a classic of children's literature.

lxxx.   The Taree District Eisteddfod is an annual event held in Taree, New South Wales. It incorporates competitions for singing, dance, and drama.

lxxxi.   White Ribbon Day is a male-led Australian campaign to end men's violence against women. http://www.whiteribbon.org.au/

lxxxii.   Bravehearts is an organization that aims to educate, empower, and protect Australian kids from sexual assault.

http://www.bravehearts.org.au/?gclid=CI_Z58KS6ckCFQybvAod XcMPDw

lxxxiii.   Mathews, B. and D. Scott. "Child Family Community Australia Resource Sheet."

Australian Institute of Family Studies. Sydney: 2015.

https://aifs.gov.au/cfca/publications/mandatory-reporting-child-abuse-and-neglect

lxxxiv.   "Australian of the Year: Rosie Batty Awarded Top Honour for Efforts to Stop Family Violence." Australian Broadcasting Commission. ABC News (Australia). 25 January 2015. Retrieved 25 January 2015.

lxxxv.   Olding, Rachel and Ava Benny-Morrison. "The Common Misconception about Domestic Violence Murders." Sydney *Morning Herald*, 12 December 2015. http://www.smh.com.au/nsw/the-common-misconception-about-domestic-violence-murders-20151216-glp7vm.html

Made in the USA
Lexington, KY
02 November 2019